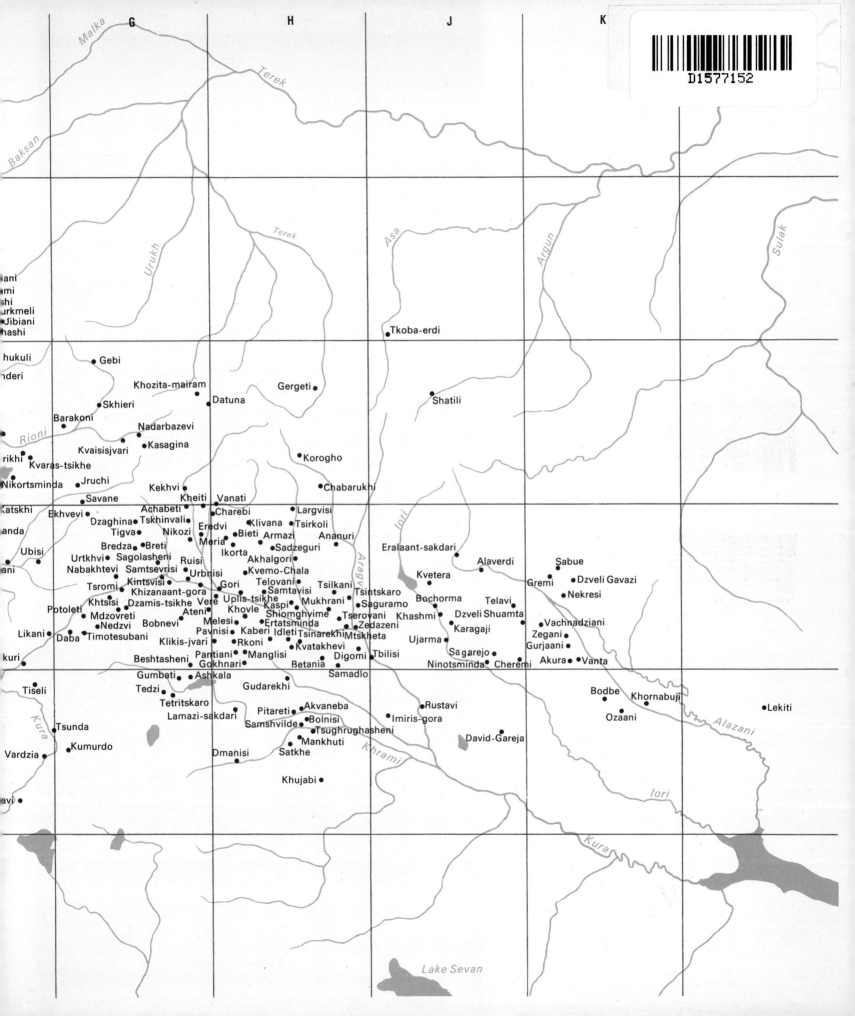

The Arts of Ancient Georgia

584 illustrations, 98 in colour

Rusudan Mepisashvili and Vakhtang Tsintsadze

The Arts of Ancient Georgia

Photographs by Rolf Schrade

Foreword by David M. Lang

Thames and Hudson

Translated from the German *Die Kunst des alten Georgien* by Alisa Jaffa

Erratum
The inscription illustrated on p. 188 appears the correct way up.

First published in Great Britain in 1979 by Thames and Hudson Ltd, London

Printed in the German Democratic Republic by Druckerei Fortschritt Erfurt

Foreword

Over the last decades, the West has begun to wake up, perhaps belatedly, to the spectacular art and architectural treasures of Georgia in the Caucasus. This land of great natural beauty is a paradise for lovers of medieval churches and icons, of sculpture, jewellery and metalwork. A small band of cognoscenti, among whom we could include such names as Sir Fitzroy Maclean and Mr David Garnett, have started to initiate the Western public into the unique qualities of Georgian civilization. However, although several monographs have been published in the West dealing with individual aspects of the subject, there has until now been a great need for a single comprehensive study surveying in detail the evolution of Georgian art from the Bronze Age to the threshold of modern times.

Georgia is the fabled land of Jason and the Argonauts, and of the enchantress Medea and her Golden Fleece; it is also the country which witnessed the fate of Prometheus, who stole for mankind the secrets of the almighty gods. Georgia is renowned for the beauty of her women and the virile dignity of her young men, for the splendour of her scenery and cultural monuments, and for her traditions of hospitality and knightly prowess, all of which continue to flourish today.

About the middle of the 19th century, a Russian Viceroy of the Caucasus, Prince Vorontsov, wrote: 'This little Georgia will become in time the most beautiful, the most durable piece of gold brocade woven into the many-coloured patchwork of mighty Russia.'

Not long after this, a British traveller and diplomat, Sir Oliver Wardrop, commented: 'There is no reason why Georgia should not become as popular a resort as Norway or Switzerland.'

These prophecies, in their various ways, have indeed come true, or are on their way to doing so. Travellers from many parts of the world today enjoy visiting Georgia, and often form a lasting attachment to the land and people. The 2nd International Symposium of Georgian Art took place in Tbilisi and at Alaverdi and Gelati in May 1977, and was attended by nearly two hundred scholars, art historians and museum curators from many countries including Great Britain, France, Italy, Greece, the Federal Republic of Germany and the German Democratic Republic, Yugoslavia, Bulgaria, Romania and the United States of America.

In recent years, the British public has had several opportunities of enjoying the performances of the Georgian National Dance Ensemble, founded by Iliko Sukhishvili and Nino Ramishvili, which has appeared at the Royal Albert Hall. Four different translations of Georgia's national epic, *The Man in the Panther's Skin*, by the medieval bard Shota Rustaveli, have appeared in English, in addition to renderings in Russian, Armenian, Japanese, Hungarian, French, German and Italian.

These are some of the reasons why I consider the publication of the present volume to be particularly timely. I have personally known the joint authors for many years, and have always admired their writings and their devotion to the cause of Georgian art. This

devotion has been evinced repeatedly by indefatigable work on the scholarly front, by energetic conservation work, and by technical expertise in making their discoveries available in published form. When I first saw the original German edition of this book, published by Edition Leipzig, I urged my friends at Thames and Hudson to secure the translation rights without delay. I was delighted that they agreed with my high assessment of the work, and that they at once took the necessary steps to acquire the English-language rights.

I would not wish to conclude this foreword without paying tribute to the founder of the modern school of Georgian art historians, the late Academician Giorgi Chubinashvili, for many years Director of the Institute of History of Georgian Art of the Georgian Academy of Sciences. It was Professor Chubinashvili who prepared the way for the present efflorescence of Georgian art studies, and he was the teacher of the authors of the present work, as well as being a friend whose encouragement and example meant much to me personally. Nor must we forget the work of his great contemporary, the late Professor Shalva Amiranashvili, for many years Director of the Georgian State Museum of Art, one of whose achievements was the formation of a collection of chased and jewelled icons which is the envy of the entire world of art.

Anyone who picks up this book is bound to be struck by the exceptional quality of the illustrations, both in colour and in black and white. The majority of these are the work of the talented photographic artist

Contents

Dr Rolf Schrade, who has visited Georgia on several occasions to photograph the architectural monuments and art objects. Of the remaining photographs, most were taken by Professor Vakhtang Tsintsadze himself, and a number of others by Dr Rusudan Mepisashvili, who in private life is Madame Tsintsadze. The authors are also responsible for almost all the excellent plans, elevations and sections of historical monuments.

DAVID M. LANG
Professor of Caucasian Studies,
University of London

Introduction

The Soviet Republic of Georgia occupies the central and western parts of Transcaucasia. Natural boundaries are formed by the Caucasus mountains to the north and the Black Sea to the west; in the south, Georgia borders on the Armenian Soviet Socialist Republic and Turkey, and in the east on the SSR of Azerbaijan. Geographically, therefore, it represents a 'frontier zone' between Europe and the Near East.

The country covers an area of 76,000 square kilometres and has some five million inhabitants. Of these, more than one million live in the capital, Tbilisi. The name for Georgia in the native language is 'Sakartvelo', and its inhabitants are known as 'Kartveli'. These terms derive from the ancient name for the eastern part of Georgia, 'Kartli', which with certain modifications also forms the root of the country's name in other languages such as Turkish, Persian and Mongolian. The Russian name, 'Gruzia', which evolved in a similar fashion, was adopted for a time even for official use. Meanwhile the form 'Georgia', frequently used in old Latin texts, is the one that has been adopted in Europe, and is consequently the most common in translations of literary works.

Georgia is a country of marked contrasts in altitude. The Likhi mountain range divides the country into East and West Georgia, and the geographical features and climate of the two are quite distinct. The eastern part comprises the basins of the Kura river (Mtkvari in Georgian), which flows into the Caspian Sea, and its tributaries, which come from the Upper and Lower Caucasus. The chief rivers of West Georgia—the Rioni and its tributaries—likewise rise in the mountains of the Upper Caucasus, but flow into the Black Sea. Thus the Likhi range is revealed as an important watershed. Moreover, West Georgia lies appreciably lower than the eastern part of the country.

The Georgian SSR has rightly been described as one of nature's blessed spots on earth. Within this comparatively small area there is an astounding variety of landscape and scenery, from the sub-tropical zones along the Black Sea, with their palm and eucalyptus trees and oleander bushes, to the eternal snows and the glaciers in the central massif of the Caucasus mountains, whose foothills are fringed with beech woods. The dry steppe-lands of the high plateau in the Iori basin, in the east of the Republic, also contribute to the beauty of the country, as do the orchards of Kartli, the vineyards of Kakheti and the tea plantations in Colchis. There are also many natural resources—marble, coal, petroleum and natural gas, as well as copper, manganese and many other ores and minerals. Because of the presence of curative springs, a number of spas have grown up, and these are just as much a part of the country's attractions as the holiday resorts along the Black Sea coast. The beauty of the landscape itself attracts many visitors from other parts of the USSR and from abroad. But although tourism is expanding rapidly, there are still large areas which are little known or visited, despite their magnificent scenery and the many important cultural monuments and art treasures that they possess.

Archaeological finds have confirmed that the natural advantages of this region favoured early human settlement: Early Stone Age settlements have been discovered both along the Black Sea coast and in East Georgia. Scholarly research and finds have established a clear picture of the development and culture of the indigenous population of this region throughout the subsequent period up to the time of recorded history. Georgia is rich in Neolithic sites. Its real importance, however, began with the Bronze Age, when the skill of the ancient Georgian tribes in the working of bronze produced a fertile exchange with other peoples.

The foundation of two slave-owning states, Iberia and Colchis, in the 6th and 5th centuries BC marked the beginning of the history of this area as recorded in ancient annals and literature. This is covered more fully in later chapters.

At the beginning of the 4th century AD feudalism developed in Georgia, and by the 6th century it had consolidated itself. It continued to determine social conditions until the end of the 18th century, and throughout this long period indigenous art was developing. From antiquity to the present day a vast array of works of art has been created. Much of it still exists today, even though the history of Georgia has not always been conducive to the preservation of its artistic heritage.

Among the various forms of Georgian art, architecture occupies a position of special importance, and the largest part of this book has, accordingly, been devoted to it, without in any way wishing to detract from the superb achievements in the metallurgical arts, sculpture, wall- and icon painting and book illumination. Each of these art forms passed through certain distinct stages of stylistic development over the centuries. It is the aim of this book to provide a historical survey of this process, outlining the main artistic phenomena from antiquity to the 18th century.

To understand the position of Georgian art history—a science as yet in its infancy—it is important to bear in mind the distance that has been covered in research into and study of the architectural monuments and works of art. The Georgian historian and geographer Vakhushti Bagrationi, working in the mid-18th century, was the first to assemble information about Georgia's monuments, to assess their importance and to give brief descriptions of them. A century later his manuscript was published in the original and in a French translation by M.-F. Brosset. The 19th and early 20th centuries were devoted to intensive collation and consolidation of the material. Initially these studies led in two directions.

One was characterized by an interest in the artistic value of the monuments (Dubois de Montpéreux, Grigori Gagarin, David Grimm and others), the other by an interest in their historical significance (M.-F. Brosset, Dimitri Bakradze etc.). A scientific approach was later undertaken by Praskovya Uvarova and Ekvtime Takaishvili.

It was his interest in the monuments of the distant Caucasus that led Dubois de Montpéreux, traveller and connoisseur of antiquities, to Georgia in the 1830s. The publication of his comprehensive factual account acquainted the world with the art of the Caucasus for the first time. Dubois did not differentiate sufficiently between the architecture of Georgia and that of Byzantium—indeed, the level of architectural research at that time was such that the differences could not have been apparent to him—and thus it was all the more difficult for him to determine the differences between the architecture of Georgia

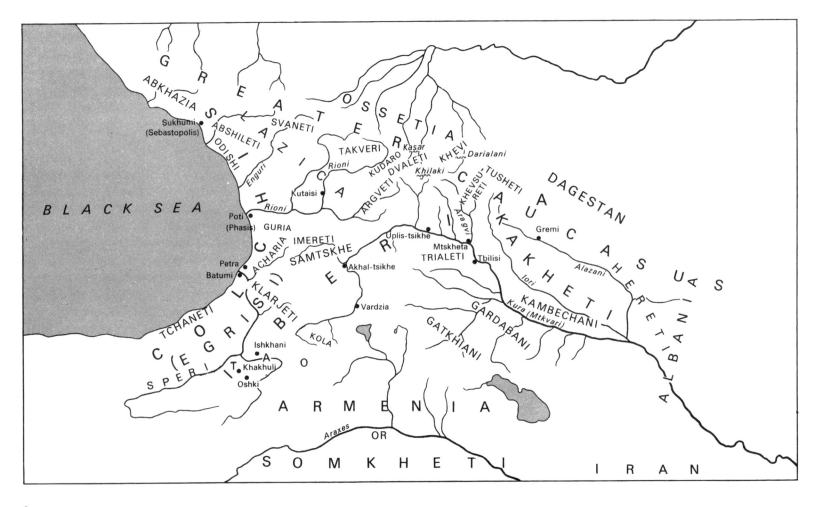

and that of Armenia. His observations resulted in Georgian art being classified as Byzantine; moreover, it was assessed as an imitator of Armenian art. This fundamentally erroneous view pervaded academic studies and for a long time hampered an appreciation of the national, individual character of Georgian art.

The artist Grigori Gagarin took an active interest in the art of Georgia; he published a large album of sketches and drawings, with an introduction by Ernst Stackelberg.

The first to make detailed measurements of the monuments—although these are not always entirely reliable—was David Grimm, who published his material with an introduction by M.-F. Brosset. For a long time the sketches and measurements by Dubois, Gagarin and Grimm remained the sole material on the basis of which hypotheses were developed and conclusions drawn.

During this same period, in the first half of the 19th century, M.-F. Brosset devoted himself to the collection of inscriptions from the monuments; he published a large number with historical commentaries, some with a brief description of the building on which the inscription occurred. Later, Dimitri Bakradze worked on the historical definition of the monuments and the periods to which they belonged.

In the last decades of the 19th century, the study of Georgian art moved into a new phase and ceased to rely solely on the initiative of individuals. The Moscow Archaeological Society, chaired for many years by Praskovya Uvarova, now took an active interest. So did local organizations such as the Georgian Historical and Ethnographical Society and the Caucasian section of the Moscow Archaeological Society; one member in particular, Ekvtime Takaishvili, produced wide-ranging and fruitful studies. A series entitled 'Findings of Caucasian Archaeology' was published in the late 19th and early 20th centuries; volumes III, IV, VII, X and XII were devoted exclusively to Georgia. A number of important publications appeared in Tbilisi which dealt with Georgian monuments. What makes the studies of Uvarova and Takaishvili distinctive is their interest in the development of the architecture and its historical value.

In the 19th century, the history of Georgian art was still completely isolated from the art history of other countries. Karl Schnaase, working in the latter half of the 19th century, attempted the first systematic appraisal of the development of art in the Caucasus in relation to the world history of art. He explicitly differentiated between the architecture of Georgia and that of Armenia, stressing the originality of the Georgian monuments by means of a series of examples, but also noted several instances of similarity with Romanesque buildings. Nikodim Kondakov, father of Byzantine art history, proposed a comprehensive schema for the evolution of Georgian art, although it was marred here and there by somewhat inaccurate dating of one or other monument. He drew on the entire mass of material available at that time, and defined a series of important tasks relating to the subsequent study of Georgian art. Kondakov's works, written in Russian, remained largely unknown to Western scholars, and a number of authors continued to make the same mistakes as had originally crept into Dubois's writing.

The beginning of the 20th century saw the appearance of the works of Josef Strzygowski, which set out to demonstrate the independent contributions of the various eastern Christian cultures to Christian art as a whole. The importance of these studies for the understanding of general developmental processes is indisputable, but they, too, were far from being totally successful in relation to Caucasian art. Apart from incorrect datings and a formalistic approach in the establishment of a systematic classification of the monuments, Strzygowski repeated Dubois's assertion that Georgian architecture was a successor to that of Armenia, even quoting from the other's books.

Thus we see that at the beginning of this century there was still no scientifically based research into Georgian art based on firm, factual data. The outlines of Schnaase and Kondakov and the studies of Strzygowski touched only on a few developmental questions, while a series of erroneous assertions pointed in the wrong direction. Systematic investigation of the development of Georgian art did not begin until the 1920s, when Giorgi Chubinashvili

Historical regions and provinces of Georgia and adjoining countries, from antiquity up to the end of the feudal era. This map is meant to serve solely to orientate the reader regarding the position of the various districts mentioned in the text; it does not afford any indication as to historical and geographical changes during the period under review.

and the assistants working under his direction began their exhaustive researches. They were able to demonstrate that Georgian art represents an independent phenomenon, with clearly identifiable features that distinguish it from the art of other lands.

Meanwhile it has become evident that Georgian art passed through distinct stages of development determined by the prevailing political, economic and social conditions in the country.

Antiquity is represented by a wealth of material discovered for the most part by archaeologists in the past few decades. Ancient oriental and Classical artistic forms occur side by side and develop alongside local folk traditions.

The following period—from the 4th to the 7th century—was the age of early feudalism, the expansion of which coincided with the conversion to Christianity. It was a period of completely independent development in architecture, an age characterized by the early flowering of its 'classical' style. During this period sculpture and other forms of art followed the general stream of development of early Christian art in the East while remaining based in deep-rooted local tradition.

The 8th and 9th centuries are generally regarded as a transitional period, characterized by the relaxation of early architectural forms and the determined striving towards a more picturesque stylistic approach. In sculpture, wall-painting and book illumination this was a time of liberation from ancient traditions, with a tendency towards the development of independent artistic forms.

The second flowering of art occurred from the 10th to the first half of the 13th century, when the definitive establishment of the picturesque style was achieved in architecture. Sculpture in stone and precious metals attained a high degree of plastic perfection. Wall-painting, which from the 11th century onwards had often completely dominated the interior of a building, followed the same course of development as sculpture. Independent schools of wall-painting grew up, each with its own particular characteristics, and reached a high level of artistic accomplishment. The second half of the 13th century and the whole of the 14th century represented a continuation of the artistic methods developed earlier.

From the 15th to the 18th century the natural process of artistic development in Georgia was slowed down. A large number of architectural monuments, together with examples of other forms of art from this period, illustrate the consequences of this process.

ART IN ANTIQUITY
Domestic dwellings and settlements — caves and megalithic structures — towns and fortresses — ceramics, metalwork and goldsmithing

The Georgian tribes are thought to be very ancient and to have formed part of the original population of the Near East. The evolution of the Georgian nation began at an early stage. The ethnic group that inhabited the territory of present-day Georgia and the neighbouring areas to the south-west broke away very early from the other Near Eastern tribes and developed into an independent unit. Following the intermingling of several tribes, the Georgian people emerged as the possessors of a unifying Georgian (Kartvelian) language.

During recent decades important sites dating back to the most ancient cultures have been discovered in Transcaucasia, some of them lying in Georgia. Archaeological excavation, which has been expanding appreciably in the past few years, has brought to light exceptionally rich material. The settlements discovered by archaeologists in Shulaveris-gora, Imiris-gora and Arukhlo (Nakhiduri) have revealed that tribes were already settled in a domestic existence on Georgian territory in the 5th and 4th millennia BC. They were farmers practising a market-garden type of economy, implying that they had reached an advanced level of social development.

We may affirm that the people of the Bronze Age Kura-Araxes culture (4th–3rd millennia BC)—so called because it originated near the river valleys of the Kura in Georgia and the Araxes in Armenia—were also forebears of the Georgians. The circular domestic dwelling characteristic of the Kura-Araxes culture, which later developed into a square form, undoubtedly derived from the prototypes of the preceding period.

The domestic complex in the 5th and early 4th millennia BC (illustrated on p. 21) consisted of a 'beehive' dwelling with outbuildings for storage which were also round in plan, the whole enclosed by a low circular fence. An opening at the apex of the hut roof admitted daylight and allowed the smoke to escape from the hearth below.

The floor area of these houses was not more than 16 square metres, the height as a rule about 2.5 metres, occasionally more. They were built of curving mud bricks with an admixture of straw and a clay mortar. The floor was of reddish-yellow beaten earth, and the walls were daubed with clay on both sides. The construction method and the materials used meant that the houses were necessarily very small, and consequently in order to accommodate a family it was essential to build a whole complex of them.

In some parts of Georgia a type of house was found which combined the domed roof with a square ground-plan. The dwellings from the 3rd millennium BC in Khizanaant-gora, Gudaberdkiya, Kvatskhelebi and Ami-ranis-gora already had a simple, angular form, with the square ground-plan rounded off at the corners. The flat roof had an opening for light and smoke as described above for the earlier houses.

A pillared porch was added to the dwelling-house at a very early stage; there are examples at Kvatskhelebi and Khizanaant-gora, and a later instance, from the early centuries AD, at Uplis-tsikhe.

In his treatise on architecture written in the 1st century BC, Vitruvius gives a fairly detailed

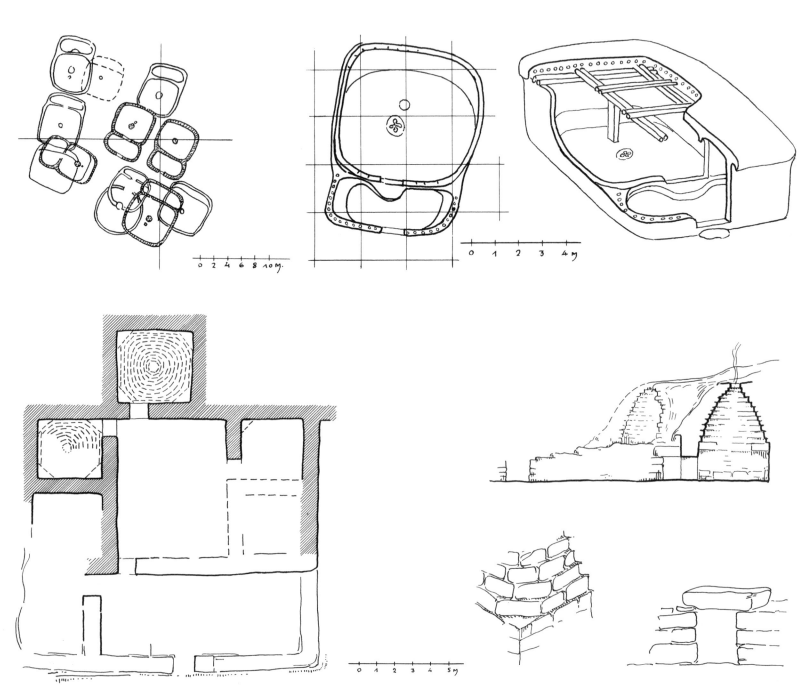

Top: Kvatskhelebi. Remains of an ancient settlement of the 4th–3rd millennium BC. Part of the site-plan, ground-plan of a dwelling, conjectural reconstruction (after A. Javakhishvili).

Bottom: Likani. Domestic complex. Plan, section and constructional details.

Peasant dwellings of the darbazi type,
19th century AD:
a Plan of a house in Ertatsminda.
b Plan and façade of a house in Digomi.
c Section through a house in Karagaji.
d Carved decoration on posts and beams in
Akhalkalaki and Mtskheta.
e Gvirgvini of a house in Mtskheta.

13

description of the Colchian domestic dwelling. This description leads us to conclude that the type of house with a domed roof and an entrance porch was retained for centuries. It accompanied the Georgian tribes throughout their history, and was in use right up to modern times in the *darbazi*-type peasant dwelling.

This house, square in plan with a central hearth, was built of stone; above a certain height wooden beams were arranged in overlapping concentric layers to produce a beehive dome *(gvirgvini)* with a light and smoke aperture. The supporting and load-bearing timbers, especially the main pillars *(dedabodzi)*, were richly adorned with carvings, introducing a wide variety of decoration to the interior.

The Greek general Xenophon, who passed through Georgia with his troops in 400 BC, left descriptions of two other types of dwelling. The first was a wooden tower of several storeys. The tradition of tower-dwellings was likewise an enduring one: stone towers, their form no doubt determined originally by defence requirements, are still built and lived in today (pp. 22–5) in the mountain regions of Svaneti, Khevsureti and Zemo-Racha. Town dwellings, too, retained a vertical emphasis until the beginning of this century. Apart from this tower-type, Xenophon also describes houses with several rooms arranged in a row. Buildings of this kind survive in old groups of dwellings in a gorge near Borzhomi.

The walls of these buildings consist of stones laid in overlapping courses without the use of mortar to bond them. In front of each house is a small courtyard fenced round with solid, upright stones. The houses, which are almost square, are roofed with high, egg-shaped domes with the usual openings for light and smoke; the domes are constructed of concentric and gradually converging courses of stone. The walls are relieved here and there with niches.

Archaeological material from the earliest Georgian settlements consists of implements of obsidian, stone, bone and pottery. Pottery was already widely used at this early stage; the forms are archaic and simple, but occasionally very expressive. A more original form of ceramic ware characterizes the culture of the Copper Age in Transcaucasia. Terracotta vessels of varying dimensions served as pots or broad, shallow jugs. Most have handles attached. The surface of the vessels is a shiny black, and many are already decorated with complicated geometric patterns. Older vessels, found in settlements like Amiranis-gora, are decorated with bands, volutes and circles. Many cult statuettes depicting human or animal forms (bulls, rams, horses and birds) have survived. Their extremely simple form is typical of the ceramic sculpture of that epoch.

By the 2nd millennium BC the Transcaucasian tribes, especially the mountain-dwellers, had amassed property in the form of livestock and pasturage. Consequently they became the target of raiding marauders, and had to defend themselves continually against surprise attacks. This new factor in their lives is reflected in the character of the settlements, which increasingly take on features associated with fortifications, being surrounded initially by a ditch and subsequently by defensive walls.

Other structures surviving from this period are built of vast megalithic blocks—dolmens, menhirs and cromlechs. They must have been used in religious rites or for burial purposes.

There are also some strange megalithic monuments known as *vishapi* and *vishapoids*.

These are stone stelae in the form of fish, found in the high mountain pasture areas, and appear to have had some connection with the irrigation systems.

Reference has already been made to the high standards attained in metalworking at an early period. By the 3rd millennium BC the Caucasian region had already become one of the most important centres of metalworking, and in Georgia and indeed the whole of Transcaucasia the art continued to develop intensively throughout the 2nd millennium.

Nearly two hundred Bronze Age *kurgans* (tumuli) have been excavated during the past few decades in Trialeti (Kvemo-Kartli). The large tumuli, on average about 6 metres high, occupy an area of up to 100 square metres each. The burial chambers are divided up by wooden props, which help to support the roof timbers laid across the top of the walls. The size of the graves, their rich contents (p. 34) and the complicated funerary rituals (chariots with the charred remains of the deceased were found in a number of graves) demonstrate the wealth and power of the buried warriors and tribal chieftains, who constituted an aristocracy ruling over the fate of a tribal community.

The hallmark of this period was a great cultural upsurge in the lives of the inhabitants of this region. At the end of the 2nd millennium and the beginning of the 1st millennium BC, Bronze Age culture reached the peak of its development. The monuments of the Middle and Late Bronze Age are so many in number and so individual in form that they deserve an important place in the history of cultural development. The first iron implements appeared at this time. The abundance of copper-ore deposits in the southern Caucasus was

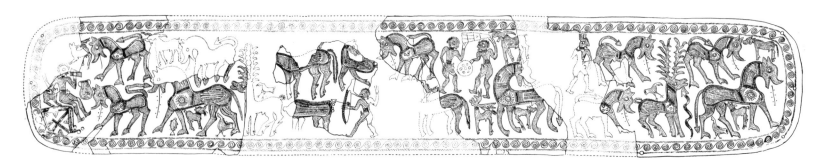

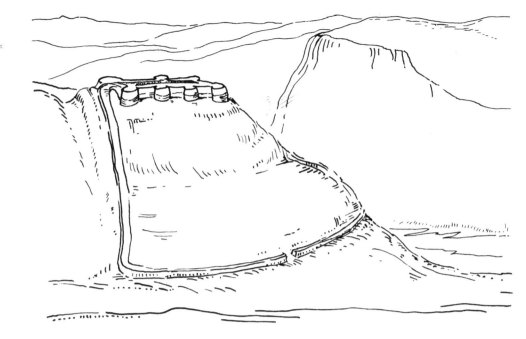

widely exploited by the local tribes, and bronze, silver and gold were also known to the Georgians, who manufactured axes, bodkins, daggers, blades and lances, clubs, pendants and many other things.

A huge quantity of metal and earthenware vessels with intricate decoration has been found in Trialeti. All these articles indicate that during the 2nd millennium BC the minor arts flourished in a variety of forms in East Georgia, and that diverse techniques such as smelting, forging, soldering, embossing and stamping were employed. The artistic working of metal at this period was the product of a high level of technical skill. The shapes of the craftsmen's tools themselves are most attractive. Of the articles found in the Trialeti tumuli, one gold and one silver goblet and a small bucket with relief portrayals of ritual scenes deserve special mention.

Also from this period are the unusual belts, long and broad and made from a single sheet of bronze, which were worn by the warriors. Their surface is decorated with engraved patterns, scenes of hunting or ritual sacrifice, and mythological figures.

In the field of pottery, vessels glazed in various colours now appeared. Of particular interest are the groups of statuettes consisting of ten highly stylized figures, made in honour of the fertility goddess.

Jewellery is found in far greater variety than in the earlier periods, and is more delicate in form and more carefully executed. The contents of the graves is an immediate pointer to the existence of different social levels within society.

Archaeological evidence and information from written sources such as Graeco-Roman and ancient Georgian records indicate that town-dwelling began in Georgia around the 8th–7th century BC. Along the trade route from India that led through the lowlands of the Kura and Rioni valleys to the Black Sea and further westwards, towns grew up and developed as centres of trade and manufacture —towns such as Rustavi, Mtskheta, Kaspi, Gori, Uplis-tsikhe, Urbnisi, Shorapani, Kutaisi, Vard-tsikhe and Poti. Less important townships—Tskhinvali, Akhalkalaki—were founded in the gorges that led into these river lowlands.

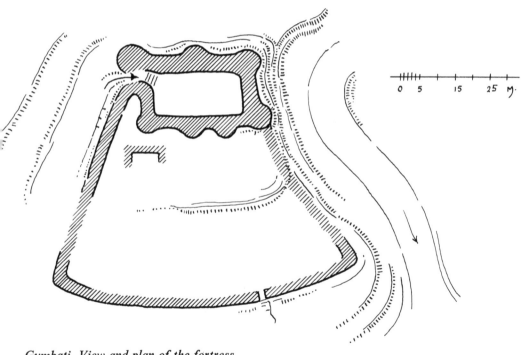

Gumbati. View and plan of the fortress, dating from the 2nd–1st millennium BC.

Bronze belt from Chabarukhi, late 2nd or early 1st millennium BC.

15

Urartian inscriptions dating from the 8th or the 7th century BC refer to fortified settlements in the Transcaucasian region. They were built on hilltops, in places protected by rivers, or at the entrances to narrow ravines. The walls of these fortresses were built without mortar, the lower part of stone and the upper of unbaked brick. Very large stones were used for this purpose, their sides measuring from 1.5 to 3 metres. The walls were between 3 and 5 metres thick and were strengthened at the corners and in the middle.

In Georgia this 'fortress' type of settlement occurred mainly in the Kvemo-Kartli territory, leading examples being Beshtasheni, Lodovani, Gumbati, Tedzi (Rekha) and Ashkala. It consisted of two parts: an upper section encircled by massive walls, and a larger lower area, often occupying the slope of the hill, likewise surrounded by walls. Each part had its own entrances. These fortresses with their massive walls must have been very imposing. Xenophon describes some further settlements in West Georgia; these were also built on hills, he tells us, and surrounded by moats and palisades.

It was inevitable that the Georgian population, which was highly advanced in economic and cultural terms, should progress to the next stage of social development at a comparatively early period, and indeed during the 6th and 5th centuries BC a class system grew up and two political states emerged, the oldest in the Caucasus: Kartli or Iberia in the east and Colchis or Egrisi in the west. Their growth was promoted by the decline and fall of the mighty state of Urartu, which for a long time had dominated vast areas of Caucasia; the Georgians participated in its overthrow, just as they did later in the destruction of the Persian empire by Alexander the Great. The Iberian kingdom, later known as Kartli, covered the major part of present-day East Georgia as well as some of the territory of West Georgia. It possessed a developed agriculture and various crafts and manufacturing industries.

The state of the Colchians, which comprised a substantial territory along the south-eastern shores of the Black Sea as well as areas in the interior of West Georgia, is mentioned in works by the Greek writers of Classical antiquity. The legends associated with Colchis were popular themes in literature. The first accounts of the Georgian-Caucasian region occur in Greek writings such as Homer's epic works, the *Iliad* and the *Odyssey*. Archaeological finds and later written accounts confirm that the Greek myths of the 8th and 7th centuries BC about the Golden Fleece of King Aietes of Colchis—the fabulous treasure sought by the Argonauts—give an accurate indication of conditions in the country at that time. Herodotus, Hippocrates, Aristotle, Xenophon and Vitruvius all refer to Colchis. Here, as in Iberia, agriculture and various forms of craft production were very advanced.

The high level of economic development in Colchis, its favourable geographical position and its natural riches increasingly attracted the attention of the Greeks. In the 6th and 5th centuries BC the Greeks began to set up trading stations such as Phasis (present-day Poti), Dioscurias, Pitiunt (Pitsunda or Bichvinta), Trapezous (Trebizond) and Gvineos (Ochemchire) along the Georgian Black Sea coast, not far from the old-established agricultural and manufacturing centres which lay along the trade routes and close to good harbours.

The new Greek settlements played an important role in the evolution of the coastal towns. In Colchis, however, the Greeks were unable to gain complete supremacy, as they had along the north and south coasts of the Black Sea, since independent traditions were very firmly rooted among the ancient population. The influence and power of the indigenous element were responsible for the special character of the socio-economic structure, and also for the individual quality of the culture. In Dioscurias and other towns the local manufacturers and farmers occupied the leading positions, and they also supplied the bulk of the army.

These Georgian towns, which were advantageously sited in both strategic and economic terms, were securely fortified and well equipped. The basic layout was derived from deeply rooted traditions of fortification that had been observed for centuries. There were two major parts: the citadel on the higher ground, encircled by a wall, and the town proper, built for the most part on terraces around the slopes of the hill, and likewise protected by a wall.

Towns which lay at the confluence of two rivers, where the water acted as a natural defence on two sides, only needed defences for the third side which was more easily accessible.

The town walls, between 2.5 and 3 metres thick and further strengthened by buttresses, were built up of dressed rectangular blocks, tightly wedged together without the use of mortar. The upper part of the walls was faced on both sides with unfired bricks with a reinforcing layer of wooden piles between them to give additional strength and stability against earthquakes and the blows of battering rams. These construction methods were in the main peculiar to the region, but they include some features that are similar to those employed in other Near Eastern countries, for instance Tel-Halaf and Urartu.

One of the cities of antiquity was Uplistsikhe (pp. 28–30), the administrative and political centre of Kartli, built over several centuries of the 1st millennium BC. It was sited on a mountainside, hewn entirely out of the rock, surrounded by moats and protected on the south side by the river Kura. The original layout has been preserved, and many domestic dwellings and several public buildings survive.

Of the townships which grew up not on the Black Sea coast but in the interior of Egrisi, the most important were Vani, Nakalakevi (the Archaeopolis of antiquity), Skanda and Shorapani. Remains of their city walls and other installations still exist today. These were built of square-hewn blocks, dovetailed by means of dowels and cramps. The towns that had nothing whatever to do with Greek colonization, like those in Iberia, were built on high ground with a complex relief.

Mtskheta (pp. 31–2), which was a small settlement in the Bronze Age, became the capital of Kartli in the Hellenistic period, and retained this status until Tbilisi took over the function in the 5th century AD. Mtskheta was the seat of the Georgian kings and their families, and of the dignitaries who were next in command—the *eristavis* ('heads of the people' or 'dukes') and the *pitiakhshes* (an Iranian title approximating to 'satrap').

The main citadel of Armazis-tsikhe—the acropolis of the capital—stood on the right bank of the river Kura, on the slopes and summit of Mount Bagineti. In the Bagineti locality numerous remains of large buildings have been found, including ruins of the 'pillared hall' from the 4th–3rd century BC. This rectangular hall, covering an area of 185 square metres, had the lower walls built of cleanly hewn, squared stone blocks, while the upper parts were of unbaked bricks. The thickness of the walls varied from 145 to 170 centimetres. Inside, a row of columns ran down the middle of the building, made of wood but having carved stone bases and decorated stone capitals of simple section. The inner surface of the walls was plastered.

An additional defence ring was constructed in Armazis-tsikhe in the 1st century BC. The new walls were as much as 4 metres thick in places. The masonry of the lower parts consisted of exceptionally well squared blocks, dovetailed together with the aid of wooden pegs. On the outer face only the edges of the blocks were carefully cut.

Greek and Roman writers have left accounts of Armazis-tsikhe. Dio Cassius, for example, mentions the destruction of the fortress in 65 BC by Pompey, the Roman general. Later, however, during the 1st and 2nd centuries AD, the town grew and developed once again.

In Mtskheta, at the foot of a steep, rocky incline, a tomb has survived which has been dated to about the 1st century AD. It measures 2.4×1.8 metres, with a height of 1.9 metres. The entrance, at the eastern end, is adorned with a moulded frame. The walls are built of large, squared, smoothly aligned slabs of stone, and the barrel vaulting over the grave is likewise very precisely executed. The interior of the walls is covered with plaster, and the floor with flagstones. The east façade terminates in a gable with a neat, narrow cornice. The roof consists of large, flat, ribbed tiles, which are commonly found in Mtskheta.

In another part of the city can be seen the ruins of the residence of the *eristavis,* dating back to the 2nd–3rd century AD; these include the palace itself, a bath-house and a number of other buildings. The palace was sacked and burned to the ground, and all that remains of it is a small part of the lower courses of the walling and a few architectural details. The

bath-house is far better preserved, and its arrangement is typical of late antiquity. It consisted of several rooms and had a pool with niches, supplied with hot and cold water from a system of earthenware pipes. The floor rested on brick pillars, and the chambers between them were filled with hot air from the heating installations. This system of heating by hypocausts is familiar from several examples in Rome and the Roman provinces.

Various branches of the arts reached an advanced level of development at Mtskheta, and there were craftsmen's quarters within the town itself and in the surrounding districts. The town had its own architect, and a master painter.

In West Georgia, the town of Vani has recently yielded archaeological material of exceptional interest. From the 7th to the 1st century BC, the place pulsated with vigorous life; in the 1st century BC it was burned to the ground and totally destroyed by enemy hand.

High up on a hill, where the local aristocracy resided, a series of architecturally remarkable buildings and a vast quantity of gold, silver, bronze and ceramic articles have been discovered. This material from the 5th–4th century BC proves that at this time Vani was one of the most important political and economic centres of Colchis.

Between the 3rd and the 1st centuries BC—the second phase of the history of Vani—the town was fortified with massive walls. The statue of the patron goddess of the city probably stood before the city gate (p. 32). On the inside, a temple with a stone altar adjoined the gate. Hellenistic influence is tightly interwoven with indigenous religious and architectural traditions in this complex.

A stepped altar has survived on the hilltop, where sacrifices were presumably carried out. On the central terrace are the remains of a round temple, and there was also a rectangular temple not far from the entrance gate. Ruins of other buildings with interesting architectural details are also scattered about the site.

Only a part of the ancient settlement of Vani has been excavated so far. The archaeological findings show that, between the 6th and the 4th centuries BC, an autonomous region had developed within Colchian territory which had its political centre in Vani, a hundred kilo-

metres from the Black Sea and therefore far away from Phasis and the other coastal towns. It has been suggested that Vani is identical with the ancient temple city of Leukothea recorded by Strabo. There are others who equate Vani with the ancient Colchian capital, Aea, or with the town of Surius described by Pliny.

The excavations at Vani have provided scholars with the basis for a new and interesting theory in regard to the penetration of Hellenistic culture into Georgia. The Vani culture shares certain features with that of Iberia of the ancient period, and these arrived, not by way of the Colchian Black Sea coast, but from Asia Minor. They were brought in by the ancient Georgian Moshkian tribes (Meshkians), who had contacts both with the ancient oriental civilizations and with the Hellenistic world.

Iberia and Colchis were powerful states in the 5th and 4th centuries BC. They maintained economic and political links with the Greeks, with Achaemenid Iran, with the Seleucids and also with the rulers of Pontus.

As a result of a series of conquests and alliances during the last centuries before the birth of Christ, the Colchians and Iberians were exposed to the most diverse foreign influences, which clearly varied in intensity. At the beginning of the 3rd century BC Farnavazi succeeded in liberating Iberia from foreign domination, and he became king of Kartli. In 63 BC Pompey conquered the Colchians; Aristarkhus was made regent, and Colchis became a Roman province.

The overall outcome of Roman rule was the disintegration of what had once been a united territory into tribal principalities of no great significance. In spite of this the Georgian people fought persistently for their independence, and in the seventies of the 1st century AD Aniketus, a Colchian slave, organized a major uprising as a result of which Roman influence was considerably undermined.

During the 2nd century AD, in the reign of Farsman II, a contemporary of Hadrian and Antoninus Pius, the kingdom of Kartli expanded considerably, acquiring possessions in the south-west in particular which extended as far as the Black Sea coast. Rome tried by every means to uphold the alliance with Iberia. Farsman II visited Rome with his consort and a great retinue, and Antoninus Pius received him with great honour and acknowledged the newly extended frontiers of the kingdom. The Colchians, meanwhile, remained under Roman sovereignty.

In the 1st century AD new cities were built to replace the old towns of the coastal region and its vicinity. Whereas in the Hellenistic period the Colchian coastal towns had been centres of trade and manufacture, during the Roman supremacy their significance was predominantly strategic, with extensive harbour installations and strong fortifications. The emperor Justinian built the citadel of Petra (present-day Tsikhisdziri), and another of the centres of Roman sovereignty was the fortress of Absaros, now known as Gonio.

Dioscurias, destroyed by floods, and Sebastopolis, later built on the same site, were comparatively large and important towns. Timosthenes, the historian of the 2nd century AD, writes that three hundred tribes gathered at Dioscurias to trade, and that they all spoke different languages. In the 3rd century AD Sebastopolis was a comfortable fortified town, with thick city walls strengthened by buttresses; it had broad streets and many public buildings, of which only ruins, such as that of a bath-house, now remain.

Accounts of the town of Phasis create an impressive picture which shows it to have been an important Colchian centre not only for trade, but also for culture and religion. Themistios, the 4th-century Byzantine philosopher, records that a Colchian Academy existed not far from Phasis, and that many local people as well as visiting students from the eastern Roman empire attended this centre to obtain an education in philosophy and rhetoric.

Shukhuti. Fragment of a floor mosaic from the palace baths, 5th–6th century. The colours of the mosaic are white, grey and brown.

Bichvinta. Fragment of a floor mosaic from the church dating from the 5th–6th century. It shows birds grouped around a Fountain of Life, a goblet-like vessel with a pine cone emerging from it. In general character, the portrayal resembles Middle Eastern art of the Hellenistic period, but the use of local stone, certain stylistic details and the fact that mosaic fragments from this period have been found in West as well as East Georgia suggest the existence of indigenous mosaic workshops.
Georgian State Museum of Art.

Bichvinta. Plan of the church dating from the 5th–6th century.

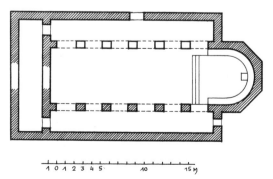

Not far from Phasis, at a place now known as Shukhuti, the remains of a bath-house with a mosaic floor have been excavated, together with remains of a dwelling. In the 4th century a villa stood here which apparently belonged to some long-established resident of the area, either a farmer or a merchant. Also in the Phasis area, at a place named Vashnari, an old town has been discovered with a basilica, a mausoleum and various other buildings. The town and citadel of Bichvinta (Pitiunt) were carefully planned, with diverse buildings arranged in streets around a square. Fragments of mosaic floors from the 5th and 6th centuries survive in some of the buildings. The streets were paved, and below the paving was a drainage system for the removal of rainwater and sewage. There was also a piped water supply.

The surviving architectural material in towns such as Sebastopolis, Bichvinta and Phasis indicates that in late antiquity the south-western part of Colchis was one of the most culturally advanced areas of Georgia. In the 4th century, however, these cities lost their former importance and dwindled into small fortified townships.

In Iberia, the capital city of Mtskheta towers above the rest in importance. These cities, employing slave labour, played a most important role in the socio-economic, political and cultural life of the land.

During the second half of the 1st millennium BC—the period of city foundation—craft production in this area received a fresh impetus. The open-work bronze buckles (p. 39) made between the 2nd century BC and the 3rd century AD have a distinctly national character. They represent the final stage of artistic metalworking in the pre-Christian era and the culmination of the ancient traditions of this art form. In the centre of the buckle is portrayed a fantastical creature representing the queen of the animals in the form of a stag, ibex or horse, accompanied by its acolytes (a bird, snake, bull or dog). These figures, closely linked with indigenous notions about the goddess of animals and fertility, at the same time show connections with the ideas and forms of the animal art of the steppes. The influence of Classical antiquity on Georgian art of this period was very strong, but long-established independent traditions likewise emerge emphatically. The bronze buckles display very forcibly a feeling for flexibility and linear expressiveness that is typical of Georgian art.

The arts of the goldsmith and the jeweller attained a very high standard even in early antiquity. Opulent pieces of jewellery worked in precious metals are indicative of varying levels of affluence among the populace, and of the clear predominance of the urban population and the ruling class.

Many examples of rich burial sites can be given: Sadzeguri (p. 35), Kazbegi, Tsintskaro, the necropolises at Mtskheta (pp. 36–8), Urbnisi, Ureki (p. 36), Kldeeti (p. 36), Vani (pp. 38, 40) and so on. The large collection of jewellery from Sadzeguri, known as the 'Akhalgori Treasure', includes outstanding pieces of metalwork from the 5th and 4th centuries BC such as gold and silver rings, earrings, torques, pendants and many others. All the main manufacturing processes—forging, embossing, stamping, soldering and granulation—are used here with the highest degree of skill, and certain elements adopted from Achaemenid art have been given a new and independent interpretation by the native artists. Items of jewellery found in the graves of the Vani settlement include golden earrings, and silver and gold diadems with pendants. In the centre of the diadems, fitting on the forehead, are thin, diamond-shaped plates decorated with animal figures and other designs; such pieces were a popular head ornament in Colchis. Fillets and earrings predominate among the products of the Colchian goldsmiths, and they include pieces in delicate filigree work displaying exquisite artistic taste. All these works are characterized by a firm stylistic unity; this is unquestionably the work of an indigenous artistic school.

Various branches of the minor arts evolved successfully along the Black Sea littoral and in the mountainous areas of Colchis (Kldeeti etc.). Military weapons, rings and earrings, bangles adorned with precious stones and portraits, silver bowls, beakers and dishes in delicate embossed work, pottery and glass products have all survived.

The material found on burial sites, particularly in the stone sarcophagi of the Iberian rulers at Armazis-khevi in Mtskheta, provides an impressive picture of Georgian art in ancient times. These objects, with their unity of style and diversity of form, provide evidence of advanced stylistic feeling and refined taste. They likewise testify to the artistic accomplishments of Georgian goldsmiths.

Many of the works in precious metal make their impact by the use of colour. This polychromy was first introduced into the art of the Georgian goldsmith during the 2nd millennium BC, and continued in use throughout antiquity. In the first centuries AD, after extensive effort and experimentation, the metalworkers succeeded in developing a decorative pictorial style which subsequently became very widespread. Surviving material also proves that schools of glyptic art existed in the major Colchian and Iberian cities, such as Mtskheta and Urbnisi, which preserved ancient native traditions regardless of foreign influences. Many pieces containing carved gems have come down to us, but perhaps the most interesting item is a finger-ring with a man's portrait, characteristically in profile, and bearing the inscription 'Asparukh—Pitiakhsh'. The gem in another ring has a double portrait of a man and a woman, and the Greek inscription reads 'Zevakh—my life. Karpak'. Zevakh lived a generation earlier than Asparukh the *pitiakhsh*. In all probability the gem was ordered by his wife, Karpak, after the death of her spouse, in his memory.

Three silver bowls with engravings inside deserve special attention. The first shows an eagle with a staff in its talons, the second a horse before a sacrificial altar with one of its forefeet slightly raised, and the third a stallion before a sacrificial altar. The two latter representations are connected with the indigenous cult of the sun deity Mithras.

The large quantity of material surviving, particularly from Mtskheta, shows to what extent rings, bangles, earrings, fibulas and chains of various materials were in use among the populace.

Coins appeared very early in Colchis: several types of silver coins minted here in the 6th century BC are among the oldest in the world. In technical and artistic quality they are in no way inferior to the best examples of coins from elsewhere dating from this period. They circulated mainly between the 4th and the 2nd centuries BC.

Imiris-gora. Remains of an ancient settlement, 5th–4th millennium BC. Site-plan of the eastern area of excavations, plan of a domestic dwelling, conjectural reconstruction of the house (after A. Javakhishvili).

Remains of a group of domestic dwellings, 5th–4th millennium BC.

Mtskheta, Armazis-khevi. Gem portrait of the pitiakhsh *Asparukh, from a gold signet-ring. 2nd–3rd century AD. S. Janashia Museum (State Museum of Georgia).*

Mtskheta, Armazis-khevi. Gem portrait of the pitiakhsh *Zevakh and his wife Karpak, from a gold ring. 2nd–3rd century AD. S. Janashia Museum (State Museum of Georgia).*

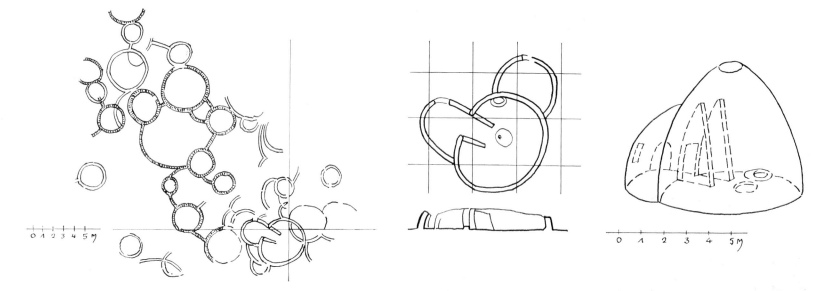

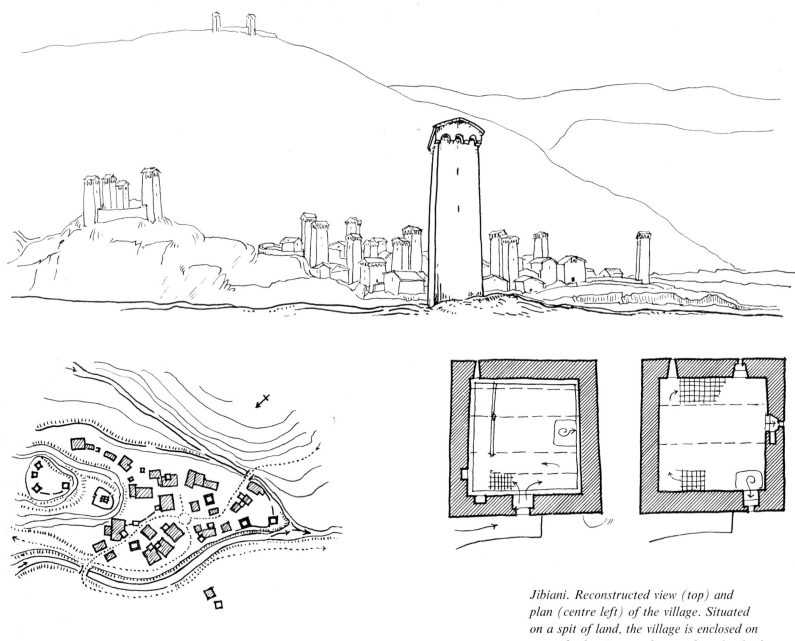

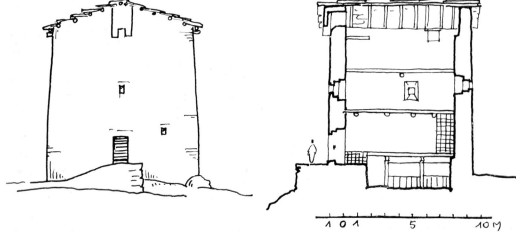

Jibiani. Reconstructed view (top) and plan (centre left) of the village. Situated on a spit of land, the village is enclosed on two sides by rivers and secured on the third by the lower fortress and a trench.

Dwelling of the tower type. Plan of the ground and first floors (centre right), elevation and section (bottom). The building has four storeys; the ground floor houses cattle and serves as winter living quarters for the occupants, while the upper levels are used for food storage and as living quarters during the summer months. Over the single door is a machicolation for defence purposes.

Ushguli. View of part of the Jibiani settlement.

Shatili. View of the village, consisting of tower houses. The fortified dwellings were designed solely for individual defence.

Ushguli. The Jibiani and Murkmeli settlements.

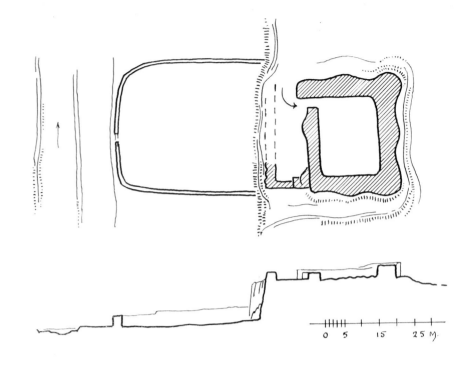

Nordevani. Fortified dwelling of the 2nd–1st millennium BC. Plan and section (right); ruins of the house and the enclosing wall (below).

Below: Pantiani. Entrance to a fortified dwelling from the 2nd–1st millennium BC.

Right: Tedzi (Rekha). Fortified dwelling of the 2nd–1st millennium BC. Site-plan and remains of megalithic masonry.

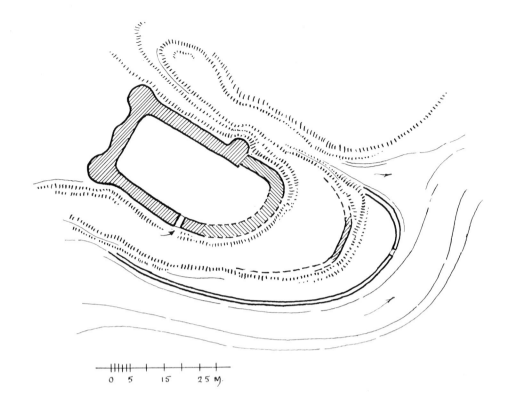

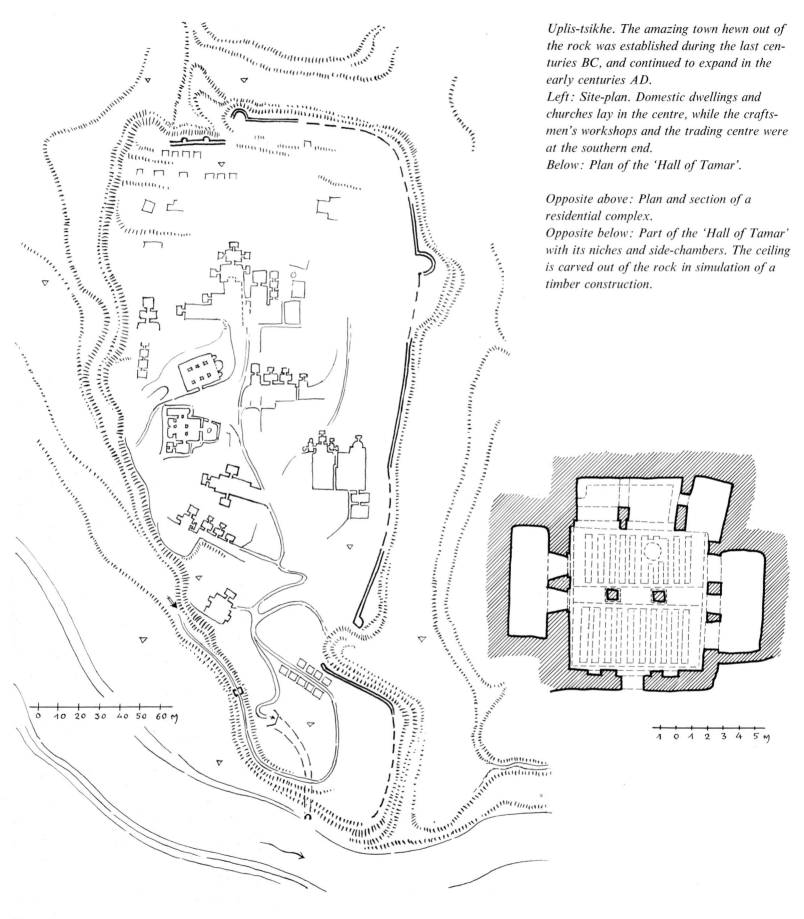

Uplis-tsikhe. The amazing town hewn out of the rock was established during the last centuries BC, and continued to expand in the early centuries AD.

Left: Site-plan. Domestic dwellings and churches lay in the centre, while the craftsmen's workshops and the trading centre were at the southern end.

Below: Plan of the 'Hall of Tamar'.

Opposite above: Plan and section of a residential complex.

Opposite below: Part of the 'Hall of Tamar' with its niches and side-chambers. The ceiling is carved out of the rock in simulation of a timber construction.

0 10 20 30 40 50 60 M

1 0 1 2 3 4 5 M

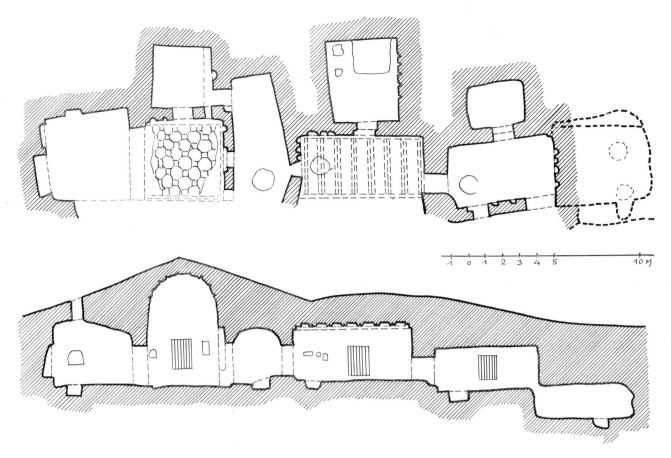

29

*Uplis-tsikhe. View of part of the cave-town
and the early medieval church.*

*Mtskheta, Armazis-tsikhe. Remains of the
ancient city wall on Mount Bagineti. Rising
high above the bank on the far side of the
river Kura is the Jvari church.*

*Mtskheta, Armazis-tsikhe.
Ruins of a pillared
hall of the 4th–3rd
century BC.*

*Vani. Remains
of the city gate dating
from the 3rd–1st
century BC.*

Khovlegora. Ram's head in clay from a heathen altar. 12th–10th century BC. S. Janashia Museum (State Museum of Georgia).

Natsargora. Ceramic vessels of the late Bronze Age. S. Janashia Museum (State Museum of Georgia).

Samadlo. Wine-jar with hunting and battle scenes and patterns in red slip. Height 180 centimetres. 4th–3rd century BC. S. Janashia Museum (State Museum of Georgia).

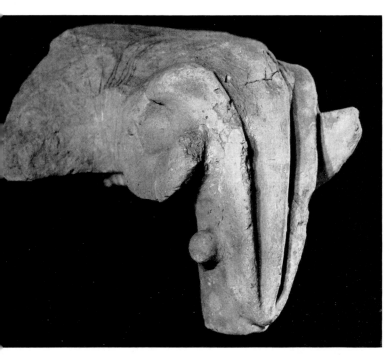

Trialeti. Golden necklet with inlaid plaques, and golden spiral earrings. Late Bronze Age. S. Janashia Museum (State Museum of Georgia).

Trialeti. Gold beaker with coloured stones and filigree work. Silver beaker with cult scenes. Around 1500 BC. S. Janashia Museum (State Museum of Georgia).

Sadzeguri. Jewellery from the Akhalgori Treasure. Golden ear pendants and neck ornaments from a burial find. The uniformity of style and the masterly skill of the workmanship are characteristic. 6th–5th century BC.

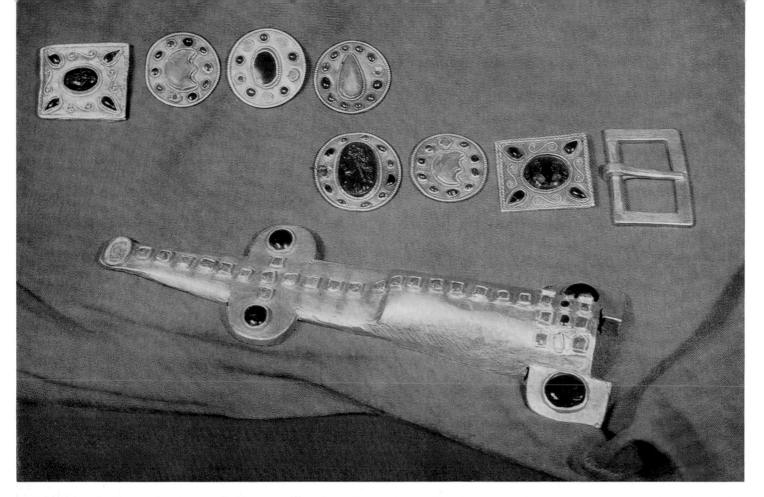

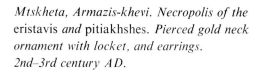

Mtskheta, Armazis-khevi. Necropolis of the eristavis *and* pitiakhshes *of Kartli, 2nd–4th centuries AD. Treasure from the grave of the pitiakhsh Asparukh. Golden dagger sheath, belt buckle and belt plaques with gems and coloured stones.*

Kldeeti. Items of gold jewellery with birds, coloured stones and granulation; earrings and clasp. 2nd century AD.
Ureki. Gold pendant and ring. 3rd–4th century AD.

Mtskheta, Armazis-khevi. Necropolis of the eristavis *and* pitiakhshes. *Pierced gold neck ornament with locket, and earrings. 2nd–3rd century AD.*

Mtskheta, Armazis-khevi. Necropolis of the eristavis *and* pitiakhshes. *Gold necklace with a small jar and scent bottle. Decorating the lid of the jar is an amethyst cut in the shape of a ram's head. 2nd–3rd century AD.*

S. Janashia Museum (State Museum of Georgia).

37

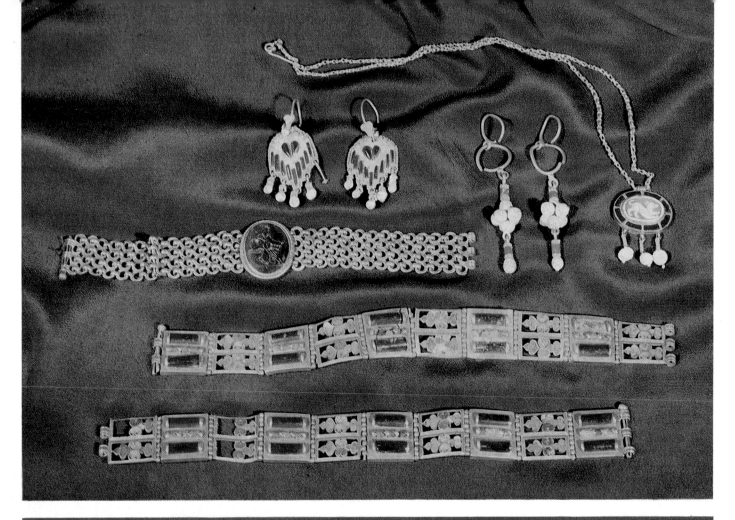

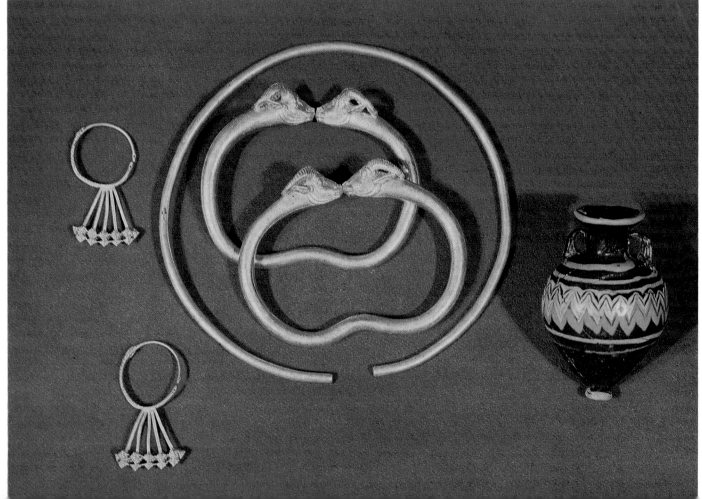

Mtskheta, Armazis-khevi. Necropolis of the eristavis and pitiakhshes. Necklace with gold pendant and agate cameo. Gold earrings. Gold bracelet with jade cameo of Pallas Athene. Two polychrome bracelets in hinged sections. 2nd–4th century AD.

Vani. Gold earrings. Cast gold necklet and bangles with animal heads. Amphora of 'Phoenician glass'. 5th century BC.

S. Janashia Museum (State Museum of Georgia).

Gebi. Bronze buckle in open work. Between 1st century BC and 1st century AD.

Manglisi. Pierced bronze buckle. Between 2nd century BC and 3rd century AD. S. Janashia Museum (State Museum of Georgia).

Vani. Part of a diadem: small gold plate decorated with animals and pendant 5th–4th century BC.

Vani. Gold pendant with cloisonné enamelling. 5th century BC.

S. Janashia Museum (State Museum of Georgia).

ART IN THE MIDDLE AGES (5th–18th centuries)
Secular buildings
Towns — fortresses — palaces

In many respects the 4th century AD represents an important turning-point in the history of Georgia and neighbouring lands connected with her. Indeed, this applies throughout the vast Mediterranean empire, for the fall of the ancient Roman slave-owning society was linked with the rise of the eastern Roman empire, later to become the feudal Christian Byzantium.

The characteristics of feudalism also began to appear in Georgia in the 4th century, but the new social order was not fully established until the 6th century.

This development went hand in hand with the spread of Christianity throughout the area, and was naturally also influenced by the political situation prevailing in the two major regions of Georgia. Kartli adopted Christianity as the state religion in the third decade of the 4th century, but found that the alignment with Rome achieved in this way did not protect the country against attack from the Sassanid Persians.

Some fair-sized Christian communities led by bishops already existed in West Georgia in the 4th century, notably at Bichvinta (Pitsunda) and Trapezous (Trebizond). Roman rule was by this time merely nominal. The Lazis were gaining increasing power over the other local principalities, a development reflected in the common use of the name Lazica (Egrisi in local usage) for the western region. Although Christianity appeared here earlier than in Kartli, it was only in the 6th century that the ruler Tsate elevated it to the status of official religion. The new religion became a prop for the central power in the continuing development of feudalism. Its spread through-

out a number of lands of the Near East and the Caucasus highlights the social situation in these countries.

By adopting Christianity, Georgia was linking her culture with that of Europe for a long time to come. Certain phenomena arising from this common background now appeared simultaneously in Georgian and European art, and these are informative as to the level of development and standards of achievement of Georgian religious art.

The spread of the new Christian ideology brought in its wake the destruction of many heathen monuments. At the same time, however, the complicated process of assimilation of elements of the old religion into the new was also taking place.

There are no examples of Georgian writing from before the 5th century AD, but these are already so mature in character that there can be no doubt as to the existence of precursors. However, the Georgian language itself could not be conveyed through the medium of these precursors—namely Greek and a local form of Semitic Aramaic writing. The latter is known as the Armazi script, from the bilingual tombstone of Princess Serapita found at Mtskheta-Armazi.

Archaeological excavations over the last decades have brought to light many examples of writing of the pre-Christian era in Georgian history, inscribed both on stone and on articles of metalwork. These inscriptions date mainly from the period between the 1st and the 4th centuries AD. The actual language of the texts written in the Armazi form of Aramaic is considered to be Middle Iranian. Thus the Georgian language itself was first written down probably in an original Georgian script after the country adopted Christianity.

Georgian script came under Greek influence. From the 5th century we have the lapidary or capital lettering, 'Asomtavruli' in Georgian, and from about AD 900 the minuscule lettering known as 'Nuskhuri' was used for the body of the text. The later secular 'Mkhedruli' script was, and is today, written exclusively with minuscules, and this was the writing used by the 'knights'—i.e. laymen—from the 11th century onwards.

Excellent examples of inscriptions from the early 5th century have been preserved in the Georgian monastery founded in Palestine in about AD 430 by Peter the Iberian. Another, longer inscription on the architrave of the Sion church at Bolnisi (p. 69) has been dated to the late 5th century. From this time onwards we have a large number of examples of the two, and later the three, scripts, carved in stone, metal or wood or written on parchment. The immense progress made by the Georgian people between the 5th and the 7th centuries in the development of cultural life in their country presupposes the existence at that time of educational establishments and scriptoria. From the 9th century onwards, there are direct written references to their existence. The Georgian school founded in the monastery of Bachkovo in Bulgaria by Ioane Petritsi became very famous in the 12th century.

From the earliest Christian times Georgia produced great preachers, many of whom were active outside their own country. They created a specialized literature in Greek and Georgian, and compiled treatises on the general issues of Christian philosophy. The 5th-century Church leader Peter of Iberia (born Prince Murvanos, later Bishop of Mayuma) is said to be the author of the philosophical treatises called 'Corpus areopagiticum', in which the foundations of Christian medieval philosophy are expounded. About the 6th century a series of Georgian monasteries were established at Jerusalem, Antioch, Edesa and so on.

From time to time monks would come to Georgia from these monasteries and settle in some remote region. It was in this way that David, for example, one of the so-called 'Syrian Fathers', began a hermit's life in a cave in the desert of Gareja. Another, Shio, lived deep in the mountainous country on the left bank of the river Kura, in the heart of virgin forest. Ioane settled on mount Zedazeni, on the site of an overthrown heathen idol. These men introduced into Georgia the strict, ascetic way of life that was characteristic of the Syrian monks.

Simeon of Antioch, the famous pillar-saint, also had an influence in Georgia; the edifice at Katskhi (pp. 70–71) is clearly connected with it. This structure consists of two churches built on a rock pinnacle 40 metres high, and it was used to accommodate hermits in the 5th–6th century, as a place of ascetic self-mortification. A similar rock pillar has survived in a gorge of the river Oltisis-tskali. The

Palestine. Mosaic inscription in the Georgian monastery near Bir-el-Kutt, in the Wilderness of Judaea not far from Bethlehem. The floor mosaic consists of a prayer in Asomtavruli, naming the Abbot Antoni and the mosaic artist Josia. (Drawing based on a photograph by P. Virgilio Corbo.)

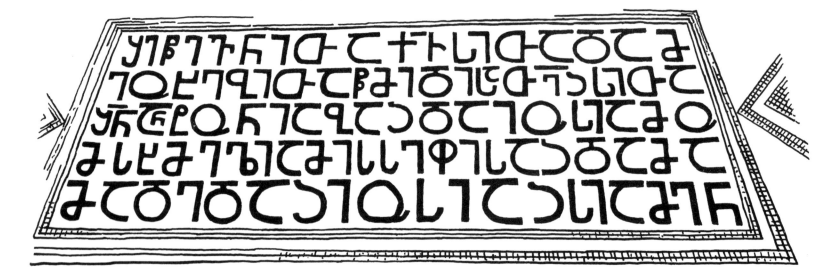

1	2	3
Ⴀ	ა	a
Ⴁ	ბ	b
Ⴂ	გ	g
Ⴃ	დ	d
Ⴄ	ე	e
Ⴅ	ვ	v
Ⴆ	ზ	z
Ⴡ	ჱ	ē
Ⴇ	თ	t
Ⴈ	ი	i
Ⴉ	კ	ķ
Ⴊ	ლ	l
Ⴋ	მ	m
Ⴌ	ნ	n
Ⴢ	ჲ	j
Ⴍ	ო	o
Ⴎ	პ	p̣
Ⴏ	ჟ	ž
Ⴐ	რ	r
Ⴑ	ს	s
Ⴒ	ტ	ț
Ⴣ	ჳ	y
Ⴓ	უ	u
Ⴔ	ფ	p
Ⴕ	ქ	k
Ⴖ	ღ	γ
Ⴗ	ყ	q
Ⴘ	შ	š
Ⴙ	ჩ	č
Ⴚ	ც	c
Ⴛ	ძ	ʒ
Ⴜ	წ	c
Ⴝ	ჭ	č̣
Ⴞ	ხ	x
Ⴤ	ჴ	q
Ⴟ	ჯ	ǯ
Ⴠ	ჰ	h
Ⴥ	ჵ	ω

Georgian characters:
1 Georgian capital lettering, 5th century AD.
2 Modern Georgian print.
3 International transcription.

practices of the pillar-saints still continued in Georgia at the height of the Middle Ages, but by that time, as will be explained in more detail later, they had acquired a totally different character. The monasteries founded in the early Christian period continued to develop and expand, gradually growing into powerful socio-political and cultural centres.

At the end of the 5th century Kartli, under the leadership of Vakhtang Gorgaslani, was able to shake off Sassanid domination for a short while. The region gained in economic and political strength, with a corresponding increase in the need for a solid secular and religious administration. Gradually the Georgian church strengthened its internal organization, emancipating itself from the influence of the patriarchate of Antioch to acquire full independence.

After years of fighting to repress the influence of their rival Byzantium, the Persians by the late 6th century were so weakened that they neglected their supervision of Georgia. In the second half of the century a feudal uprising took place in Kartli, led by the *eristavi* Gurgen; as a result of this upheaval, the aristocracy of Kartli installed Guaram as *eristavi*. The effect of these changes was to create a supreme sovereign power based on the feudal system. In the eighties of the 6th century, this new state further strengthened its independent position by minting its own coins.

In the religious field, the policies of the new state were mainly directed towards the fight against the fire-worshippers. In this it made common cause not only with Armenia, but also with Byzantium, which in turn resulted in the conferring of Byzantine titles on Georgian rulers.

These political and religious developments gave rise to a great expansion of building activity in both the religious and the secular spheres, which brought with it a flowering of many branches of the arts.

TOWNS

With the development of feudalism in Georgia, a number of new towns developed, while the ancient ones changed their character.

The towns of the early Middle Ages (4th–10th centuries), such as Tbilisi, Ujarma, Kutaisi, Tsunda, Khornabuji, Samshvilde, Rustavi, Dmanisi, Artanuji and Petra (Tsikhisdziri), usually grew up in places that were politically and economically important, but their actual size was fairly limited.

The basic layout of these townships, with the citadel on an elevated site and the town itself below, dates from very early times. It is related to the fortified settlements of Kartli in the era pre-dating social stratification, which were discussed in the previous chapter. Although these oldest settlements were, by their nature, neither fortresses nor towns, nevertheless the principle of their structure, oriented towards defence and tested over the centuries, was widely adopted and further developed in accordance with the requirements of each particular time and place.

Like its predecessors, the town of the Middle Ages was characterized by the choice of an inaccessible, strategically advantageous site. Frequently this would be a spit of land washed on two sides by a river. The city was fortified with walls of stone and unbaked brick and surrounded by ditches. A tunnel, often camouflaged, led down to the river for the purpose of fetching water; there were also public baths. Trade and crafts were concentrated in their respective districts outside the walls, but bondsmen artisans were compelled to live within the town boundaries. Markets sprang up near the walls, either inside or outside the town, and outside the walls were the suburbs and gardens.

The churches rising up between the low houses made a significant contribution to the overall effect. In Mtskheta there was the majestic church of Sveti-tskhoveli, in Kutaisi the cathedral of Bagrat, and in Tbilisi the Sion cathedral and the Metekhi church.

Of course, the diverse geographic locations of these towns, as well as their varying historical development, gave to each its individual character. A more detailed look at a number of interesting and characteristic examples will fill out the picture.

Tbilisi. Conjectural reconstruction of the town as it was when the capital was established here (5th century AD). The citadel was prominently sited on a ridge of land between two rivers, the Kura and the Taboris-tskali. Walls led down from the citadel to the banks of the river Kura, and the area they enclosed was called Kala. The older settlement of Tbilisi was situated on the far side of the Taboris-tskali, in the neighbourhood of the hot sulphur springs. West of Kala lay the Kala plain. On this side of the river Kura, which was spanned by a bridge, was Isani, site of the royal palace, an area of the city which was to expand considerably in later years.

Ujarma (p. 51), a fortress town from the 5th and 6th centuries, survives largely in its original form, providing a fine example of early medieval urban architecture in Georgia. The citadel, rectangular in plan and fortified with walls and towers, occupies a long, narrow hilltop. At its eastern end can be seen the remains of a three-storey palace, and a church which was rebuilt at a later date. Massive walls run from the citadel down the slopes to the river Iori, forming an outer fortification in the shape of a square; nearby stands a separate tower. The walls are built of small stones of uniform size laid in regular horizontal courses, and town walls and citadel alike were further fortified by rectangular towers with no openings on the outer face. On the town side only, the towers had horseshoe-shaped doors and windows. A steep tunnel leads out of the town down to the river. The plan of Ujarma is compact and unified in its artistic conception.

According to the accounts of a medieval chronicler, Ujarma was for a time the residence of Vakhtang Gorgaslani, and in the 12th century Giorgi III set up his treasury here.

Several brick buildings, mainly of a subsidiary nature, have survived from the late medieval period. Archaeological excavation of the town will provide the missing details of the hitherto incomplete picture.

Ancient Tbilisi was built on either side of the river Kura. To the south is an arm of the mountain range enclosing the Kala lowland, while on the north the Isani plateau rises up over the river bank. It is as if the river, forcing its way through, had stopped the two in their headlong flight towards each other. Along the banks of the Taboris-tskali, a small river that joins the Kura at this point, hot sulphur springs gush out of the earth. To this day the story is still told of a pheasant, shot during one of Vakhtang Gorgaslani's hunts, which is supposed to have fallen into the hot springs and been completely cooked. This fortuitous discovery is said to have prompted the king's desire to shift the capital from Mtskheta to Tbilisi. Archaeological findings, however, have established that this ideal location had in fact attracted settlers as early as the 5th or 4th millennium BC, and that it has been inhabited continually ever since that date. The oldest settlement was located right by the springs, on a naturally protected site which in antiquity was called Tbilisi (*tbili* in Georgian means 'warm') and which subsequently became known as the 'old town'.

The meagre surviving remains of the walls and of a tower, dating from the 5th century, are enough to show that the construction method was similar to that used at Ujarma.

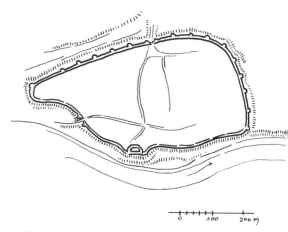

Urbnisi. Remains of the township of the 5th–7th centuries.
Above: Site-plan of the settlement.
Opposite, top to bottom: Plan of the citadel; plan of a tower in the city wall; section of the tower; schematic reconstruction (after P. Zakaraia).

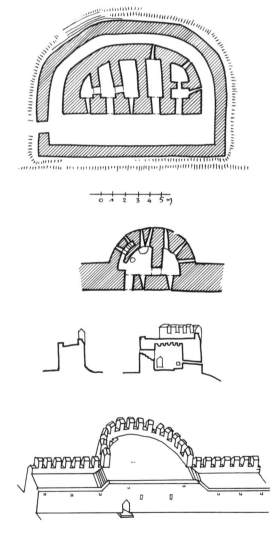

0 1 2 3 4 5 m

Tbilisi's citadel stands in the area known as Kala, and the walls ran from here down to the Kura. The town gate must have been situated in the vicinity of the bridge, near the later church of Metekhi. The crossing of the bridge was controlled from nearby watch-towers. In the 8th and 9th centuries a new sector, Isani, was added to the town, and the fortification system was extended with a double wall and a ditch. Tbilisi continued to expand, particularly in the 12th century, after David the Builder had driven the Arabs out of the town in 1122 and 'assured his descendants of their entitlement to their property for all time'. The royal residence, which during the early feudal period had been situated in Kala, was now moved to Isani. In Isani was the royal palace where Queen Tamar married David Soslani, and in the 13th century Demetre 'the Self-Sacrificer' erected the domed church of Metekhi on the Isani promontory and 'furnished it with great splendour'.

From the day when it became the capital until the 19th century, Tbilisi did not undergo any significant social change; in its everyday life, trade and industries it followed the pattern of a medieval feudal town. The development and growth of Tbilisi were not the result of any plan, and because of this the town, its various quarters connected by narrow, winding streets and squares, never had the effect of an artistic entity. It was a product of the sustained activity of many generations of builders, and as such it illustrates the traditions of Georgian architecture as affected by changing social and economic conditions.

We pass now to the ancient capital of West Georgia, Kutaisi. Fragments of walls surviving in the area known as Gora ('the mountain') or Ukimerioni make a reconstruction of the ancient town possible. Two walls led down from the citadel on Gora to the river, but they did not meet there; the river formed a natural boundary along this side. The walls protected the access to the bridge and controlled the road leading to Svaneti.

At the lower end of the town, a stone bridge had been built across the river Rioni. On the far side of the river lay the market, the artisans' districts, the caravanserais and the warehouses. By the bridge, on the left bank, were quays for merchant ships 'following a great trade route'. The town walls, built of cobblestones set in regular horizontal courses, are not laid out on a geometric plan, as at Ujarma, but follow the lie of the terrain. The older part of the town, to the west of the citadel, evidently dates from the 5th and 6th centuries. It is surrounded by its own wall, which has rectangular towers.

In the 8th century, when the Arabs had conquered Tbilisi and the capital had been removed to Kutaisi, King Archil, who had established and entrenched himself there, began extensive building projects. Kutaisi remained the capital until the 12th century, when David the Builder liberated Tbilisi, and during this period the town was appreciably extended by the addition of new fortified areas. In the late 10th and early 11th centuries the Bagrat cathedral, built in the citadel, became the most outstanding feature of the city.

In the late Middle Ages, the administrative centre was shifted to the left bank of the river Rioni, to the so-called 'lower town' by the bridge. This 'lower town' was likewise enclosed by a wall with buttresses on which artillery pieces were sited. The palace, with its wall-painting depicting battle scenes, stood here; there were also six churches and a tilt-yard.

The town of Urbnisi existed long before the 1st century AD, and unlike the majority of pre-Christian Georgian cities it continued to expand and develop in medieval times. It lay on flat ground on the high bank of the river Kura, in a commanding position with a sheer drop to the river below. The town was surrounded by a high wall with towers placed at regular intervals, and later a broad ditch was dug outside the wall. Archaeological excavations have uncovered a large number of residential and subsidiary buildings. As in other towns, the dominating architectural feature is the church, which here dates from the 5th–6th century.

It has been established that a great upsurge of building activity took place in Georgia during the 12th century; one of its products was the complex of rock-dwellings at Vardzia (pp. 200–201). Here, in a massive rock face rising above the river Kura, are caves arranged on several levels and extending over some 500 metres.

In the second half of the 12th century the Turkish sultanate, which bordered on south-western Georgia, attempted to annex Georgian territory. This prompted King Giorgi III to create a stronghold in this part of the country, and he chose to make it in the form of a cave complex. The work was carried out according to a plan and in a uniform style. So far 550 dwellings have been found, together with the remains of a water conduit 3.5 kilometres long. The majority of the caves were used for accommodation, but there are also churches, a bell-tower, a refectory, a wine cellar, a 'refuge room' or shelter with secret passages, an assembly hall, 'Queen Tamar's Room', and others which remain unidentified.

The caves were hewn out one next to another and their individual porches or balconies connected by means of doors and passages, which created as it were a floor of apartments with its own roofed walkway. The entire complex consisted of these units arranged like the storeys of a block of flats. The different levels were connected by steep inner passages cut in the rock, and by hatches in the ceilings against which wooden ladders were propped. In order that the caves could be reached from the ground far below, steep tunnels and steps were cut through the rock, complete with doors which could be barred with beams.

Giorgi III was not able to complete the construction of Vardzia, and after his death his daughter Tamar used the caves to house a monastery. The central part of the complex was converted into a huge monastery church,

Vardzia. 12th-century complex of rock-dwellings. (Drawings based on material by K. Melitauri.)
Far left, top to bottom: Part of the complex in the extreme east; plans of the upper, middle and lower levels.
Left: Examples of cave interiors.

46

its walls partially constructed of dressed stone; the interior was painted, and the name of the artist—Giorgi—is recorded on an ornamental band in the apse. Vardzia was severely damaged by the earthquake of 1283; repairs were carried out in the late 13th and early 14th centuries under Beka Jakeli, a feudal lord, and it was probably at this time that the bell-tower was erected. Building work on the Vardzia monastery continued through the late Middle Ages.

Another measure of Georgian architecture is provided by the few surviving examples of bridges built across racing mountain torrents. The bridge over the river Besleti is faced with dressed stone and bears a 10th- or 11th-century inscription in Asomtavruli characters. Other bridges still standing today include those across the rivers Ajaris-tskali, Dandalo and Purtio, the one in Rkoni over the river Tedzami and those at Artanuji and Berta and near Okrobageti. Beside the existing massive stone bridge across the river Khrami, a second one was constructed in the 17th century on a number of brickbuilt piers. Multi-arched bridges have survived in a number of other places, including Taparavani.

There are still a few examples of caravanserais—the inns along the caravan routes which are frequently mentioned, together with hospitals, in the literary sources—but they are in a very poor state of preservation.

FORTRESSES

Exposed as it was to constant attack, Georgia fought tirelessly to preserve its independence and protect its people. It was compelled to expend vast quantities of manpower and materials in the construction of defence installations.

Much attention was paid to the location and exploitation of the most advantageous geographical positions: the Georgians were constantly preoccupied with the guarding and fortification of gorges, plateaux and roads. In each ravine, at each point of strategic importance, they built a tower or a fortress, and all these fortifications together made up a far-reaching system of defence that played a vital role over the centuries in keeping enemies at bay.

The fortresses that survive today represent only part of the complicated military defences established over several centuries. A lot of the buildings have been destroyed, and although the majority still exist in some form, many have been heavily damaged or considerably altered.

There were two kinds of fortification: those of overall state importance, erected along the frontiers to secure the main roads leading out of the country, and those intended for the defence of individual feudal units. Certain variations emerge in the historical development of these installations which were determined by the particular features of individual stages in the evolution of the feudal system.

An important element in the fortifications of state importance were the massive curtain walls which controlled access from the north by way of the narrow river valleys of the Caucasus. Walls 3.5 metres thick and 6 metres high, with towers, were erected across the entire breadth of the valley at Kasar on the river Ardon and Khilaki on the river Phiagdon. They were built of cobble-stones sorted according to size, laid in regular courses and packed with limestone rubble and mortar. In the Terek valley the way was barred by the Darial wall. Such installations in narrow passes, of course, exploited to the utmost the natural advantages of the terrain. In addition to the walls, solitary watch-towers were also erected.

Most of the fortresses of the early and middle feudal periods were situated high up on inaccessible sites overlooking the roads. Every feudal lord had his castle, which also represented the administrative centre of his territory. The typical complex of the feudal era housed the feudal lord, his family and his troops.

The feudal fortress at Dzamis-tsikhe (pp. 54–5) is still relatively well preserved today, and provides a typical example of early medieval building of this particular type. It stands on a high, sheer cliff, flanked on two sides by rivers. A tower on the very edge of the cliff creates a magnificent silhouette. The high walls are reinforced with semicircular buttresses, and on the accessible side there is an additional defensive wall. The castle walls are built of medium-sized, roughly dressed stones aligned carefully in neat, even courses and leaving an occasional observation slit. A small gateway leads into the fortress, where a number of buildings forming a compact group have been preserved. Some of them, with their large arched niches and broad openings, are reminiscent of the palaces of the 8th–10th centuries which will be discussed in the next section. Narrow, sloping passages connect the rooms. A round tower, the oldest structure, is linked to a spacious, three-storey dwelling which formed the residence of the feudal lord. In one corner stands a building which has on its first floor a small chapel of dressed stone, and between the chapel and the feudal residence are two- and three-storey buildings which presumably housed the guard. Built into the second floor of the outer wall is a latrine. In the central part of the fortress are the remains of a pool which was used as a reservoir, the water being conducted in through earthenware pipes. There are also pits for the storage of grain and other foodstuffs, a pit-oven for baking bread, and other features. The first written reference to Dzamis-tsikhe dates from the 10th century, but it is safe to assume that the fortress was built considerably earlier than this.

Ruins of fortresses similar to the one at Dzamis-tsikhe, built at more or less the same time and likewise used as residences by leading feudal lords, can be seen at Skhvilos-tsikhe, Opreti, Chapala and elsewhere. In each case the layout is largely determined by the terrain, and thus, despite an overall similarity in the building plan, each fortress has its own individual character.

Kvaras-tsikhe castle (pp. 52–3), which dates from the 11th–13th centuries, is smaller than Dzamis-tsikhe, but resembles the latter in its choice of location, the principle of its planning and its constituent parts. Situated on a rocky peak and reached only by a narrow path following the crest of a cliff, the fortress was virtually impregnable; furthermore, the entrance lay 2.5 metres above the ground, so that it was impossible to gain access without a ladder, which had to be let down from above when required. In addition, the gateway was flanked by two semicircular battlemented towers, so that the area in front of the entrance could easily be defended.

On the inside, the gateway extends far into the courtyard. The vaulted entrance broadens towards the end, and here the remains of a wall-painting can be seen; there must have been an icon here where people stopped to pray before entering the fortress. The guard was housed on the second floor of the building.

The inner courtyard is arranged in terraces, on which the remains of various buildings are dispersed. In the centre was a massive building, rectangular in plan—the residence of the feudal lord. A two-storey structure built against the outer wall at the northern end had a prison on its first floor. To the east, at the highest point, stand a round tower and a small church, and there were also domestic buildings here. Along the entrance side there was a wall-walk for defensive fire.

Certain parallels can be drawn between Kvaras-tsikhe and some European fortresses, for example the one at Maglič, which dates from the 13th century.

Other seats of feudal and religious dignitaries which are worthy of mention include those of Ateni, Vere, Vakhani, Kekhvi and Akhtala.

In the late Middle Ages, as Georgia disintegrated into petty feudal principalities (satavado) and firearms became widespread, fortresses were no longer built on clifftops, but on lower ground at the centre of the feudal lord's possessions, among the settled areas. This change corresponds exactly with the contemporary tendencies in western European defensive architecture. The buildings were now generally rectangular in outline, with round towers at the corners and occasionally also in the centre. They were also larger than before, in order to afford protection during attacks to as many as possible of the lord's vassals. Examples of this type include Mukhrani, Mdzovreti and Akhalgori in the Ksani gorge.

A new type of fortification, known as a galavani, appeared in the 18th century. This was a rectangular cordon of walls providing communal defences for the lord's household and the population of the surrounding areas.

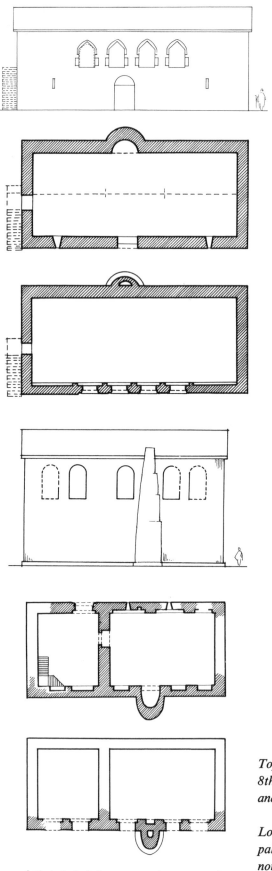

Top three figures: Khashmi. Bishop's palace, 8th–9th century. Elevation of the west façade and plans of the lower and upper floors.

Lower three figures: Samtavisi. Bishop's palace, 10th–11th century. Elevation of the north façade and plans of the ground and first floors.

PALACES

As already mentioned, there are in Georgia remains of a number of palaces dating from late antiquity: Armazis-tsikhe—Bagineti, Shukhuti, Uplis-tsikhe, and others. All we have from the 5th century is a written description of a palace that had a hall with eight niches separated by half-columns.

It is interesting to note that religious and secular buildings, despite their different functions, had various features in common; this is hardly surprising when one considers that both these branches of architecture had their roots in the folk tradition and were products of the same social conditions. Thus the Georgian word *tadzari* had the two meanings 'church' and 'palace', though derived originally from the concept of a palace.

A group of 8th-, 9th- and 10th-century palaces of a distinctive architectural type has survived in Georgia: it includes Cheremi, Kvetera (p. 57), Vanta, Vachnadziani, Nekresi, Khashmi, Samtavisi and Nikozi (pp. 56–7). These are large, two-storey buildings; on the lower level were the service quarters, with a fireplace, while the upper floor formed the living area, consisting chiefly of a large hall lit by high, broad arched windows. As a rule there were four windows in the main façade and two at each end. A number of smaller rooms led off from the hall. The roof of the palace was supported by wooden rafters. The interior was richly decorated with wall-paintings, wood-carving, carpets and embroidered tapestries and door-curtains. Palaces of this type were owned not only by secular rulers, but also by church dignitaries.

The architectural style of these Georgian buildings of the 8th–10th centuries is similar in some respects to that of later west European palaces built during the Romanesque period, for example the recently excavated Spudenbrod Palace and others in Prague, and, in Germany, the palace on the Wartburg. Individual details such as the shaping of doors and windows show that the builders of these palaces must have been familiar with oriental art.

The King's Palace at Geguti (pp. 57–8) is an outstanding building of exceptional significance for our understanding of secular architecture of the 10th–12th centuries, not merely in Georgia but in all the countries of the early Christian world. The monument is in ruins, but the excavation and research work undertaken on the parts that remain have made it possible to reconstruct the palace in its original form, and to date it.

Geguti is a complex site, with various buildings dating from different periods. A so-called 'hunting lodge' was built here in the 8th century. In the 10th century the great domed palace was built, incorporating the original hunting lodge into the structure. During the 12th and 13th centuries a number of side rooms were added on to the main building.

The palace stands on a plinth 2.5 metres high, faced with dressed stone; the walls themselves are of brick. The outline of the building is rectangular, with round towers projecting at the corners and in the middle of each side. The entrance is sheltered by two projecting semicircular walls, and between them a stairway leads up to a hall, cruciform in plan, which occupies the major part of the palace. The southern end is almost twice the depth of the remaining 'arms' of the cross. The central chamber has a dome 14 metres in diameter resting on massive squinches; the roofing that remains over the southern end is vaulted. The side wings of the palace contained various rooms: the southern arm of the hall was flanked on one side by a bedchamber with an alcove and on the other by what may have been the treasury, while at the other end of the building, to the right of the stairway, was a bath with a boiler for heating the water, and next to the bath a latrine. The palace was furnished with a hot-air heating system set into the plinth. To the left of the entrance were the domestic quarters.

The 'hunting lodge' is of particular interest. It is built on two floors, each with a large fireplace clearly intended for the roasting of boars, stags and other game caught in the hunt. It was probably built by King Archil when he had his residence at Kutaisi. Basili Zarzmeli, the chronicler, refers to a similar lodge that belonged to the regent of Samtskhe, the *eristavi* Chorchaneli, in the 9th century.

It was not merely its size and architectural form that made the palace of Geguti a remarkable monument of its time. It also played an important part in the public life of the region. The local assembly met here, and receptions of various sizes were held. The arrangement of the rooms and the accounts of eye-witnesses make it possible to reconstruct the course of various ceremonies that took place in the palace. For example, it was laid down from which point the king should enter the hall and how he should proceed to the throne at the southern end, and we also know exactly where the ministers sat. A noteworthy feature is the external door at the southern end of the hall, which is placed 2.5 metres above the ground outside. It was an established ceremony at the Byzantine court, as described in surviving accounts of the period, for the king to appear on certain occasions before the people or the army, wearing ceremonial dress and standing on some elevated spot where he could be clearly seen; although there are no surviving Georgian sources on this subject, it seems safe to assume that one of the places where the rulers of the land appeared before the people was this south door of the palace of Geguti.

The west rooms, added during the 12th and 13th centuries, are now badly damaged. This part was originally two storeys high. The lower floor had a richly decorated vestibule in the middle, and rooms with fireplaces and wall-niches built in. The upper storey was reached by a covered stone staircase.

Like other royal palaces, the one at Geguti must have been richly and beautifully furnished. The interior walls were covered with mural paintings, of which fragments were revealed in the course of work on the palace. These paintings must have portrayed battle scenes and historical characters, as noted by medieval Georgian sources. Describing the royal apartments of King Giorgi III and of Queen Tamar at Isani, for example, a 12th-century chronicler writes: '... we saw the walls of the palace, likewise covered with battle scenes—with divisions, an army, and troops of slaves, with towns and fortresses abandoned and devastated. And we saw the king himself in a posture like Gorgaslani, his right hand raised like Achilles, his countenance radiant—a man truly worthy to be seen as a hero.'

Apart from the wall-paintings, the rooms at Geguti were adorned with carpets, hangings of costly fabrics, decorated furniture with gold and silver fittings, oil lamps and many other things. The windows were glazed; one pane of this glass has survived, measuring 18–20 centimetres across and ornamented with a rosette in relief.

Before the entrance to the palace was a small canopy, beneath which stood the cross which was carried in front of the king and the troops as they went into battle. All around the buildings were gardens with fountains.

In the late Middle Ages, another type of living complex evolved, in the form of a house with an adjoining tower. Such complexes were usually owned by representatives of the ruling class, who might be either secular or ecclesiastical feudal lords.

The manor house usually consisted of between three and five rooms. The central room was used as a reception hall, and it had a projecting balcony; smaller rooms such as bedrooms were arranged on either side of it. The rooms had fireplaces and wall-niches, and the interiors, particularly that of the hall, were decorated with wall-paintings and details in carved wood and alabaster. The lower floor of the house was of secondary importance.

Adjoining the house was a tall tower of several storeys: there were usually three at the very least, but often as many as five or six, with the lower ones connected by doors to the house itself. The top floor could be used for defence, while the remaining levels were employed for domestic and residential purposes. In some cases, for example at Dzaghina, the upper levels of the tower have arched openings. Such a tower, with its open archways, its decorated rooms on the upper floors, and a latrine, represented a comfortable, if not luxurious, type of dwelling. In the event of an enemy attack, the owner moved up to the tower with his family, and it then served as a fortress.

This juxtaposition of two architectural forms, the one emphatically horizontal, the other vertical, occurs not only in secular architecture, but also in religious buildings. The complex of Kvemo-Chala provides an example of an aisleless church with a bell-tower built on to the west side.

Dzaghina. Feudal palace of the 17th century. Schematic reconstruction, section and plan.

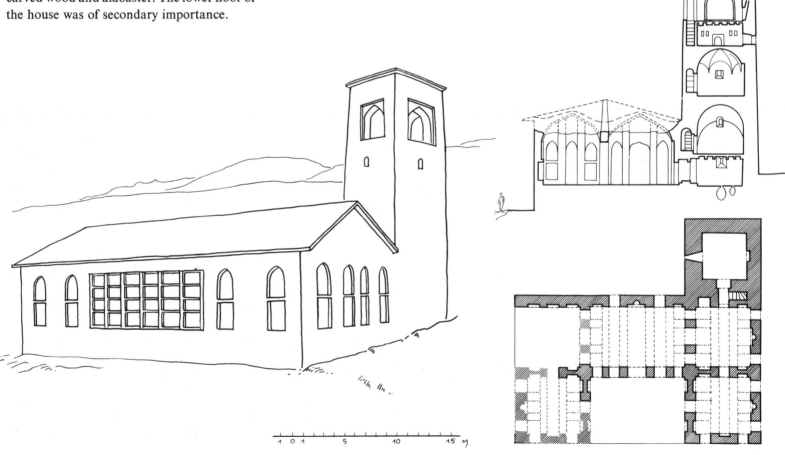

Ujarma. Remains of the former town,
dating from the 5th century.
Right: Conjectural reconstruction
of the city (after I. Tsitsishvili).
Centre: Plan of one of the citadel towers,
known as the 'Tower of King Vakhtang'
(it is thought to have been used by King
Vakhtang as his residence).
Bottom left: Elevation of one of the
towers, viewed from the city side.
Bottom right: Remains of the so-called
'Tower of King Vakhtang'.

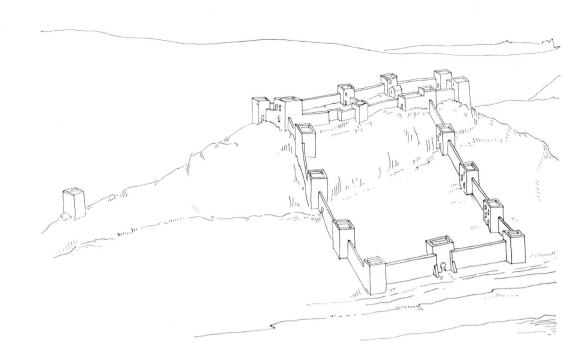

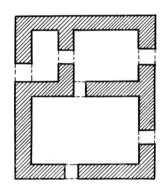

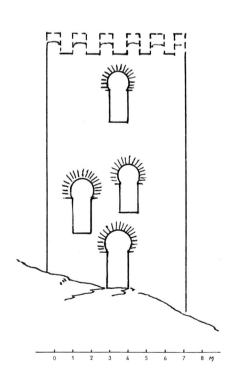

51

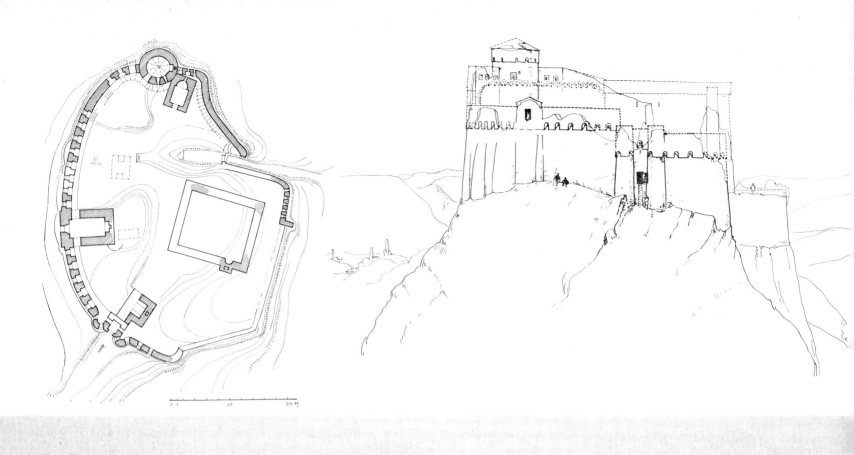

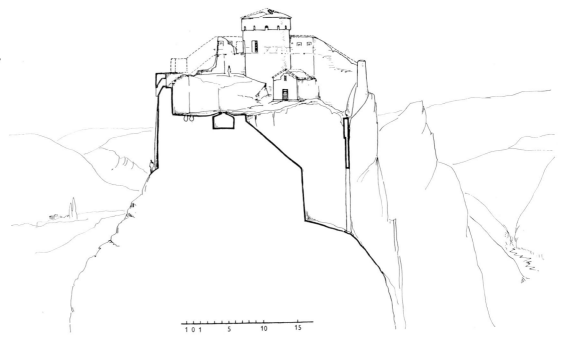

Kvaras-tsikhe. Fortress of a feudal lord, 11th–13th century. Plan (far left), reconstructed view from the entrance side (left), section (right) and general views (below).

1 0 1   5   10   15

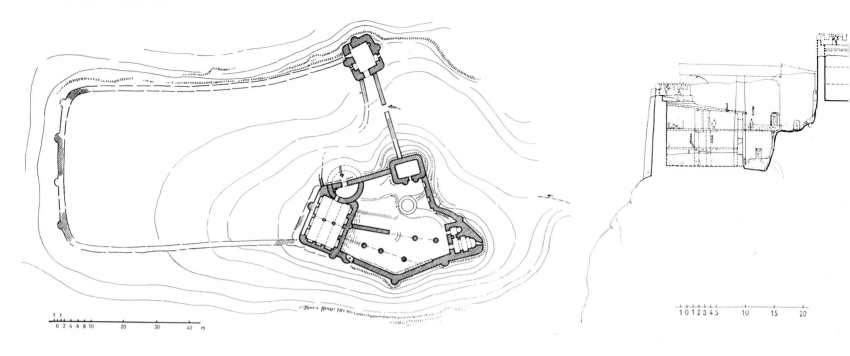

*Dzamis-tsikhe. Early medieval fortress
of the* eristavi *Dzameli.
Above, left to right: Site-plan;
section, looking west;
section, looking east.
Right: Ruins of the fort, from the west.*

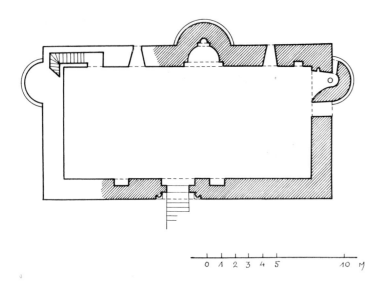

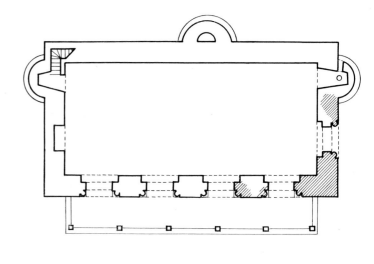

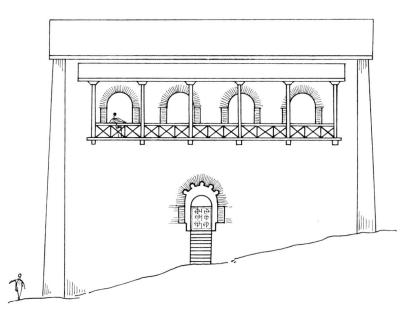

Overleaf: Geguti. King's palace, 10th century.
*Plan (top left), sections (top right),
conjectural reconstruction of the entrance
front (centre) and view of the ruins from the
entrance side. The converted 8th-century
'hunting lodge' with its huge fireplace can be
detected in the plan and section. The aisleless
church to the south of the palace is most
probably contemporary with the 12th- and
13th-century extensions on the west side.*

*Nikozi. Bishop's palace,
9th–10th century.
Above, left to right:
Plan of the ground floor;
plan of the upper floor;
conjectural reconstruction
of the north front.
Left: Ruins of the bishop's
palace, built of rubble masonry
and squared stone. Bricks were
used for the decorative shaping
of the arches.*

*Kvetera. Ruins of the palace
of a feudal lord, 8th–9th century.*

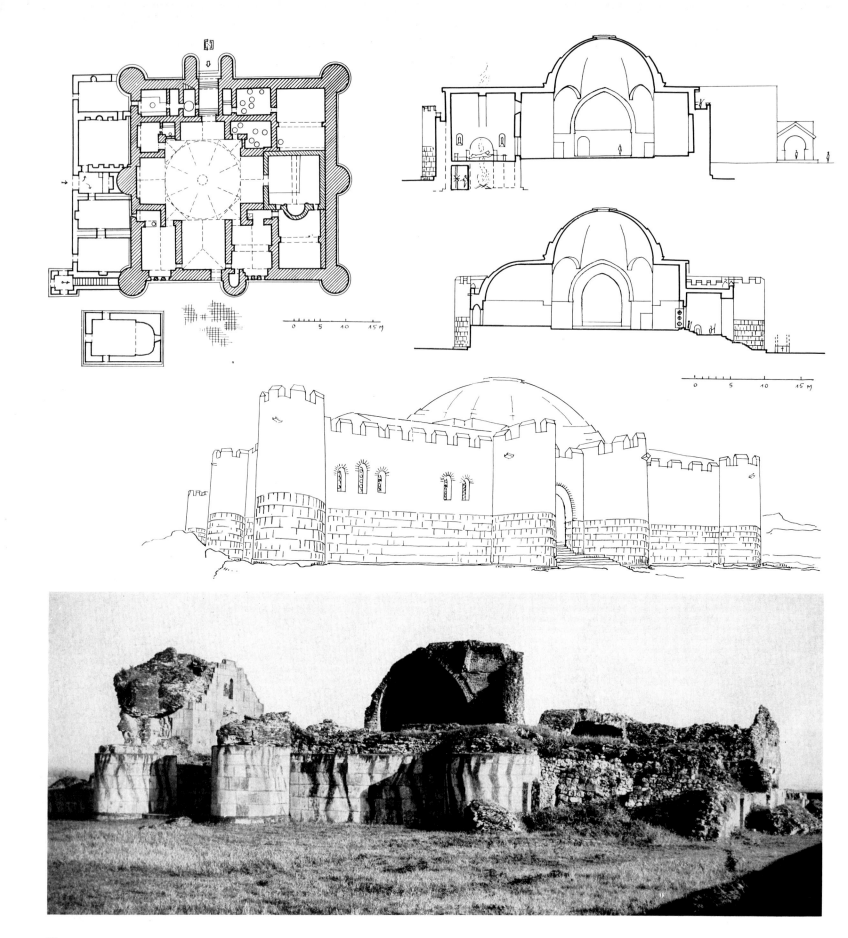

ART IN THE MIDDLE AGES (5th–18th centuries)
Religious buildings
First flowering — transitional period — second flowering — late period

Apart from the secular buildings such as palaces and fortresses described in the previous chapter, Georgian architecture of the medieval period survives mainly in the form of religious buildings such as churches and monasteries. The many surviving church buildings provide a clear picture of the development of Georgian architecture, and make it possible to determine the place of the latter in European art.

Written sources that mention the early churches of Georgia indicate that religious monuments existed at an early stage in almost every part of the country. The chronicles refer to the construction of houses of worship in Erusheti, Manglisi and Bodbe. We learn, furthermore, that Bakur, son of King Mirian, built churches in Tsilkani and in Rustavi, that Bakur's brother Trdat built one at Nekresi, and that his son Mithradates constructed the church and fortress at Tukharisi and continued the building at Erusheti and Tsunda. Under Varaz Bakur, the father of Peter of Iberia, the church of St George was built at Mtskheta and work continued on the churches at Nekresi and Cheremi.

But alas, only a few of these early churches have remained intact to this day, and those purely by chance. The first Christian churches were, for the most part, erected at important centres of the old heathen religion. In the words of Vakhushti Bagrationi, the 18th-century historian and geographer, 'In the 4th century King Mirian destroyed all the idols in his kingdom and set up in their place the life-giving crosses of Christ, the Lord, for the destruction of his enemies.'

Judging by the surviving material, Georgian churches of the 4th century were small and did not have any set architectural form. They were also built of differing materials. Thus the church of Sveti-tskhoveli (p. 67), founded by St Nino—a Cappadocian nun who converted Georgia—was made of wood and had a rectangular ground-plan, while the Samtavro church (p. 72) was built of stone and crowned with a dome resting on a low drum. At Cheremi the church is really only a stone baldacchino with a domed vault. The church at Nekresi is the most complex structure: it consists of a raised central portion, and lower side sections which open outwards through horseshoe arches. But for all this variety, the ancient architectural traditions, the predominant use of stone and the principles of vaulted construction persisted unchanged.

In the past, various foreign influences have been suggested as the sources from which domed architecture developed. Yet the findings of archaeological research show plainly enough that both the technique of vaulting and the dome form had been widely anticipated on Georgian soil in pre-Christian times. It was this national tradition, and also technical innovations from neighbouring lands such as Armenia, Iran and Syria, that provided the necessary basis for the further evolution of domed architecture in Georgia.

There are no clearly defined examples of domed churches from the 4th century AD, but by the 5th century this style had already developed considerably in Georgia and acquired individual features.

The basilican type of church, a legacy of the Roman and Hellenistic world, was also quite widely adopted in Georgia, although modified to a local form. The most striking example of this is the Sion church at Bolnisi.

The Sion (pp. 68–9), built in the reign of Vakhtang Gorgaslani between 478 and 493, is a large, three-aisled, vaulted basilica, with five pairs of tall, slender pillars, cross-shaped in section, spanned by horseshoe arches. The side aisles are almost the same height as the nave, and all are vaulted and drawn together under a pitched roof.

Here the rows of slender pillars do not create the clear division into aisles customary in a basilica, but are seen rather as vertical supports for the roof which rises over the hall-like space. As a result, the typical basilican orientation of the interior along a longitudinal axis is very much reduced. This impression is further emphasized by the positioning of the entrances not at the western end, but in the north and south walls, that is, along the transversal axis of the building. Only the open galleries with their lower roofs give Bolnisi the graduated silhouette characteristic of the basilica.

Capitals with relief carvings of animal motifs and geometric and plant decorations usually derive from oriental patterns, but those at Bolnisi, on the piers of the triumphal arch and the baptistery, also originate in native artistic traditions.

The architectural solution presented by the three-aisled basilica of Bolnisi, and in particular the articulation of the interior space and the exterior mass, cannot be viewed altogether in isolation. Other three-aisled basilicas were built during this period, some of them contemporary with Bolnisi and others somewhat later. These, however, employ the solution usually adopted for structures of this type: they are divided up into three distinct aisles, the central one being considerably higher than those on either side. The nave, accordingly, has a pitched roof, while the lower side aisles have sloping roofs (see Anchiskhati in Tbilisi, Urbnisi, Akhshani, etc.).

There is an analogy in the small basilica, likewise called Sion, which was built in the Ertso region several centuries after the building of Bolnisi.

Halfway through the 6th century, there evolved out of the fundamental concept of the domeless basilica-type structure an independent solution in keeping with the basic tendency of Georgian architecture at that time. This was the so-called 'triple-church basilica', consisting of three parallel barrel-vaulted

The earliest Georgian churches, dating from the 4th century:

a Mtskheta, Sveti-tskhoveli. Plan of the wooden church.
b Mtskheta, Samtavro. Small domed church, thought to have been built by King Mirian. Plan, and elevation of the south façade.
c Cheremi. Plan and elevation.
d Nekresi. Plan, elevation of the east façade and view from the north-west.

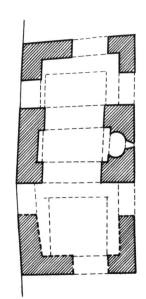

d

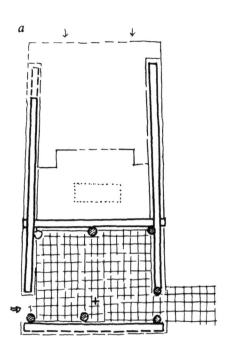

a

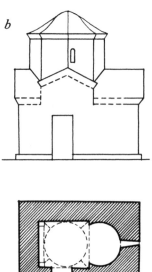

b

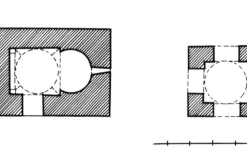

c

naves connected by doors through solid walls. The central 'church' was larger and higher than those at either side. This form, which probably corresponded to the requirements of the developing religion, is exemplified by Kvemo-Bolnisi (p. 76), Vanati, Sabue, Saguramo and Cheremi. By the 7th century, the triple-church basilica had acquired an artistically refined appearance, as for instance at Zegani and Nekresi. During the 9th and 10th centuries this type of building became quite common in certain regions of Georgia, but it ceased to be generally used after the first half of the 11th century. However, an example of this type of structure dated to the latter half of the 13th century, has recently been discovered.

Domed churches had already developed clearly defined architectural forms by the 5th century: the central section of the building was square in shape and served as a foundation for the dome, which always rested on a drum. The transition from the square to the circle was made by means of squinches, which in Georgia attained an extraordinary degree of stylistic and technical maturity at an early stage, whereas those parts of Asia under Hellenistic influence adopted the pendentive, a feature which did not appear in Georgia until the 9th century.

An interesting example of these early domed structures is the small 5th-century church of Zegani. Its ground-plan is cruciform, with arms of equal length, and the the whole structure including the cupola, is covered by a pitched roof.

The 6th and 7th centuries produced a number of variations on the centralized domed church: the so-called 'free cross', for instance, where the ground-plan of both exterior and interior is cruciform with an inscribed semi-circular apse—Idleti (p. 77), Shiomghvime (p. 73), Eralaant-sakdari—or the triconch and tetraconch buildings such as are found at Sukhbechi, Dzveli-Gavazi and Manglisi. Monuments of this kind continued to develop during the following centuries in Georgia. The 7th-century church in Samtsevrisi (p. 79) deserves special mention for superlative artistic mastery. It is outstanding for its harmonious proportions, the even regularity of its masonry and the transition to the dome by means of two rows of squinches. The variety of the squinch forms that occur both here and in other buildings is conclusive proof that Georgia was one of the countries which achieved a constructive and independent solution to the problem of the transition from the square substructure to the circular form of the cupola.

Nekresi. Monastery complex with 4th-century church, 7th-century triple-church basilica, and domed church and bishop's palace from the 8th–9th century; the tower of the palace was added in the 17th century.

The 6th-century cathedral of Ninotsminda (p. 78) is an interesting example of early Christian architecture; it represents the first large centralized building in the religious architecture of Georgia. The chief features of the building are that it originally had a domical vault, and that each of the recesses inserted between the four main apses has two tiny apses of its own.

The struggling progress of the 5th and 6th centuries towards a truly independent national art culminated in the unique flowering of architecture in the late 6th and early 7th centuries, when Georgia had finally adopted feudalism and the erection of monumental buildings had thus acquired the status of a state commission. From an artistic standpoint, this was a thoroughly mature stage in the development of Georgian architecture, which now attained a classic perfection. We are indebted to Giorgi Chubinashvili for his profound characterization of the monuments of this classic period: they 'possess perfect clarity of geometric form, both in their ground-plans and in the construction of the buildings; they display a clear articulation, a wealth of content and an attention to proportion, and make an impression of calm and balance which results in great dignity. The fusion of the independent, individual elements can be felt, and the building is experienced as a unified whole, organized as a natural organism. The perfect clarity of the forms is expressed both in the creation of harmonious proportions and in the decoration. This decoration is plainly visible right down to the last detail, yet it is only applied where it is absolutely essential to the overall effect. In this way all the interrelationships between the different elements become inevitable; nothing could be altered or removed without detriment to the composition.'

This era has left an abundance of magnificent monuments which are landmarks both in Georgian architecture and in the architecture of the world as a whole. The most outstanding examples are at Jvari near Mtskheta (church of the Holy Cross), Tsromi and Bana.

Jvari (pp. 80–87)—one of the epoch-making embodiments of the artistic genius of the Georgian people—stands on a cliff in the foothills of the Caucasus massif, where it blends with the landscape in exceptional harmony. The church tops a steep incline above the point where the Kura and Aragvi rivers meet; the city of Mtskheta, with its great and noble building of Sveti-tskhoveli, lies spread out below. Jvari is incomparably beautiful by day, when the swelling outline of the building, caught by the sun's rays, stands out against the backdrop of the blue sky. The sight of the church against a flaming sunset is equally impressive, its silhouette, completely black, is once again cut out against the sky, now appearing sombre and lowering.

6th-century domed churches of the 'free cross' type. These early examples are characterized by the relatively large square crossing area under the dome.

Below: Idleti. Plan, section and elevation of the east façade.
Opposite below: Eralaant-sakdari. Plan, section and elevation of the east façade.

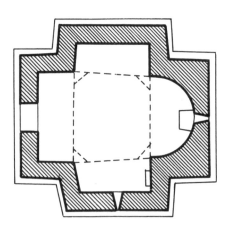

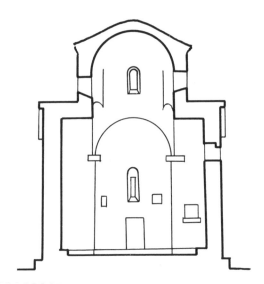

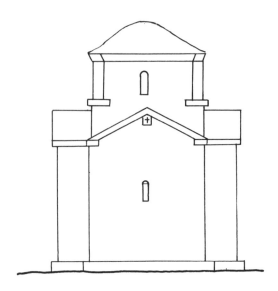

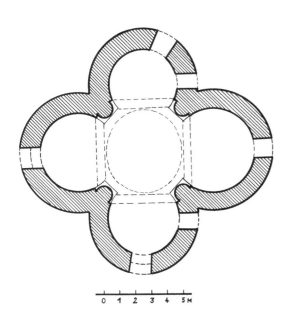

Dzveli-Gavazi. 6th-century tetraconch with deep horseshoe-shaped apses. The arches under the dome, the doors and the windows are also horseshoe-shaped. An interesting feature is the presence of entrances on the eastern side of the lateral apses.

Jvari has fortunately been spared destruction or substantial alteration. It is easy to understand why generations of pilgrims have made their way up the steep path leading to the church. From the very beginning, Jvari enjoyed great popularity, and not only Georgians but Christians from the whole Caucasus region and even further afield made their way here. On this peak, as the ancient chronicles tell us, a cross was erected in the fourth decade of the 4th century on the initiative of Nino, the herald of Christianity. The base of this cross, in the shape of a large octagon, is preserved in the central part of the church. In the second half of the 6th century Guaram, the ruler of Kartli, ordered a small church to be built beside the cross. This beautifully constructed building of dressed stone had a crypt and was roofed with a groin vault. A mosaic adorned the apse.

The great church was erected by Guaram's son Stephanos I, Demetre, the brother of Stephanos, and Stephanos's successor Adarnese. The construction of Jvaris-sakdari—as it is also known in the region—has been dated to the years 586/7–605/6.

Both outside and in, Jvari is faced with neatly dressed stone blocks, uniform in size and of a warm yellow colour. The eastern apse was originally decorated with a mosaic. The uniqueness of Jvari lies not only in the way it blends with its natural surroundings, but, more significantly, in the harmonious control of complex architectural forms and the artistic construction of the façades. The broad, open, domed interior, with its four semicircular conches with deep niches set between them, has four separate rooms in the corners. The transition to the dome is made by means of three tiers of squinches. The visitor to Jvari is immediately struck by the clearly defined disposition of interior space. No one entering the church can fail to be aware of the sublime grandeur of this perfectly balanced design.

The structure of the interior is visibly expressed in the exterior mass of the monument. In the centre rises the dome, surmounted by a low cap roof. The projecting arms of the cross have pitched roofs, and lower roofs indicate the position of the separate corner rooms. Arched niches link the various surfaces of the façade, which are decorated with relief figures representing the founders of the church, and with ornamentation whose composition reflects the fine taste of the master. The decoration forms a harmonious unity. Nothing here is accidental or imperfect.

The architect had no direct example on which to model Jvari, either in terms of general architectural forms or in the decorative scheme. The design was determined by the evolution of Georgian architecture up to that point, and the builder tackled the archi-

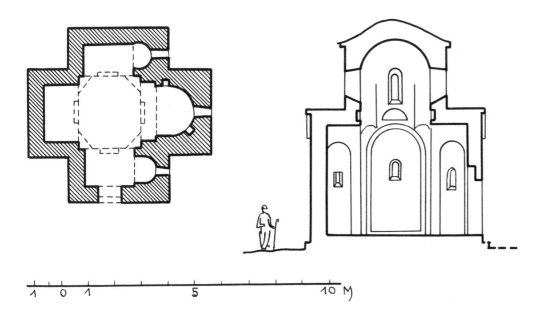

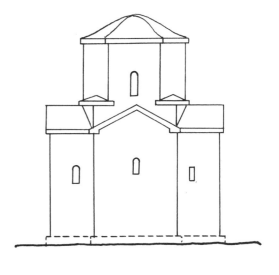

tectural and artistic problems in total accord with national traditions. He thereby created a monument that deserves a place in any survey of world art.

Buildings of the Jvari type soon became widespread in Georgia. Examples survive which are so similar that the original on which they were modelled is instantly recognizable: from the 7th century, for instance, we have Dzveli Shuamta, Ateni (pp. 88–9), Martvili and, with considerable variations, Dranda, which is built in brick and stone in the Byzantine manner and has a drum relieved by numerous broad windows. A comparable church in Chamkhusi, now in ruins, also traces its origins back to Jvari, though this building clearly dates from the 8th–9th century.

The second stage in Georgian architecture of the so-called 'classical' period is illustrated by a monument at the centre of the village of Tsromi (pp. 90–93) which was built between 626 and 634. An inscription on the south façade refers to Stephanos, the feudal lord of this area. The church is built of neatly dressed stone, yellowish in colour, and the joints between the blocks were filled with a white substance, making the lines of the courses stand out. This effect was further heightened by the bevelled edges of the stones. The accented joints can still be seen today around the window arches, where white, red and black colouring was applied in alternation.

The architect of Tsromi introduced a new element in the construction of the interior:

four free-standing piers on which the drum and dome rested. The transition to the dome —which has not survived—was achieved by squinches. The interior, which extends beyond the square bay under the dome in all four directions, terminates at the eastern end in a semicircular apse, with small chapels to either side of it. The west front has a narthex attached, surmounted by a gallery.

At Tsromi, as at Jvari, the external mass follows the interior construction very closely. Each of the façades is meticulously planned down to the last detail, and in terms of composition each is an independent unit. Their ornamentation is restrained, serving to accentuate the door and window openings. The delicacy and elegance of the ornamentation and of the crosses, and their sculptural quality, add to the expressiveness of the façades.

The architect of Tsromi contrived to reconcile the semicircular internal apse to the straight external façade in a manner that was pleasing from both the aesthetic and the structural points of view: he introduced niches, which not only relieved the massiveness of the walls, but were also satisfying to look at. The effect of the east façade, where the two deep recesses combine with the window arch to form a triple arcade, is austerely majestic, as indeed is the effect of the entire structure. This grandeur, the clarity of line and the composition of the architectural elements indisputably endow the church of Tsromi with an appearance of aristocratic dignity.

Buildings of the Jvari type. The tetraconch in its mature form, complete with side-chambers, first appeared in Jvari (586/7–605/6) and subsequently spread into several of the ancient provinces of Georgia, for example at Ateni, Dzveli Shuamta (7th century), Martvili, Chamkhusi (probably 8th century) and Dranda (7th century). Chamkhusi and Dranda are variations of the basic type.

a Jvari b Ateni c Dzveli Shuamta
d Martvili e Chamkhusi f Dranda

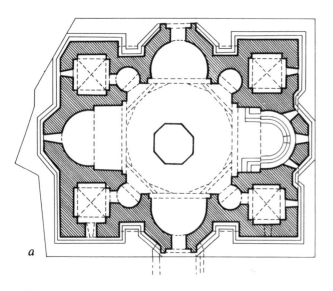

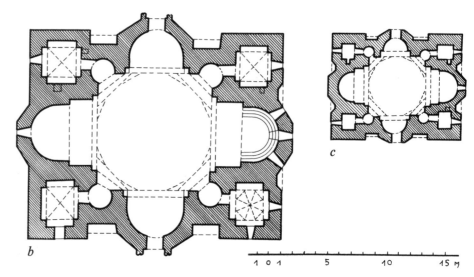

The architect of Tsromi thus solved several important problems simultaneously in the fourth decade of the 7th century: on the ground-plan of an inscribed cross, he courageously introduced four free-standing clustered columns under the dome, an innovation at that time quite unknown in Byzantium and the Near East; and he found a method of articulating the east façade that was inspired and influential in terms of both construct on and aesthetics. Clearly, Tsromi was built by a master of artistic experiment. Like the architect of Jvari, he determined the subsequent course of Georgian architecture in a number of ways.

Originally the altar recess, the most important part of the church from a liturgical point of view, was accentuated by means of a mosaic. Parts of the mosaic from the apse vault survive, with fragments of figures and bands of leaf ornament. Seeing the remaining pieces, it is not difficult to visualize how well the colours and the gold background must have blended with the yellowish hue of the stone, or to imagine the effect on the beholder of the harmon ous accord between the architectural and the mosaic decorations.

The decoration of the Georgian church interior between the 5th and the 7th centuries was the object of lavish attention: the altar conches were decorated with mosaics, and the walls were enlivened by lines of red, black and white between the stone blocks. Huge crosses stood out in relief from the stonework of the

domes, as at Jvari, Ateni and Samtsevrisi (p. 79). At Ateni the red colouring on the cross can still be seen. These decorative techniques were used to help concentrate the worshipper's attention on the altar area and the dome.

Several of the buildings also possessed mosaic floors. In recent times, mosaics have been found in religious buildings and palaces in various parts of Georgia, for example at Bichvinta and Shukhuti, and in Georgian monasteries in Palestine and near Antioch.

Further examples of the spectacular flowering of Georgian architecture in the first half of the 7th century are provided by Ishkhani and Bana in the south-west of what was then Georgia. Ishkhani, however, has been drastically rebuilt, and Bana was badly damaged by shelling in the mid-19th century. Built of carefully dressed stone with ornamental details, Bana (pp. 94–7) is a tetraconch of colossal dimensions, with corner rooms set between the apses; the whole composition is enclosed by a circular ambulatory. The apses are high, and open out into the ambulatory through horseshoe arches set on pillars with relief capitals. The corner rooms rise to the same height as the apses, and have three floors.

The tetraconch with corner rooms, introduced into Georgia with monuments of the Jvari type, is the composition on which the Bana church is based, but with certain modifications: the interior is broken up by numerous arches, and the ground-plan of the

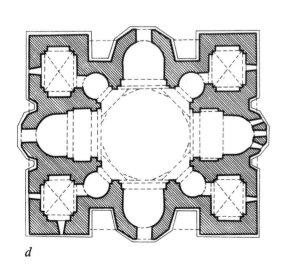

d

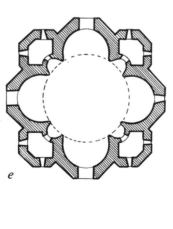

e

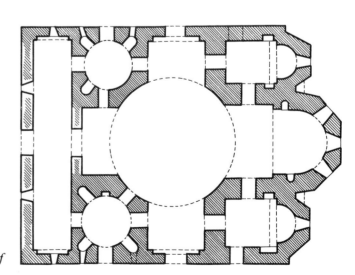

f

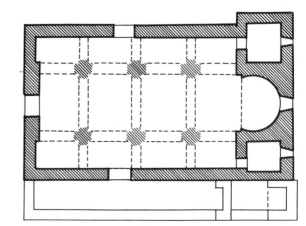

exterior is circular. From the limited material available to us, it seems that Bana must have looked somewhat as follows. The ambulatory was probably originally single-storeyed, its walls faced on the outside with dressed stone and adorned with blind arcading and vine tendrils, a motif commonly used here in the 6th and 7th centuries. Blind arcading likewise ran all the way round the interior. Here, however, the arches sprang from boldly projecting pilasters, making the arcading an important feature of the construction. The upper storey of the ambulatory is built of coarse, rough-hewn stones, and contrasts starkly with the lower level; it was probably added in the 9th century, when, according to historical documents, the church was rebuilt under Bishop Saban. The niches in the ambulatory were presumably also bricked in at this time. The diagrammatic reconstruction of Bana as it originally looked is based on the assumptions outlined above.

Ishkhani (p. 98) was rebuilt in the 9th century, and then again in the 11th century by the architect Ioane Morchaisdze. All that remains of the 7th-century building is the richly decorated arcading of the eastern apse. Besides Ishkhani and Bana, there is another small church dating from the 8th–9th century in Lekiti, in the historical province of Saingilo.

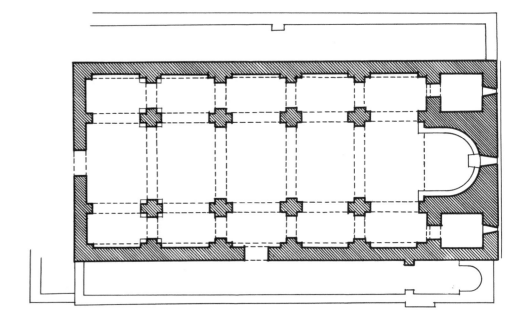

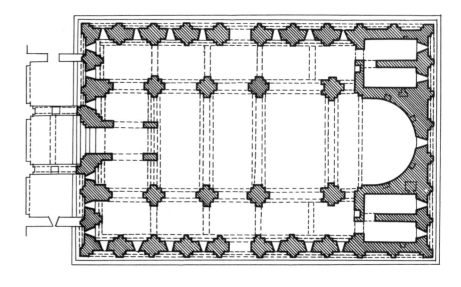

Three-aisled basilicas. Top to bottom: Anchiskhati in Tbilisi (6th century); Urbnisi (5th–6th century); Otkhta-eklesia (10th century). These buildings represent the basic type of three-aisled basilica without significant variation.

66

Mtskheta, Sveti-tskhoveli. Plan and remains of the 4th-century wooden church excavated in 1970 at the south end of the cathedral. The archaeologists found imprints of paired foundation beams which had been sunk into a limestone mortar, holes to take the wooden wall supports, and remains of the flooring, with slabs measuring 31×31 centimetres and 18×31 centimetres.

According to the chroniclers, 'the chiton [tunic] of Christ, inherited by Georgia' lies buried beneath the 15th-century stone altar canopy called Sveti-tskhoveli ('the life-giving pillar').

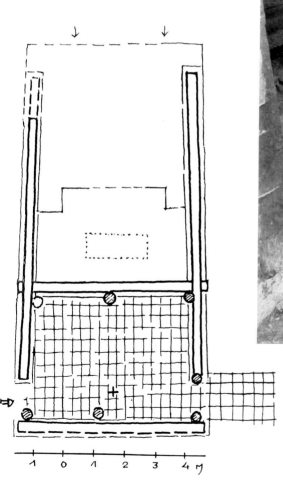

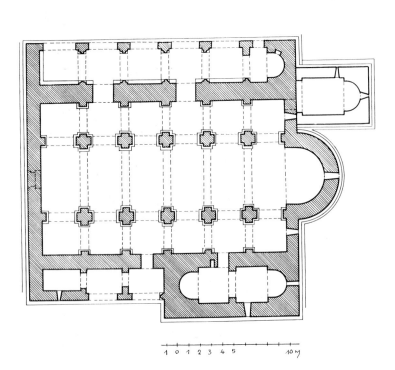

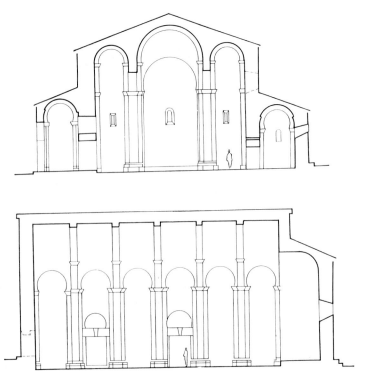

1 0 1 2 3 4 5   10 M

Bolnisi. The Sion, a three-aisled basilica from the late 5th century.

Far left: East façade. The smaller stones and bricks of the upper portion are the result of a restoration.

Left: Capital of a half-column in the south gallery.

Below left: Plan, cross-section and longitudinal section. A small aisleless church was added at the north-eastern end in the 8th century. The shape of the original roof is reconstructed in the cross-section.

Below: Pilaster capital in the 5th-century baptistery. On the front face of the capital only the lower part of the carving remains, showing a gable with a cross and two peacocks, The heathen motif of the bull's head has been converted into a Christian one by the addition of the cross.

Above right: Inscription on the architrave of the north door, dating from the year 493/4. Written in Asomtavruli, the inscription reads as follows: 'With the help of the Holy Trinity, the building of this church was begun in the twentieth year of King Peroz and completed fifteen years later. Whosoever bows down here, God will pardon, and whosoever prays here for David, Bishop of the Church, him also will God pardon. Amen.' The original is now in the S. Janashia Museum (State Museum of Georgia).

Right: View of the interior, looking north-west.

Katskhi. There are many legends about the 40-metre-high rock pinnacle, some of them dating from pre-Christian times, which suggests that the place had some religious importance even then. In the early Christian period it was inhabited by a pillar-saint, as a result of which it became known as 'the life-giving pillar' or 'the column of Simeon the stylite'. Two churches were built on the summit in the 5th–6th century. The first was partially hewn out of the rock, and the second included a crypt of dressed stone. Both are now in ruins. Round the top of the rock runs a wall; fragments of domestic jugs have been found embedded in it. The plateau at the foot of the rock pillar is likewise encircled by a wall, and inside the enclosure stands a small church built in the 10th century. Far right: Plan and section (reconstructed) of the churches on the peak.

70

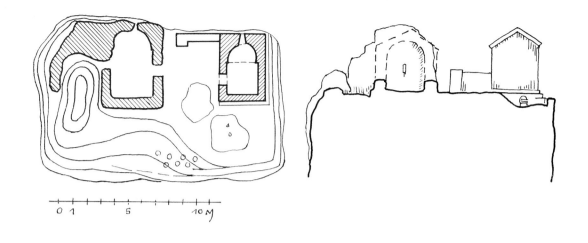

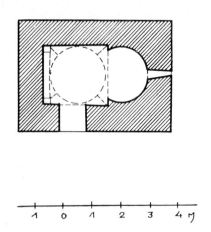 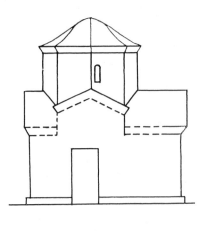

Mtskheta, Samtavro. 4th-century domed church built, according to legend, by King Mirian. Plan, elevation, and modern view from the south-west.

Shiomghvime. Monastery buildings, 6th–18th centuries. View from the south-east. The domed church was built in the 6th century, though the west wing was later lengthened considerably. The caves in the rock face were used by the monks as cells.

Mtskheta, Sveti-tskhoveli. Excavations carried out between 1968 and 1972 revealed important traces of the 5th-century three-aisled basilica built by Vakhtang Gorgaslani to replace the 4th-century wooden church. These findings made it possible to reconstruct the exact layout of the 5th-century church. Its polygonal choir was found under the floor at the altar end of the 11th-century church. Parts of the foundations of the walls, and 5th-century pillars discovered at the core of the 11th-century piers, provide clear indications of the ground-plan (above right). An unusual feature is that the three aisles are almost exactly equal in width.

Parts of the figurative and ornamental decoration from the earlier church were incorporated into the 11th-century structure in various places; they include the two bulls' heads on the east front (right) and a fragment of capital on a pilaster in the sacristy (far right, top). Various pillar mouldings and decorations were uncovered, for example the ornamental decoration on the base of the second pillar in the south-east (far right, centre) and the profiled base of the second pillar in the north-east (far right, bottom).

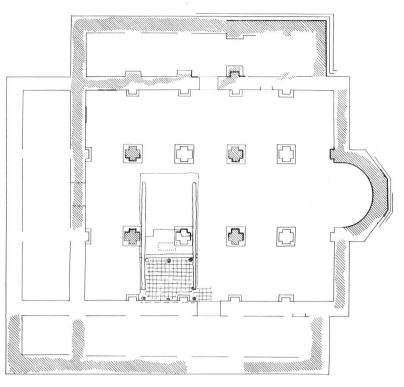

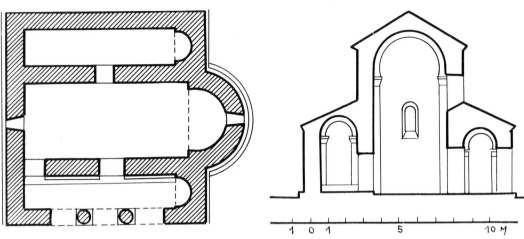

Kvemo-Bolnisi. 6th-century triple-church basilica. Plan, section, and view from the south-west. The south front originally had a triple-arched entrance.

Idleti. One of the earliest cruciform domed churches in Georgia, dating from the 6th century. The virtually unadorned building is constructed in simple rubble masonry. Inside it is dimly illuminated by means of a few small windows. The drum is square, with the corners cut off, and small squinches are used for the transition to the dome. Surviving fragments of wall-painting date from the 12th century.

Plan, section, east elevation and view from the north-east.

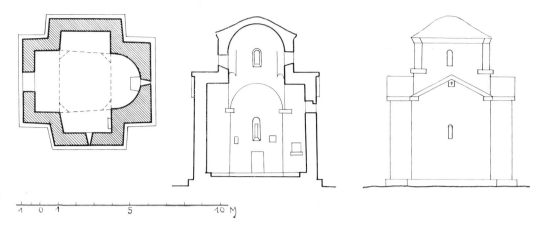

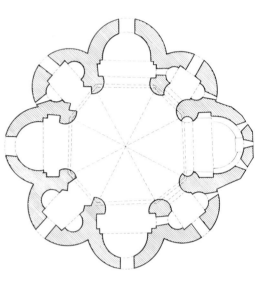

Ninotsminda. 6th-century cathedral. The first major Georgian church to be built to a centralized plan, Ninotsminda is a tetraconch with side-bays set between the apses.

The square central bay was probably surmounted by a domical vault, as indicated by the dotted lines on the plan.

Below left: Remains of the eastern end. The upper arches, the squinches and the remains of the drum date from the 10th century, when the building was restored. The side-bays were also restored and altered.

Samtsevrisi. 7th-century central-domed church. Plan, section and east elevation (below); view from the south-east (right), and interior of the dome, showing the relief cross.

Mtskheta, Jvari. Built between 586/7 and 605/6.
Left: Tympanum relief of the south portal, showing the Exaltation of the Cross.
Below: View from the south-east. Remains of the surrounding wall can be seen in the foreground. The complex structure of the interior is reflected in the form of the exterior.
Opposite: View of the interior, facing east. In the centre is the base that supported the original wooden cross erected at the beginning of the 4th century.

Mtskheta, Jvari.
View from the south.

Plan, east elevation and section; partial view
of the south front, showing the portal and the
remains of the portico.

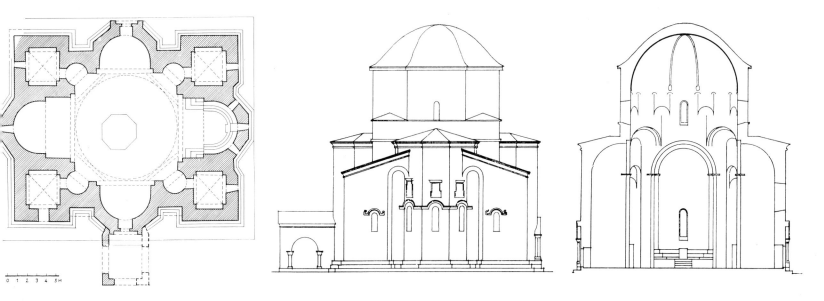

Mtskheta, Jvari.
Left: Head of the founder Adarnese, from the right-hand founder's relief on the east façade. Plaster cast and relief detail as restored by S. Maisuradze.
Below: Founders' reliefs on the east façade. The compositional harmony of the scenes, and the decorative window hood running all the way round, are evidence of the sculptor's unifying intention. The central panel shows the standing figure of Christ blessing the founder, who kneels at his feet; in the side panels the founders, and the angels hovering above them, all reach out towards the figure of Christ.
Right: Overall view of the relief of Adarnese.

Mtskheta, Jvari.
Left-hand founder's relief
on the east façade,
showing the founder
Demetre.

Founder's relief above the portal on the south front.

Ateni. The 7th-century church of Sioni. The building was erected on a tongue of rock jutting out into a ravine, and shored up by a mighty retaining wall. In both the arrangement of the architectonic forms and the composition of the façade decoration, Ateni has obvious links with Jvari.

Left: Relief on the tympanum over the north door, showing stags drinking water from a spring.

Below left: View of the church, seen from the south-east.

Above right: Reliefs on the west front showing stag-hunting.

Right: Still distinguishable under a flaking 11th-century wall-painting in the west conch is the original painting, a pattern of geometric shapes in black, brick-red and lighter colours. The north and south conches may well have been decorated in a similar fashion.

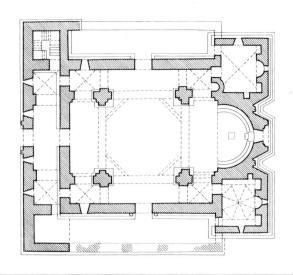

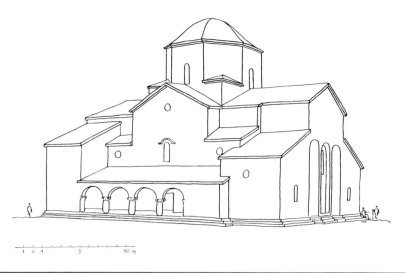

Tsromi. Cruciform domed church, built in
AD 626–34.
Opposite above: Ground-plan, showing the
four detached piers supporting the dome, and
diagrammatic reconstruction with the original
dome and south gallery.
Opposite below: View of the church from the
south-east.
Below: The east front with the archetypal
niche formation.

Tsromi.

Left: Interior view, looking into the altar apse.

Below: Drawing of the interior, facing westwards.

Right: Sketch of the remains of the mosaic in the apse.

Surviving ornamental fragments of the apse mosaic.

Georgian State Museum of Art.

Bana. Cathedral, first half of the 7th century.
Top left: Reconstructed plan of the entire
building, showing the ambulatory and the
inner tetraconch, with the lower part of its
apses opening out into the ambulatory through
arcades.
Bottom left: Reconstructed plan of the upper
level.
Top right: Reconstructed section, looking east.
Bottom right: Reconstruction of the west
elevation.
(These reconstructions are based on the work
of E. Takaishvili.)

1 0 1 2 3 4 5 6 7 8 9 10

Bana. Detail of the blind arcading on the outside of the ambulatory, and (below) view of the ruins.

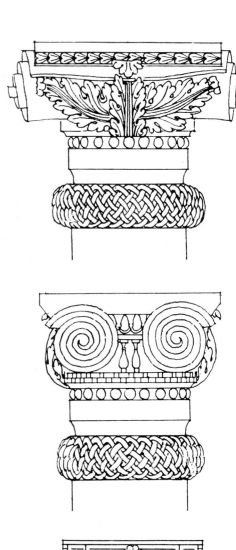

Bana. North-east corner of the interior (left), bricked-up arcading in the eastern apse (below left), and various examples of capital ornamentation from the arcades.

Ishkhani. Details of capitals from the colonnade in the eastern apse, and (below) view of the colonnade.

98

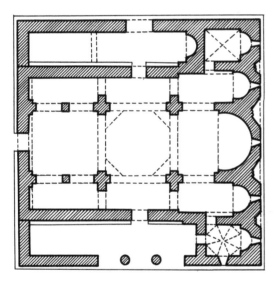

Samshvilde. Centralized domed church,
AD 759–77.
Certain similarities between this building and
Tsromi are evident in the adaptation of the
basic plan, the general architectural structure
and the composition of the details of the de-
sign on the east façade. As a whole, however,
the building bears all the typical marks of its
time. (After Niko Chubinashvili.)

Halfway through the 7th century, the Arabs entered the world arena as a menacing power. After occupying Syria, Palestine and Persia, they gradually extended their power across the entire Caucasus region. Byzantium at this time was entering the period of the Iconoclast controversy (8th and 9th centuries).

The Georgian people put up a life-and-death struggle in defence of their independence, and repelled attacks not only from the Arabs, but also from the Khazars, who were threatening them from the north. The fight against the Arabs was long and hard. The latter eventually secured a foothold in the interior of Kartli, but meanwhile several feudal principalities or *saeristao* around the periphery of the region were gaining strength, and in a comparatively short time—by the beginning of the 9th century—had established themselves as *de facto* independent states. These were Kakheti, Hereti, Egrisi-Abkhazia (West Georgia) and Tao-Klarjeti in southwestern Georgia.

When the Arabs conquered the country, Georgia had a strong cultural foundation and great artistic traditions to sustain it. The interests of the Arabs were concentrated above all in the economic sphere. In the cultural field, local traditions persisted, and the artistic development of Georgia did not undergo any radical changes.

The creative powers of this people were revealed afresh in the 8th and 9th centuries in a series of important architectural works. There is, for instance, the magnificent domed church of Kvela-tsminda in Vachnadziani, which already shows signs of a more picturesque stylistic feeling and arouses great admiration in visitors. Further examples are the twin-domed church of Gurjaani, the domed building in Telovani, the cathedral in Samshvilde, the palaces in Vachnadziani, Vanta and Cheremi referred to earlier, important church buildings at Taoskari, Shatberdi, Opiza, Sveti and Vashlobi, and many others in the southwestern part of Georgia. All these date from the period in which the foundations were being laid for the great flowering of literature, art and philosophical thought in the 10th–12th centuries, as exemplified in the work of the brilliant poet Shota Rustaveli. It is customary to present the 8th and 9th centuries as a tran-

sitional period in the history of Georgian architecture, as a time of tireless quest, a bridge linking the classic period of the 6th and 7th centuries to the second peak, which lasted from the 10th to the 13th century and represented one of the most interesting stages in the development of ancient Georgian architecture. The efforts of the Georgian architects, who were now working in the independent principalities, were persistently directed towards the search for new solutions. New stylistic forms and original features were already emerging quite clearly at this stage. Classical perfection was superseded by a host of new approaches to structure and the decoration of façades, representing attempts to develop more picturesque forms. In the 8th and 9th centuries this trend frequently appeared side by side with elements of the preceding stage; its final phase came in the 10th and 11th centuries.

Buildings of the 8th and 9th centuries are also distinguished by the construction materials employed. They were seldom built of smooth, dressed blocks, but mostly of stones with a roughly-hewn surface, and rubble, boulders and porous tufa were also used.

The four-pier church of Samshvilde, erected between 759 and 777 on the model of the classical structure at Tsromi, is built of splendidly aligned, smoothly dressed blocks of yellowish sandstone. All that remains of the mighty dome is the eastern part, but following the excavation of the site the ground-plan is now plainly visible.

The east façade was furnished with four triangular niches, which obviously contained sculptures. The windows in this façade, with their decorated arches, are linked by a long band of lettering; the characters are in Asomtavruli script, and are filled in with red paint. The inscription states that the local rulers, Varaz Bakur and Iovane, were the founders of the church, and that building began in the reign of the emperor Constantine V Copronymus and was completed under Leon IV, the Khazar.

The grandiose 9th-century domed church at Vachnadziani (present-day Shroma) in Kakheti represents a new departure in Georgian art, and one that was significant in the context of the new concept of the picturesque. It is a complex and highly individual composition of the so-called domed hall type, which combines the idea of the triple-church basilica with the dome motif. This signifies that the fundamental concept is firmly rooted, in every essential feature, in the Georgian architectural tradition.

The hall-like main part of Vachnadziani is articulated by wall-piers that carry the dome over the central bay. The transition to the round dome is here achieved by means of pendentives, an element of construction new to Georgian architecture which was to become more widespread in the course of the 9th century. By contrast, in the niches of the subsidiary bays formed by the piers, the vaulting is built up on squinches.

On either side of the apse there are small triconch chambers, which can be recognized as such from the outside of the church. The western end is enclosed by a three-sided ambulatory. The gallery opens out into the domed hall through large, horseshoe-arched openings.

All this, together with the arrangement of the various interconnected rooms clearly visible on the ground-plan, produces broader and more relaxed spatial effects very much in the spirit of the new picturesque tendency that characterizes the transition to medieval archi-

Vachnadziani. 9th-century church of the so-called domed hall type. This is a highly finished example in artistic terms, and firmly rooted in the developing traditions of Georgian architecture, as revealed particularly in its fusion of two basic types, the domed building and the triple-church basilica. Interior view facing north-east, elevation of the east façade, and plan.

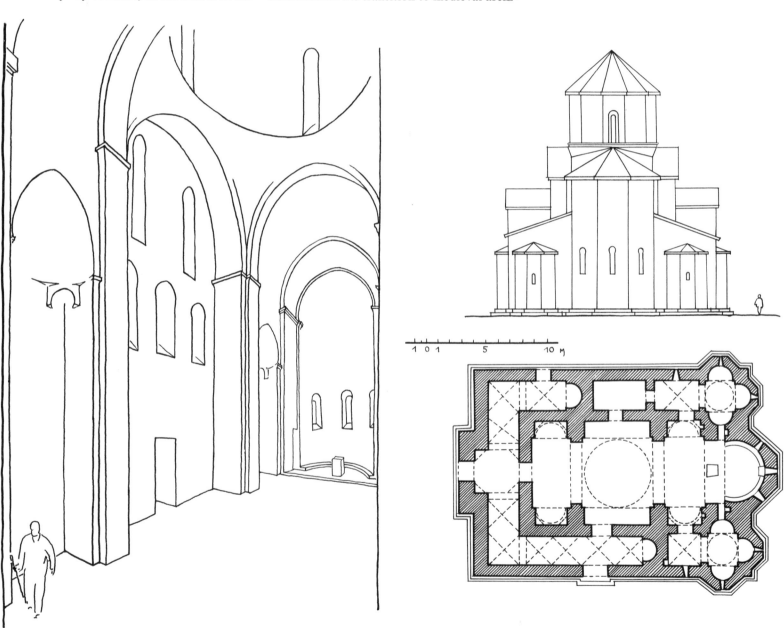

Kabeni in Kanchaeti. Early-9th-century church. The church as it now stands is extensively restored and enlarged, but excavation of the monument has made it possible to reconstruct its original form. It is interesting to note that the entrance to the small southeastern chapel is just as splendid as the entrance to the church itself. The drum is decorated with blind arcading. Section, plan and view from the south-east (reconstructed).

tecture. In this respect—and also in terms of the high artistic standard of its execution—Vachnadziani is a remarkable monument.

Built in the restless, questing 8th century, the two-domed brick and rock basilica at Gurjaani (pp. 120–21) is unique in Georgia. The aisles of the basilica are separated by low, weighty piers. At the west end is a narthex. The high nave carries two relatively small drums topped with domical vaults. In spatial terms, the domes do not play the dominating role here that they do elsewhere in Georgia, and as a result the nave retains the character of a hall. The gallery extending along three sides of the upper level is highly individual: on the south and west sides this upper ambulatory can be reached by large external staircases, and in the south wall it has large, round-arched windows.

The architectural forms of Gurjaani, particularly the external staircases and the construction of the south façade, are features peculiar to the 8th and 9th centuries, and

find echoes in the secular architecture of that time.

The solution adopted at Gurjaani, in the churches at Armazi, Tsirkoli and Likhne which will be discussed later, and in other, similar Georgian churches, is a precise indication of the social differences that divided the worshipping congregation. The gallery, reached by its grand external staircase, was reserved for members of the ruling family; the nave was kept for the lesser nobility, and the lower orders—the peasants and domestic servants—were restricted to the narthex and the side aisles.

The 8th-century domed churches in Nekresi and Telovani (Ksovrisi) (p. 125) are distinguished firstly by certain peculiarities in their structure, and secondly by details of their façade decoration.

The domed church of the Nekresi monastery (p. 123), more or less contemporary with the buildings discussed above, is, like Vachnadziani, a domed variant of the triple-church

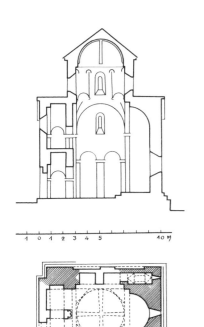

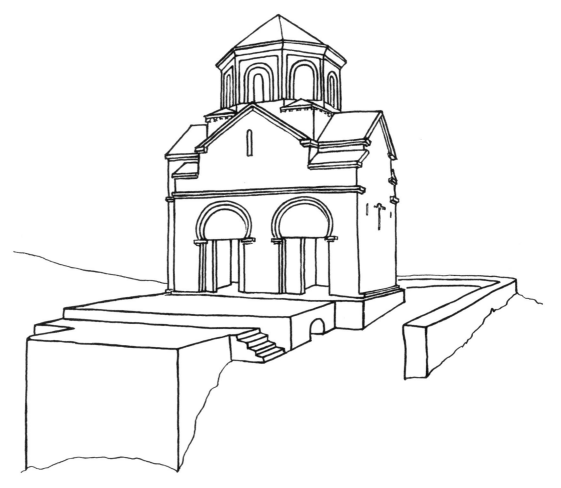

basilica. The modestly proportioned square interior is surmounted by a dome on a tall, slender drum which rests on the walls and on the triumphal arch at the eastern end. The transition from the square to the circular drum is achieved on the eastern side by slabs placed across the corners and on the western side by horseshoe-shaped squinches. The apse, too, is horseshoe-shaped. The external ambulatory, built at the same time as the church, terminates in altar niches at the eastern ends, and its south and west façades have entrances in the form of paired horseshoe arches. The drum is articulated by niches, though these are not joined up into a uniform arcade, as they are in later monuments. The architect has emphasized the unusual features of the structure, thus endowing them with added significance.

Three smaller churches in the valley of the river Ksani, at Armazi, Tsirkoli and Kabeni in Kanchaeti, are clearly the work of a single master. They were built in the 9th century from simple materials—rubble and porous tufa—but their construction is so unusual that they attract very special interest.

Armazi, the most recent of these three monuments, was built in 864, as recorded in an inscription surviving on the south façade. Its plan is rectangular, with four interior pillars. The dome never had a drum, its weight resting directly on the arches that spring from the four columns. The transition to the circle of the dome is achieved by squinches, the arches

Tsirkoli. Domed church, mid-9th century. View of the interior facing north-west; section; elevation of the south façade; plan. The domed church has a pitched roof. The outlines of the blind arcading on the north and south façades are picked out in red paint.

of which have a slight ogee point. The building has a pitched roof, concealing the presence of the dome from outside.

In domed structures the vaulting of the dome, which usually rests on a drum, raises the central part of the building. The interior makes a strong impression of verticality, which is further emphasized by the light entering through the windows of the drum. A dome without a drum is largely denied this effect, and resembles a simple vaulted roof, which makes the interior as a whole seem more like a hall. This is why the Georgian architects devoted so much attention to tectonics, seeking harmonious proportions and normally avoiding the use of a dome without a drum. Domical vaults springing directly from the walls were as a rule used only in areas of secondary importance, as for example in a narthex.

Having created a very individual architectural composition in Armazi, the architect endeavoured to match it with a particularly decorative interior. He emphasized the east end by means of a painted altar screen. The walls were coated with stucco, and etched with parallel and intersecting lines which were then painted in.

In terms of its construction, the church at Tsirkoli differs somewhat from the one at Armazi. From the outside it looks like a rectangular block, but inside it is an original and complex organism. The central part, as at Armazi, is roofed over by a dome without a drum, but here the dome rests on the walls and not on columns. The west end of the building has an upper level, and a pitched roof surmounts the whole structure.

The new artistic techniques are clearly illustrated on the façades, for example in the alternation of broad and narrow rows of facing stones, the two horizontal bands of relief, and—most important—the articulation of the south and north façades by triple blind arcades. The accentuation of the windows by means of their framing should also be mentioned, as should the use of red paint to pick out certain decorative features.

The oldest of the three works by this master is the church of Kabeni in Kanchaeti. It has a complicated history. Partial excavation and

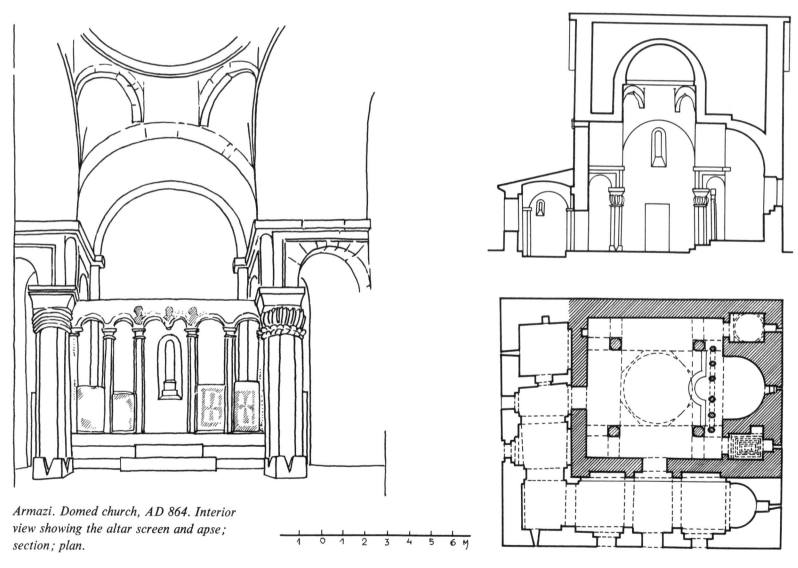

Armazi. Domed church, AD 864. Interior view showing the altar screen and apse; section; plan.

1 0 1 2 3 4 5 6 M

a thoroughgoing analysis of the building have shown that the domed church erected at the beginning of the 9th century was considerably smaller than the one that exists today. In the 10th century an ambulatory was built round three sides of the church. In the 13th century the whole of the eastern end was extended, and openings were made in the three remaining walls, thus combining the church interior with the ambulatory. In this way the whole structure was given an entirely new form.

Originally built on a rectangular plan with a semicircular apse, this church, like the one at Tsirkoli, had a gallery at the western end, with arches looking into the interior. As at Armazi and Tsirkoli, there are small rooms on either side of the altar. The arrangement of the stone slabs in the vaulting of the southern room is reminiscent of the conical roofing of the *darbazi*-type peasant dwelling with its concentric layers of wooden timbers.

Unlike those of Armazi and Tsirkoli, the dome of the Kabeni church rests on a low drum. The exterior of the octagon is decorated with blind arcading; Kabeni is the third church to display this feature, following the 8th-century examples of Nekresi and Telovani. Surviving fragments of a red painted inscription on the south wall mention Latavri, daughter of Adarnese Bagrationi, *eristavi* of Kartli.

Tao-Klarjeti, which the Arabs did not succeed in taking, increased greatly in political and economic importance during the 8th and 9th centuries, and the people's indefatigable creative talent now shifted to this region. The area is exceptionally rich in architectural monuments, their construction linked with the names of such famous personalities of Georgian history as Gregory of Khandzta and Grigol Oshkeli, or with rulers of Tao-Klarjeti such as Ashot Kuropalates, David the Great, the Kuropalate, and others of the house of the Bagratids. The walls of the church interiors are covered with paintings.

Many fortresses have survived in this area which for centuries served the people as bulwarks against the invaders. Inside these fortresses, palaces and churches were built, whose walls bear chiselled inscriptions with the names of their founders.

During the 8th and 9th centuries an abundance of the most diverse architectural forms appeared in these regions. There is, for example, the polygonal structure of Taoskari (p. 122), where eight deep rectangular recesses radiate outwards from the octagonal central bay, or the church in Sveti, which has four apses opening from its hall-like vaulted interior. From outside the observer sees a polygonal lower level articulated by niches and a row of round arches, above which the rectangular core of the building rises up, stark and undecorated. There is also the tetraconch of Bobosgeri, where four pillars carry a dome; from outside the edifice appears to be built up in steps. Similar in some ways is the monument of Kalmakhi, which also has a dome supported by four pillars, but with a simplified rectangular exterior. Finally there is the group of triconch buildings with an accentuated longitudinal axis, beginning with Otkhtaeklesia at Kola, Isi and Zaki (or Zegani) and including also Ortuli, Bakhchali-Kishla and others.

The Christian Church, which had acquired considerable power at an early stage, played an important role in defending the interests of the country in the face of the foreign conquerors. During the 8th and 9th centuries, monastic life expanded on a large scale. The leaders of the movement were mainly figures from Tao-Klarjeti, the so-called 'Georgian Sinai', including Gregory of Khandzta, his disciples Saban, Tevdore and Kristephore, and others who were active in Kartli, in West Georgia at Nedzvi, Kvirike-tsminda and Ube (present-day Ubisi), and elsewhere. Gregory of Khandzta was a highly educated man. He was as important for his time as was Peter of Iberia for 5th-century monastic life in Palestine, and his particular achievement was the founding of monasteries and the organization of monastic life.

Gregory of Khandzta was connected with the erection of the monastery at Shatberdi. A domed church and a large number of buildings, indicating the monastery's former size and importance, survived there until modern times. Niko Marr wrote of it: 'I imagined that I was Gregory Khandzteli's guest, in the presence of the compilers and scribes of the 10th-century Chronicle of Shat-

Sveti. Church of the 8th and 9th centuries. The square, barrel-vaulted hall interior with its four small apses is scarcely reflected at all in the polygonal exterior. Only the rectangular structure beneath the pitched roof indicates the shape of the inside.
Plan; section in a north-south direction; section in an east-west direction; elevation of the north side. (After E. Takaishvili.)

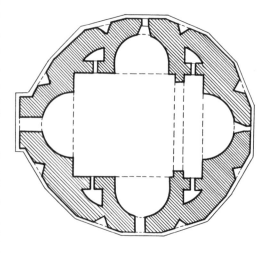

berdi, and my physical fatigue appeared to vanish in the company of the creators of the once flourishing Georgian culture. I had already been overcome by a mood of such remoteness from the world of today, and had begun to feel so close to the bygone reality of this secluded corner, that I would not have been surprised if Gregory Khandzteli had appeared in person to answer the question which had brought me here: "Where is Shatberdi?" Although Gregory referred to himself as "from Khandzta", and Khandzta was his first creation, yet in my mind Shatberdi seems somehow more closely bound up with him, and I believe that he cherished it more.'

The church of Shatberdi is a cruciform domed building, with the dome resting on the corners of the apse walls at the eastern end and on two free-standing pillars at the west. It was the first church built on this plan, which became widely used later on.

Shatberdi resembles Opiza, which dates from the same period, firstly in its situation on the slopes of a mountain, and secondly in the treatment of the drum with its blind arcading, zig-zag cornice and fluted roof. In some other monuments, too, the drum is dodecagonal in shape and carries a domical vault instead of a hemispherical dome.

According to surviving inscriptions, the monastery of Opiza (p. 126) was rebuilt by Ashot I in the first decades of the 9th century. Apart from the church, several other buildings still stand today, including a three-aisled hall—the seminary—and the scriptorium. The scriptorium, square in plan, has a dome with an opening to admit light. The hall is large, and is lit by four broad windows in the façade. Such buildings exist in many of the major monasteries of Tao-Klarjeti, as for example Shatberdi, Berta, Khandzta, Otkhtaeklesia and Oshki.

The church at Opiza, with its large, high dome, is remarkable for its elongated western arm and the blind arcades on one surface only of the east face. Blind arcading, as we shall see in due course, later extended across all the façades of a building and became one of the dominant decorative features.

A significant monument of the 8th and 9th centuries is to be found in another historically important province, Egrisi-Abkhazia. The great triple-church basilica in Ambara, on the shores of the Black Sea, is built of a variety of materials. The central section, which is large and high, has three doors at the west end and rows of niches with windows at the top along the north and south walls. Above the narthex is a gallery which communicates with the church by means of large openings arranged in two tiers as in Gurjaani. Three large round-arched doors in the centre of the south fa-

çade, further emphasized by a triangular gable, invest the south entrance of the church with the character of a great portal. At the same time, the narthex at the west end, with the three doors leading into the inner church, gives the whole west entry a special air of importance. Two different artistic approaches have here been combined: the arrangement of three doors at the west end, which is characteristic of Byzantium, and the typically Georgian motif of an arched main entrance on the south side. Preference is clearly given here to the latter.

The church of Sioni—today the neighbouring village bears the same name—stands on a fortified mound on the road that runs beside the river Terek to Kazbegi. Nearby is a slender tower, and the two buildings make a striking picture standing together in the mountain scenery of the Greater Caucasus. The church is a three-aisled basilica, built at the end of the 9th and the beginning of the 10th century. The tall, slender nave is connected to the side aisles by arches, though the normal rhythm of this kind of building is somewhat impaired here by the fact that the arches become narrower towards the west. The north and south annexes, likewise linked to the basilica by arcades, are badly damaged.

The altar screen, which dates from the same time as the church itself, consists of a row of

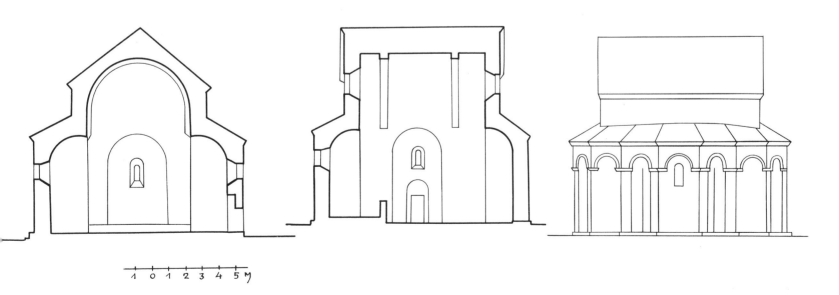

slender, beautifully decorated columns with arches springing from them, and shares the same expressiveness that characterizes the whole building. The Sioni basilica is one of the late and rare examples of its type in Georgia. Near the building on the south side stands a stele which once ended in a small cross; an inscription, and some relief carvings in a poor state of preservation, can be seen on the stone.

The rulers of Georgia established links with other states through the medium of the Christian Church. They supported the expansion of existing monasteries and the foundation of new ones, and in these monasteries the Georgians engaged in many kinds of intellectual and artistic pursuit, thereby selflessly furthering the interests of their homeland.

Whereas in the 5th and 6th centuries the promotors of the Georgian cause had looked towards Jerusalem, the first home of Christianity, as time went on their attention turned increasingly to the west. In many ways the mighty Constantinople had greater advantages than Jerusalem, for whereas the latter was in Moslem hands, Byzantine culture on the other hand was now acquiring world importance. In the 9th century Ilarion of Georgia founded a monastery on Mount Olympus in Asia Minor, and before that he had established a settlement at David-Gareja. Many

Georgians were involved in prolific activities in Constantinople during the 11th century, and great work was also performed in the Georgian monastery on the island of Cyprus.

The work of the Georgians in the great community on Mount Athos in Greece was particularly important: the famous Iberian (i.e. Georgian) monastery built there in the 10th century subsequently became a great centre of religious learning. Grigol Bakurianisdze, the 'Grand-Domestic of the West' (general of the Byzantine army in Europe) founded a Georgian monastery, the Bachkovo monastery, at Petritsoni in Bulgaria, but all that survives intact from this period is a cemetery church with wall-paintings inside which include a portrait of Grigol himself. Grigol Bakurianisdze left a typikon—the house rules of the monastery, setting out the daily routine and the programme for the seminary. Ioane Petritsi spent many years at Petritsoni as an active representative of a new philisophical movement, and later continued his work at the monastery of Gelati.

The establishment of the Georgian colony in Europe exercised a great influence on the evolution of the national literature. The works written in these centres and handed down to us—some of them having been brought back to Georgia at a later date—enable us to reconstruct the literary activities of Georgians

Ambara. 8th-century triple-church basilica with narthex and gallery.
Plan, and elevation of the south façade.

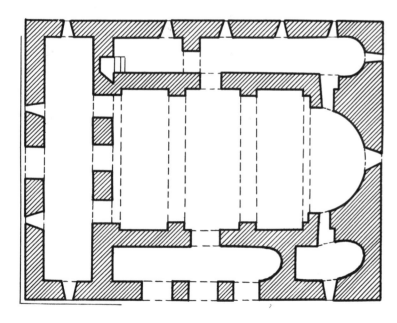

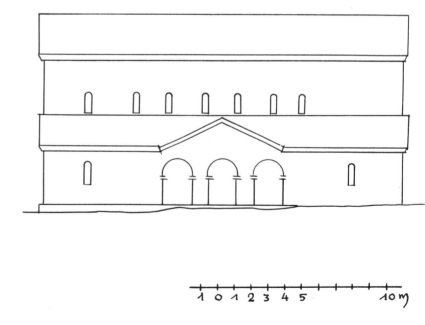

abroad. As regards their building activities away from home, however, the information we have is extremely limited.

In this respect, the majestic ruins of the monastery church (pp. 164–5) on the Black Mountain 40 kilometres from Antioch—one of thirteen Georgian monasteries in this region—are of very special value. It is a cruciform domed structure with four supporting piers, the walls faced inside and out with neatly dressed blocks. Originally, the church was richly decorated, and the little that survives of this decoration reveals a beauty of detail and a high standard of craftsmanship worthy of great admiration. Even the fragment of an inscription written in Asomtavruli characters is outstanding for the beautiful, decorative formation of the letters. The startling similarity of various details in this Georgian church on the Black Mountain with details of the cathedral of Samtavisi have led Vakhtang Djobadze, who has been making an intensive study of the former for some years, to believe that it was built by a disciple of the Samtavisi architect.

At this time the interest of the ruling powers in Georgia was focused on the north, on Dvaleti and, in the northern Caucasus, on Ossetia, Ingushetia and Dagestan. The Georgians endeavoured to introduce Christianity to these regions, and this is why there are still churches in these countries today which bear Georgian inscriptions and have ornamentation, reliefs and wall-paintings of distinctly Georgian character: at Khozita-mairam, for example, and at Tkoba-erdi, Datuna, Tli, Kalaki and Nuzal.

The 10th and 12th centuries represent a period of the highest achievement in Georgian culture, particularly in art. The 10th century saw rapid progress towards the unification of the separate feudal states, and on the threshold of the 11th century Bagrat III succeeded in uniting them under central rule, thereby accelerating the economic and cultural development of Georgia. The economic revival was accompanied by greatly expanded trade: Georgian coins found in Russia, the lands of the Baltic, Germany and Scandinavia demonstrate the extent of the country's trade links.

Halfway through the 11th century, Georgia was struck by a catastrophe of massive pro-portions. Nomadic Turkish tribes, who had conquered first the Arabian and Persian lands and then Byzantium, now moved into Georgia. The period of economic and cultural expansion was succeeded by one of stagnation. The Georgians, however, displayed great endurance and courage in the defence of their homeland, and refused—unlike others—to submit to this foreign power. During this troubled time, when both the Turkish rulers and the west European Crusaders were waging a calamitous policy of conquest of foreign territory in the Near East, the Georgian people not only defended their political independence, but actually consolidated it. In the first quarter of the 12th century King David, known to the people as 'the Builder', completed the unification of the country. During his reign, the frontiers were pushed back until Georgia stretched from the Black Sea to the Caspian, and southwards as far as the river Araxes. The political weight of the country grew to such a degree that in the early 13th century Queen Tamar played an active part in establishing the kingdom of Trebizond. The rulers of Trebizond became vassals of Georgia.

The period from the 10th to the first half of the 13th century was the high point of Georgian culture, particularly in the fine arts (architecture, sculpture, metalwork, wall-painting and book illumination). In the 12th century, often described as the 'Golden Age', religious and secular literature reached their zenith. Great works of religious poetry were written at this time, some with musical notation.

The architecture of this period developed the ideas of the transitional period and transformed them into accomplished artistic formulae. Structural and decorative forms were now determined by the desire to produce rich effects of light and shade. The squinch was generally replaced by the pendentive, which provided lighter, more fluent transitions. The component parts of the building lost their individual significance and became subordinate to the overall artistic conception. The decoration and ornamentation of the buildings were constantly enriched by masterly workmanship and endless invention. Chubinashvili has characterized this multiplication of complex in-terior arrangements and exuberant decorative elements as a 'baroque' tendency.

It is interesting to observe parallel processes in the development of architecture in Georgia and Byzantium at this time. The second flowering of Byzantine architecture occurred in the 10th and 11th centuries, and although it could not equal the splendour of the age of Justinian, and like the latter was unfamiliar with questions of façade construction, it did resolve the artistic problems in a balanced, harmonious and picturesque manner. 'Byzantine architecture did not perfect the exterior, and in particular applied no artistic decoration to it, leaving bricks, stones and mortar unadorned. Georgian architecture of this period, on the other hand, not only evolved a highly finished exterior, but also developed an exceptionally rich system of decoration, with a form of ornament quite unique in both its expressive power and the infinite variety of its motifs. So here we have evidence of parallel developments, occurring at more or less the same time and resulting partly from an exchange of forms, which in terms of stylistic conception are of the same type. These developments, however, occurred independently in each country' (Giorgi Chubinashvili).

Georgian architects of the 10th century surveyed the wealth of architectural forms and ideas inherited from previous epochs, and selected for use those which fulfilled the requirements of their own particular time.

The buildings of the first half of the 10th century occasionally display characteristics that were already important in the 8th and 9th centuries: the striving for new architectural forms, occasionally to the detriment of the artistic unity and structure of the buildings, the use of a variety of building materials, and restraint in the decoration of the buildings.

An unusual feature of the church of St George in Eredvi is the ambulatory running round all four sides—that is, enclosing the east end as well. The column at the south entrance to the building carries an inscription with the date of construction, 906. The church of Sabatsminda in Kheiti is also highly individual. With its cruciform plan it corresponds to the basic type of the domed central-plan church—except that here there is no dome. The barrel vaults over the main nave and over the arms of the cross intersect at different heights, so that there is no resulting domical vault.

The church built in Doliskana (p. 127) by King Sumbat I (923–58), son of Adarnese II, is a cruciform domed building with a projecting western arm. From outside, it appears rectangular in shape. The façades are decorated with relief figures and ornamental details, of which the most prominent is a fan-like motif above the windows, executed in different coloured stones.

The church in Zaki (or Zegani) is a triconch with an eastern apse projecting well beyond the line of the east wall, and has interesting ornamentation. Equally remarkable in this respect is the 10th-century domed church in Tskarostavi, whose west end with its horse-shoe arches is reminiscent of models from the 5th and 6th centuries.

A special place in 10th-century church architecture is occupied by the grand three-aisled basilicas of Otkhta-eklesia (Dortkilisa) (p. 128) and Parkhali, which have inscriptions mentioning David Kuropalates and other rulers of the historic province of Tao-Klarjeti. These buildings show that, despite the predominance of other architectural types, interest in three-aisled basilicas was not yet dead. Each has four pairs of pillars inside, but the distance between the pairs varies, which interrupts the regular rhythm of the arcades and produces a wealth of picturesque effects in keeping with the prevailing taste and requirements of the 10th century. Both buildings have galleries at the west end and two side-chambers at the east end—the prothesis (used for the preparation and storage of the eucharist) and the diaconicon (used for the reception of the congregation's offerings, and also serving as vestry and library).

The façades of the two basilicas are finished with squared stone, and have blind arcades which already form the dominant feature of the decoration. The lower arcade in each case is set on broad flat pilasters, while the upper one springs from slender half-columns. Some of the windows and doors are adorned with ornamental and figural reliefs, and with different coloured slabs arranged to form a fan pattern. There are several red painted in-

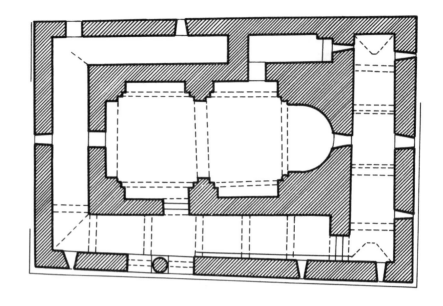

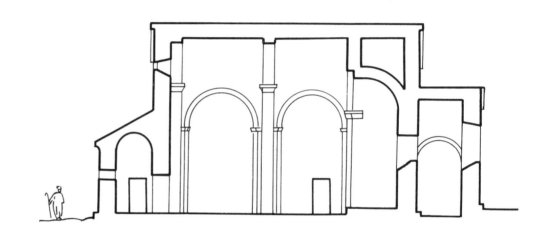

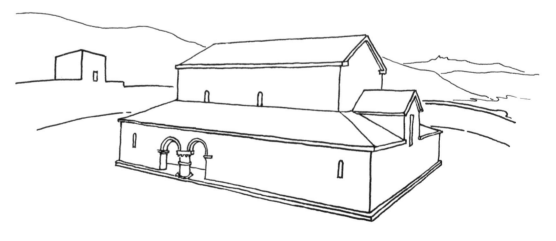

Eredvi. Triple-church basilica, AD 906.
The ambulatory running round three sides,
which is normal for this type of building, here
has an additional section to the east, a feature
which cannot be found anywhere else in
Georgia.
Plan; section in an east-west direction;
general view from the south-west.

Kheiti. The church of Sabatsminda, early
10th century. The exterior gives no hint of
the tall, hall-like interior, nor of the cruci-
form plan of the church. The ambulatory
running round the west end, and the side
rooms projecting on either side of the apse in
the east, reinforce the rectangular impression
made by the body of the building. The church
underwent minor restorations in the 13th and
14th centuries, and again later. The only other
instance of this particular type is at Khobi,
built at the end of the 13th century.
Plan, and bird's-eye view from the south-west.

scriptions in Asomtavruli and Nuskhuri scripts, and inside the churches the remains of wall-paintings can be seen.

In the second half of the 10th century, a new form of church building appeared in Georgia: the centralized structure with six apses. Buildings of this type occur in various Georgian provinces, and include the churches of Bochorma (p. 135) in Kakheti, Katskhi in Imereti, and Gogiuba, Kiagmis-alti and Oltisi in south-western Georgia. These monuments deal with the interior space in a sophisticated manner. With the exception of Gogiuba, each of them has a projecting east apse, in some cases with small side-chambers on either side of it. The outward appearance of these buildings is characterized by the contrasting effect arising from the juxtaposition of the spreading main structure with the slender dome above. The façades are decorated with tall niches and blind arcading, and Bochorma and Katskhi, like Opiza and Shatberdi, have zig-zag cornices all the way round.

The most recent of these churches, Katskhi, is also the most highly developed composition. An ambulatory, actually built in the mid-11th century but provided for in the original plans of the late 10th and early 11th centuries, lends it a certain air of dignity.

The centralized churches of Kumurdo and Nikortsminda have cruciform exteriors. The church in Kumurdo (pp. 129–30) was erected by the master builder Sakotsari, and one of the inscriptions dates it to the year 964. The basic plan of a structure with several apses is given a highly individual variation here. The apses are grouped in an unusual way; they do not radiate outwards from the central core in the usual manner, but instead there are two on the north side and two on the south, lying side by side. The east apse is flanked by two smaller side apses. The dome, which rested on six tall, slender polygonal piers engaged with the dividing walls of the apses, has collapsed. The western end no longer retains its original appearance, for in the second quarter of the 11th century an ambulatory was built round three sides of the church, and substantial parts of it are still standing today. The precision of the workmanship of the interior stonework is most attractive: the courses are continuous throughout, the blocks are neatly squared, and the stone, especially that used in the conches, has been carefully selected for its veining. Two reliefs survive on the eastern squinches; one is a portrait of Queen Gurandukht, mother of King Bagrat III, while the other shows a male figure, presum-

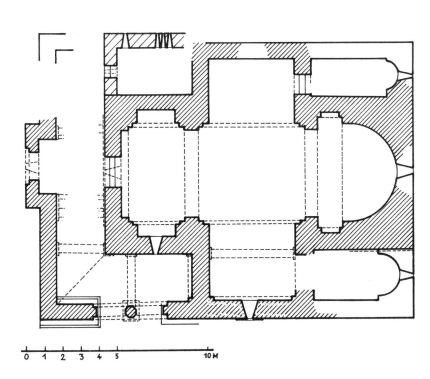

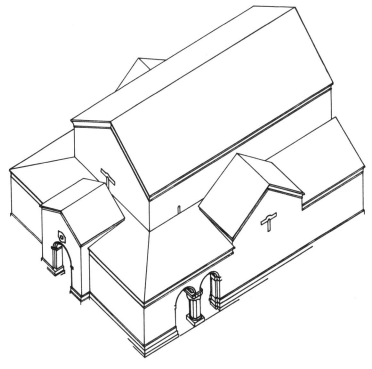

0 1 2 3 4 5   10 M

ably Gurgen, Bagrat's father. The exterior of the church is as finely executed as the interior. The decoration of the exterior is bold and simple, consisting of tall niches with ornamental details; the ornamentation is in low relief, producing a graphic effect. The solution of the given artistic task at Kumurdo makes the church an outstanding work of its time. If we compare it with the equally important monument of Nikortsminda, built at the beginning of the 11th century, the two buildings with their striking differences appear to represent completely different artistic periods.

Nikortsminda (pp. 131–4) was built between 1010 and 1014, in the reign of King Bagrat III. As at Kumurdo, the cruciform shape of the exterior does not reflect the multi-apse composition of the interior, though here the apses are grouped as in conventional six-apse structures. In section, the apses are horseshoe-shaped. A tall, broad drum crowns the structure.

From outside, the church of Nikortsminda looks completely different from that of Kumurdo. Whereas there the overriding impression was of the architectural forms and the great expanse of smooth walls, here all is subordinate to the decorative ornamentation. At Nikortsminda the observer is fascinated by the abundance—perhaps even excess—of decoration on the drum, which is completely covered with carved ornament. The façades, the window surrounds and the cornices are all equally richly embellished. Relief scenes on the drum, the gables of the façades and the tympana over the portals blend with the ornamental patterns in a unified system of decoration.

The small, elegant palace church in the citadel of Kvetera (p. 136) is entirely different in character. It has four apses, with almost wholly circular niches inserted between them. Its plan and architectural forms are reminiscent of those of the small 6th-century domed church in Dzveli Shuamta, yet it is unmistakably of its own time, the 10th century. From the outside one sees four polygonal apses, the angles between them filled by small, rounded protrusions. This gives such diversity to the external forms of the building that the basic outline is lost in their alternation and in the ensuing picturesque effects of light and shade. The church is decorated inside and out with clustered mouldings, whose profusion masks the basic shape of the building even more.

There are also a number of important buildings from the 10th century in Abkhazia, whose

Centralized buildings with six apses, from the second half of the 10th century. These represent individual variations and extensions of the tetraconch type, corresponding in their approach to the decorative trends of the period.

a Gogiuba b Kiagmis-alti c Oltisi d Bochorma e Katskhi

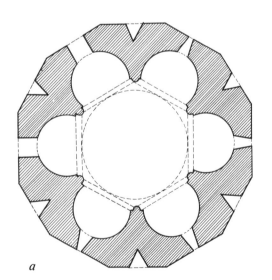

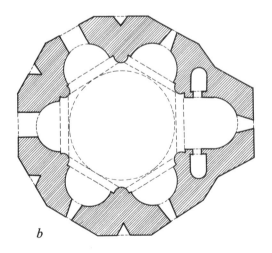

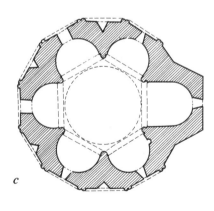

political and economic power was expanding at this time.

The church in Bichvinta represents the cruciform domed type developed in Georgia, with two detached piers supporting the dome and a narthex with a gallery above it. The interior of the building is spacious and magnificent. Outside, three semicircular apses project at the east end. The walls consist of alternate courses of stone and brickwork. A layer of stucco was removed from them only recently, revealing the construction of the 10th-century squinches and the open arches of the doorways.

The Mokvi church, built in the reign of King Leon II (957–67), is likewise an impressive structure. This central-domed building with its four free-standing piers has an ambulatory on three sides, with a gallery running above it. The general appearance of the church and some of the details suggest a familiarity with the architecture of Constantinople, although the Byzantine inspiration has been appropriately modified to conform with national traditions.

Four-piered domed churches have survived in Likhne, Bzibi, Akhali Atoni and other places in Abkhazia. These monuments are built of dressed stone and have some interesting details. Bzibi stands out for the ornamental decoration of its window arches, similar forms of which appear on other 10th-century monuments.

The tendency towards the grandiose in the architecture of the late 10th and early 11th centuries is demonstrated by the erection of cathedrals in the principal regions of Georgia: Bagrat III's cathedral at Kutaisi in the west, Alaverdi in the east, Oshki and Ishkhani in Tao-Klarjeti and Sveti-tskhoveli in Mtskheta. And in the Samtskhe region there was the mighty church of Atskuri, now in ruins.

Oshki, Alaverdi and the Bagrat cathedral at Kutaisi are all built on a triconch plan with a projecting west arm. Oshki differs from the other two in having chapels on either side of each of its apses. At Oshki and in the Bagrat cathedral the drum rests on four massive free-standing piers; at Alaverdi the piers are detached only at the bottom, whereas further up they engage with the walls. All three churches have a gallery.

Despite their common features, each of these buildings has its own distinct character. At Oshki, for example, the bases and capitals of the piers are richly decorated.

David III, the ruler of Tao, and his brother Bagrat began building the great and richly appointed church of Oshki (pp. 138–41) in the second half of the 10th century. Life-sized figures of the founders, with inscriptions picked out in red on the stone above them, are carved on the south façade on either side of the representation of the Deesis (the intercession of the Virgin and St John the Baptist before Christ). The master mason and architect was Grigol Oshkeli, who is portrayed on one of the columns in the south gallery.

The Oshki church is a large and imposing building. Its powerful structural forms blend harmoniously with the splendour of its decoration. The massive piers under the dome vary in form, the pair in the east being polygonal, while those in the west are stepped in a cruciform pattern. The decoration of the bases of the piers, which are as much as three metres high, also varies. The transition to the dome is made by means of four decorative squinches. Despite the colossal size of the building, the architect managed to keep the lines clean and the forms delicate. The interior with its vertical emphasis is filled with light, which streams in through the numerous windows and plays on the many different surfaces.

In the apse and the west arm are areas of rough stonework which were once covered

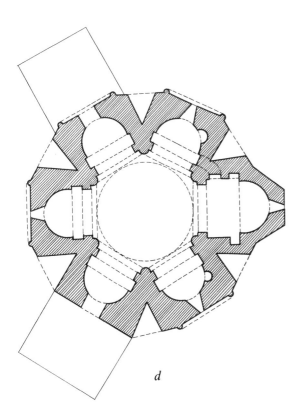

d

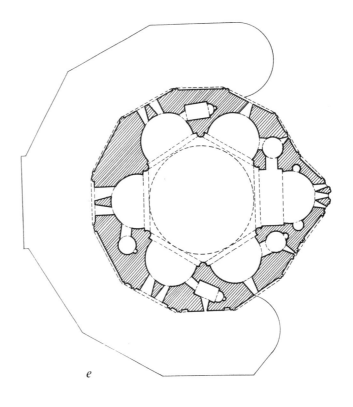

e

with plaster and painted. Surviving fragments of one wall-painting date from the early 11th century.

From outside, the structure seems to build up in steps to the mighty dome. Deep niches are let into the façades, and the south gallery, with its double row of columns and its multi-gabled roof, reinforces the overall feeling of movement.

The decorative blind arcading at Oshki stands out in pronounced relief. Against the high, smooth wall of the west arm, the gallery is sharply defined. The twelve windows on the drum are framed in blind arches with double twisted columns. Their capitals, like the windows, niches and capitals of the church itself and the details of the portico, are richly ornamented with patterns and figures in relief, the backgrounds of which still retain traces of colour. These reliefs, to which we shall return later, are clearly the work of a talented and progressive master.

Beside the church are the buildings that housed the academy and the library and scriptorium. The academy, now in ruins, was a large building divided up inside by four pairs of columns and communicating by means of a door with the library. The latter, built on a square plan, is surmounted by a dome on squinches. Both buildings are constructed of rough-hewn stone, though dressed stone is used for the structural elements. Two

Georgian bibles and several other manuscripts which later passed to Mount Athos are thought to have emanated from the monastery of Oshki. They must have been written in this scriptorium.

In the Tortumi gorge is the domed church of Khakhuli, which according to one of the annalists was likewise built by David III Kuropalates. The monument is in an excellent state of preservation. It differs from Oshki and many other buildings of the period in that its façades have no blind arcading. Instead the walls, which are faced with dressed stone, have individual decorative elements: the window frames are ornamented with fan patterns in stone, and there are reliefs on the façades. Blind arcading does, however, surround the windows on the drum. Inside, a wall-painting dating from the time the church was built has been preserved.

The church in Kutaisi (pp. 142–5) was even larger than that of Oshki. It was founded by King Bagrat III and is generally referred to by his name. Now an imposing ruin, the building stands on a hill above modern Kutaisi, where it appears as an integral part of the town's architectural character. Work on the building began in the last quarter of the 10th century and was completed at the beginning of the 11th century. An inscription on the north façade of the building gives a date, and reads as follows: 'When the floor was finished,

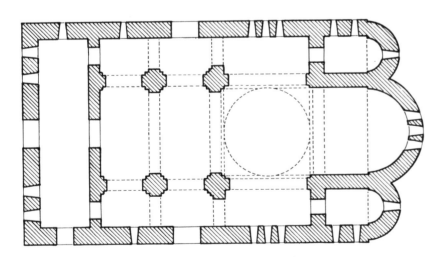

Bichvinta. 10th-century church.
Plan, and elevation of the east façade.

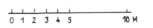

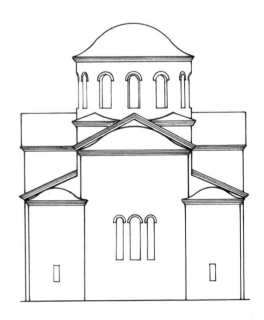

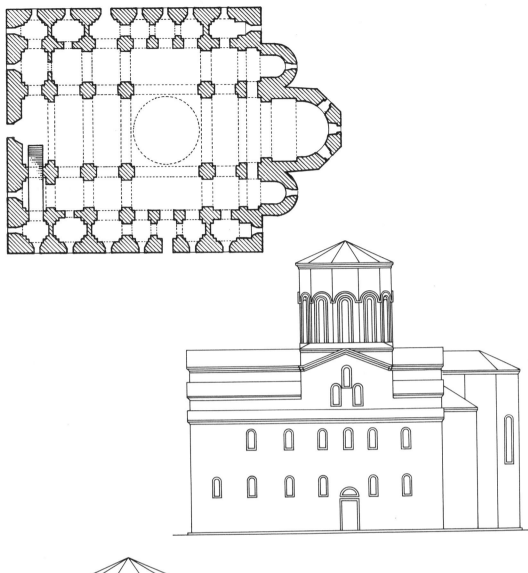

Mokvi. 10th-century church.
Plan, and elevations of the south and west façades.

it was the Chronicon 223.' In order to arrive at an equivalent date in our own reckoning, we have to add the figure 780, making the year 1003. When the church was completed, Bagrat III arranged a spectacular consecration ceremony: 'He assembled the neighbouring rulers, the patriarchs and archbishops, the abbots of all the monasteries and all the notables from the higher and lower parts of his realm and from all other kingdoms,' writes a chronicler.

At the beginning of the 11th century, a three-storey tower which evidently served as the archbishop's residence was erected at the north-west corner of the building. Then, during the first quarter of the century, richly decorated porticoes with arched openings were added to the south and west walls of the church.

Like Oshki, the Bagrat church is a triconch with four detached piers. It has a narthex at the west end, and an ambulatory round three sides with arched openings in its outer wall. The dominating features of the interior were the soaring octagonal piers and the drum, whose windows, together with those of the conches, flooded the building with light. The façades are articulated by blind arcades with deep stepped mouldings. Their rhythm gives the slender gables a feeling of lightness and dynamism, further emphasized by the pairs of slender windows with a small round window above each pair.

The ornamental decoration is partly in the flat graphic style characteristic of the 10th century, but elsewhere it is three-dimensional and sculptural, with splendid unfurled leafwork and complicated modelling of shapes such as we find on monuments of the first half of the 11th century. The reliefs on the capitals in the church and the pillared entrances are particularly interesting; they employ a wide repertoire of animal subjects, blending well with plant motifs. The flooring whose completion is referred to in the inscription survives at the eastern end of the building. The pattern consists of large circles with coloured segments of black, white and red paste inlay. Brick-red inscriptions in Asomtavruli name King Bagrat, his mother Gurandukht and the king's sons.

The Bagrat cathedral was sacked and partly

demolished in the 17th century, but work carried out over the last ten years has partially restored the building to its original appearance.

Built in the first quarter of the 11th century, the church of Alaverdi (pp. 146–7) stands proudly in the broad Alazani valley against the backdrop of the Caucasus foothills. This imposing triconch is distinguished by the quality of its internal structure. The skill with which the various elements are combined to form an effective whole can be seen at a glance from the plan: by his clear and simple arrangement of the bays, the architect has produced a spacious, light-filled interior. Pastophories (side-chambers) at the east end connect with the east conch and the side conches through small antechambers. In the west, the gallery opens on to the central space through arches.

Alaverdi no longer has its three-sided ambulatory. The dome and drum were rebuilt in the 1480s, and other restorations have been carried out since, but in spite of all this the church has retained its basic architectural form and its decorative adornment.

The façades of the church are decorated with blind arcades, and two niches at the east end set off the apse. The normal function of blind arcading—to give extra definition to the structure of the building—is here undermined by the unusual emphasis laid on its decorative aspect. The variation of the decorative forms and the arch heights on the north and south façades, and the two large rosettes on the east wall, all contribute to this effect.

Inside, the church was painted. The fragments of painting surviving in the choir date from the time when the church was built, those elsewhere in the building from the time of the restoration of the dome.

A high defensive wall surrounds the church, enclosing also the palace and the scriptorium to the south-west. Both the latter are badly damaged. The palace was on two floors, with four large archways at the front. Beside it stands a large refectory dating from the late 16th and early 17th centuries, and there is also a 16th-century bell-tower. At the northwestern end of the court is the summer residence. The bathhouse lies outside the enclosure.

The church of Ishkhani (pp. 148–9), with its wealth of superbly worked decoration, must be regarded as one of the outstanding examples from this period. According to the accounts of the chroniclers it was originally constructed in the 7th century (see pp. 65 and 66), but in the 9th century Bishop Saban Ishkhneli ordered the now ruined church to be rebuilt. The final phase of building took place in the year 1032, under the direction of the architect Ioane Morchaisdze. Ishkhani is a cruciform domed structure, with four piers, varying in form as at Oshki: the pair in the east is octagonal, while the western pair is cruciform, with curved protrusions filling in the angles. As at Oshki, the bases and capitals of these piers are richly ornamented.

The façades are dominated by blind arcades with complex graduated profiles. Apart from being decorative, these have a structural function, for the areas enclosed by the arches are considerably recessed, giving added prominence to the walls above them. The effect of this is to divide the façade into two layers, with the resulting shadows emphasizing the impression of movement. The windows are set into the arches with absolute symmetry, which emphasizes the bold lines of the arcading just as the picturesque qualities of the façades are underscored by the decorative ornamentation of the windows and doorways. The master of Ishkhani included a frame in his decoration of the windows and doors, combining it skilfully with the hood of the arch. This principle of composition, with variations, was to be employed for centuries to come.

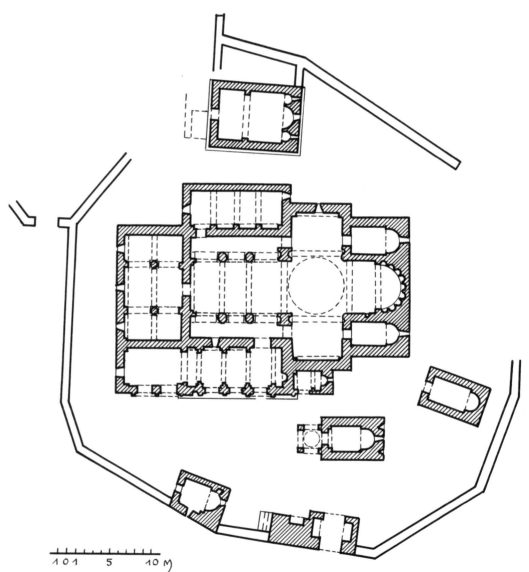

The drum is decorated with blind arcading inside and out. In its sixteen arches, eight tall slender windows alternate with eight small round ones, all with ornamental frames. The arches with their pairs of slender spiral columns, the cornice with its dentil band and the circles worked in flat relief on a dark background all combine to make the drum picturesque.

Inscriptions on the building in Asomtavruli script name rulers of Kartli and Tao-Klarjeti and bishops of Ishkhani. These inscriptions provide confirmation of other written records, and are thus of great historical importance.

Sveti-tskhoveli (pp. 150–57) has always been one of Georgia's national shrines, and there are many legends bound up with it. Its destiny was closely interwoven with that of the country. Its foundation was associated with the acceptance of Christianity and the establishment of feudalism, and though destroyed and desecrated many times it has always been built anew, a symbol of the nation's vital power. The complex history of the building left abundant evidence, much of which has been recovered as a result of excavations and research work in recent years.

Architecturally, Sveti-tskhoveli is the focal point of the city of Mtskheta. The present building dates from the first third of the 11th century. An inscription on the east façade names the founder and the architect: 'Praised be, in the name of Christ the Lord, Melkhisedek, Catholicos of Kartli, Amen. This holy church was built by the hand of thy wretched servant Arsukisdze. May God send peace to his soul.' High up in the arch on the north façade is carved a hand holding a set-square, with the inscription: 'Hand of the humble servant Arsukisdze. Grant forgiveness.'

The church is a centralized domed structure with a narthex and gallery at the west end and two-storey pastophories flanking the apse. Blind arcading, enriched by splendid ornamental work and relief figures, articulates the façades on all sides of the building. Originally the church had subsidiary buildings on three sides, but all that remains of this is the foundations.

Its immediate predecessor was the church built by King Vakhtang Gorgaslani in the 5th century. This in turn was erected on the site of a timber church, by that time already in ruins. Vakhtang Gorgaslani's structure was a large three-aisled basilica, similar to the Sion church in Bolnisi, with four pairs of cruciform piers, a projecting polygonal apse at the east end and galleries on the north and south sides. Piers of various heights, with ornamented bases, survive to this day, as do the original apse and the foundations of the galleries (pp. 74–5).

By the beginning of the 11th century, Vakhtang Gorgaslani's building was in an advanced stage of decay, and had already been partially rebuilt. Arsukisdze used the piers of the basilica for his new building, but heightened and altered them, giving them their present unusual shape. He also extended the east-west dimension of the building by moving the apse further east and adding a narthex, and later a portico, in the west.

In 1283, as recorded in one of the chronicles, the church was damaged by an earthquake. It also suffered serious harm during the Mongol invasions led by Tamerlane at the beginning of the 15th century. 'This he dared to do ... with unclean hands he set about destroying and laying waste Sveti-tskhoveli,' writes the chronicler. At that time the dome collapsed, and the entire western part of the building was damaged. Alexander I, King of Kartli, initiated the rebuilding of the church in the first half of the 15th century. He replaced the drum and dome, reconstructed the western end of the building and reinforced it. In the 17th century, however, dome and drum had to be rebuilt once more. The annexes, which were used for a variety of purposes, fell into such disrepair that in the 19th century they were removed altogether.

The decoration of the façades was likewise restored many times, but for the most part only in its details. Its original character remained unaltered. Thus the blind arcading on all four façades dates from the 11th century, as do the ornamentation of the upper part of the west front, with the sculptural group representing the Majestas Domini, and the two representations of the Tree of Life on the sides of the apse. The figures on the east front of a lion and an eagle in high relief have also survived in their original form. Lower down are two angels placed here at the time of the

Khakhuli. 10th-century monastery.
According to the chronicles, the great domed church was built by David Kuropalates, a ruler of Tao and a member of the Bagrationi dynasty, who died in 1001. The monastery precinct contains several other small churches built at different periods.

restoration. The upper part of the north façade has survived unscathed. The two bulls' heads on the east façade, however, came from the 5th-century basilica.

Sveti-tskhoveli was the burial place of the Georgian kings. The graves of Erekle II and his son Giorgi XII, the last outstanding rulers of Georgia, are here, and according to tradition Vakhtang Gorgaslani is also buried in the church.

Around the church were the palace and various domestic buildings, and the whole complex was enclosed by a high stone wall with a large gatehouse. In the south-west part of the enclosure, some 200 square metres of the remains of the palace walls have been excavated. They are constructed of rough-hewn stones, and there is evidence of a fireplace at the centre. The excavations also revealed a great state hall next to the palace, approximately 600 square metres in area. This was built of neatly squared stones. The walls had pilasters, and the only remaining window has an ornamented surround. The hall dates from the 11th century.

Following the removal of later additions, the west gate emerged as a structure unique in Georgia. The inscription on the front of the upper storey again names the Catholicos Mel-khisedek as founder. The building, as indicated, has two floors. In the centre of the ground floor is the great arched doorway, with guardrooms on either side. The first floor consists of a hall approximately 100 square metres in area, with arched openings in its west wall. There was originally an open wooden balcony at the east end, but this has not survived. The outer wall of the gatehouse is faced with dressed stone, while the side facing on to the courtyard is constructed of rough boulders, originally coated with stucco. The building displays great creative energy, and various indications lead one to suppose that it, too, was built by Arsukisdze.

The cathedral of Atskuri must be included in the list of outstanding monuments deserving examination here. Already in decay by the time Sveti-tskhoveli was devastated by the earthquake of 1283, it was later rebuilt, but today lies once again in ruins. In its time, Ats-kuri was an important centre of religious and cultural life in Georgia.

These mighty cathedrals, built in various regions of Georgia within such a short time-span, incorporated new artistic ideas quite unknown to the architecture of antiquity. They represent great creative achievements, the fruit of the artistic skill of the Georgian people. There are two further impressive monuments dating from the first half of the 11th century, when such great progress was being made in the decorative and artistic treatment of façades: Samtavisi, and the great church of Samtavro in Mtskheta.

Compared with the 10th- and 11th-century churches discussed above, both these buildings are constructed on a simplified plan. The dome is at the centre; at Samtavisi it rests on four free-standing piers, the eastern pair joined to the apse walls at the top, whereas at Samtavro it is supported directly by the apse walls in the east and by piers in the west. Adjoining the crossing are short arms, flanked on either side by lower corner sections. This type of building, which first appeared in the 9th century at Shatberdi, became more widespread from the 11th century onwards. Both these churches contain fragments of late medieval wall-paintings.

The distinguishing feature of the church in Samtavisi (pp. 158–61) is its elegant proportions. Blind arcades ascending the façades further emphasize the height of the tall, slender transepts. The design of the arcading is much richer on the east front, with ornamental additions enlivening the walls. Attention is further concentrated on the east wall of the apse by the wealth of decoration employed here. Elaborately carved foliage, with bunches of grapes and pomegranates, covers the window surrounds and the ornamental cross and diamonds on the wall. On the north and south walls, the central arch contains a tall, narrow window with a large ornamental medallion above it.

The design and execution of these decorations is brilliant, the modelling of the forms exquisite. They completely fill the window surrounds, the ornaments on the wall and the surviving parts of the cornice, and their effect is further enhanced by the use of colour. The different colourings of the ornamental surfaces, the fan patterns above the niches in the east wall and the green bosses of the two diamond-shaped mouldings stand out most effectively against the pale ochre of the smoothly dressed stone of the walls.

The inscriptions on the east façade are equally well executed in bold and beautiful Asomtavruli characters. They record that the church was built in 1030 by Ilarion Samtavneli, son of Vache Kanchaeli.

The monument originally had an ambulatory on three sides, but this no longer exists. The dome, like that of Sveti-tskhoveli, was destroyed by Tamerlane's armies, and the present dome dates from the 15th century.

In the decorative treatment of the façades, the architect of Samtavro went even further than his counterpart at Samtavisi. His compositions on the north and south walls are highly imaginative. The varying design of the decorative arches and the motifs filling them, and the great variety in the ornamentation, are most impressive, even if they do not always reach the same high standard of artistic excellence as at Samtavisi.

Samtavro (pp. 162–3) is a medium-sized church built of dressed stone of a warm yellow colour. Nineteenth-century gravestones in the western part of the building refer to King Mirian and Queen Nana, under whom the Georgians adopted Christianity.

An annexe with an ante-room dates, like the rest of the church, from the 11th century. The interior of this building is rich and elegant. The central part has decorated star vaulting, and the walls are articulated by niches. The northern annexe incorporates a chamber which dates from the 8th or 9th century.

Apart from the domed churches and basilicas, Georgia also has a number of simple churches consisting of a single nave without side-aisles. These monuments occupy an important position in the architecture of the country. They occurred from the 5th or 6th century right up to the 19th century. The simple basic form is varied chiefly by the shape of the apse, which may be either semicircular or polygonal, but differing proportions and building materials, and the addition in some cases of extra wings or chambers, all help to ensure variety. Above all, these simpler buildings always have features characteristic of their respective periods. There are certain

areas, such as Svaneti, Khevi, Kartli and Zemo-Racha, where these aisleless churches were evidently preferred to other types.

Early examples of the aisleless type from the 5th–6th century survive on the Katskhi rock pinnacle, mentioned on p. 42. One of these has a crypt. The churches in Oltisi and Tetritskaro are also important, and similar buildings include the one at Akvaneba and two churches in the region of Mankhuti (present-day Sarachlo). In certain examples from the 8th and 9th centuries, for example in Klikis-jvari, Achabeti, Bredza, Gviara and others the apse is rectangular in plan, and squinches are used for the transition to the conch.

One of the most interesting examples from the last quarter of the 10th century is the church of Zemo-Krikhi (pp. 166–8). Both exterior and interior of the building are faced with dressed stone, and, like several churches in Svaneti such as Nesgun and Chvabiani, it is very high and has a projecting polygonal apse. The interior is short, with the stress on the breadth and height. The apse and the deep bema are narrower and lower than the nave, leaving a comparatively large interior east wall which is decorated with niches, reliefs and both ornamental and figural wall-painting.

The individual decorative composition of the south façade is partially obscured by a projecting annexe added in the first quarter of the 11th century. There was another annexe on the west side, but all that remains of this is fragments and foundations. At the beginning of the 11th century the church interior was painted at the behest of local feudal lords, whose portraits can be seen on the north wall.

The sculptural decoration which was beginning to display its brilliant potential in the early decades of the 11th century was used in all its splendour by the architects of the single-nave churches in Khtsisi and Savane.

Khtsisi (p. 172) is the best example of Georgian architecture in the period of its finest flowering. The church is tall, slender and elegant. The façades are faced with dressed stone of a warm yellow hue with some areas of pink, and decorated with austere and delicate blind arcading. Windows and doors

Zemo-Krikhi. Late 10th-century church. Ornamental details from the façade and the altar screen. In motifs and execution these show similarities to the ornamentation of various monuments in Tao-Klarjeti, for example Oshki, Ishkhani and Khakhuli.

117

are emphasized by ornamentation. Crosses and other reliefs extend freely across the façades, and beautiful inscriptions complete the richness of the decoration, recording that Archbishop Anania began the building of the church in the year 1002, in the reign of Bagrat III.

The attractive and carefully decorated church of Savane was built in 1046. Although its builder was unable to attain the artistic standard of Khtsisi, Savane remains an interesting and attractive monument. Inside the church, an ornamented alabaster altar screen survives. Altar screens are frequently found in Georgian churches, and their ornamental decoration or inset relief panels make them masterpieces of stone-carving or sculpture. We shall return in greater detail to examples of stone-carving from the 11th and 13th centuries, when considering the artistic achievements of these periods.

Many aisleless churches of excellent construction have survived from the 12th and 13th centuries. The exterior of the elegant and slender church of Magalaant-eklesia (pp. 190 –91) at Tsinarekhi is striking, not least for the unusual design of the blind arcades and the ornamental surrounds of the windows and doors.

The church known as Lamazi-sakdari was a magnificent building standing in the Khrami gorge. It has an inscription naming Queen Tamar and her consort David.

A church built in the reign of Rusudan (1222–45), daughter of Tamar, is the jewel of the ancient city of Gudarekhi. The decoration of its east façade features niches similar to those we have seen on the façades of the domed churches. A bell-tower dating from 1278, one of the best preserved in the whole of Georgia, stands beside the church.

Aisleless churches.
Among the large number of buildings of this type surviving are examples of a wide variety of basic architectonic forms.

The churches of the 6th and 7th centuries are small, without pilasters or ribbed arches: Katskhi, 6th century (a), Mankhuti, 6th–7th century (b and c), Oltisi, 7th century (d).

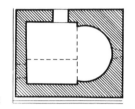

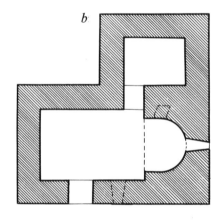

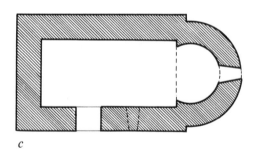

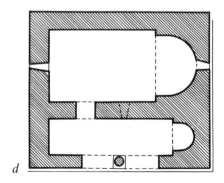

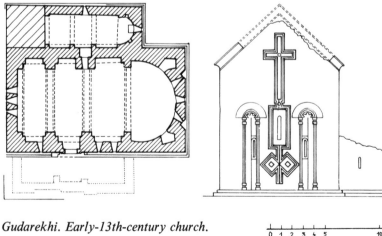

Gudarekhi. Early-13th-century church.
Plan, and elevation of the east façade.

118

The buildings of the 7th–10th centuries—Klikis-jvari, 7th–8th century (e), Tsvirmi, 9th century (f), Eli, 10th century (g), Zemo-Krikhi, 10th century (h)—are more complicated in structure. Pilasters and ribbed arches are regularly employed. Some of the choirs are rectangular, with small semicircular niches; others are polygonal on the outside, with a semicircular apse inside. Zemo-Krikhi, with its deep choir illuminated by three windows, is particularly interesting.

In the 11th–13th centuries, the dimensions of the churches are appreciably larger: Ekhvevi, 11th century (i), Savane, AD 1046 (k), Lamazi-sakdari, late 12th and early 13th centuries (l). Their general construction, however, still follows along earlier lines. They are distinguished by the magnificent decoration of their façades.

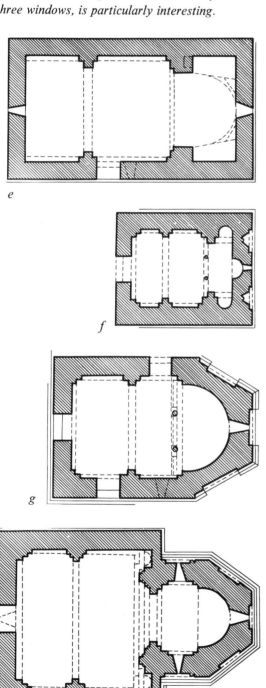

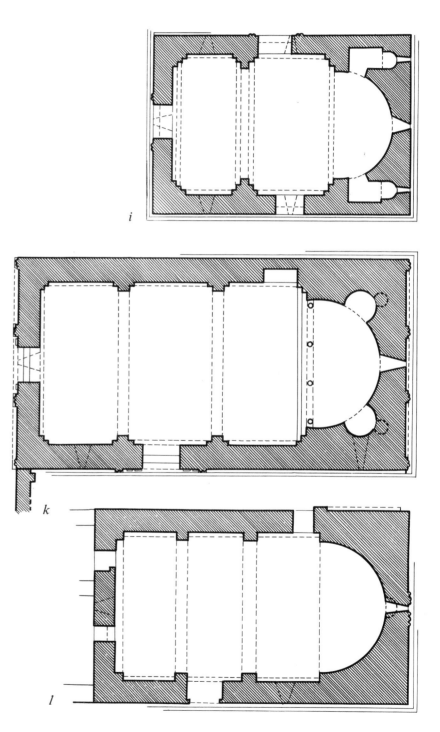

119

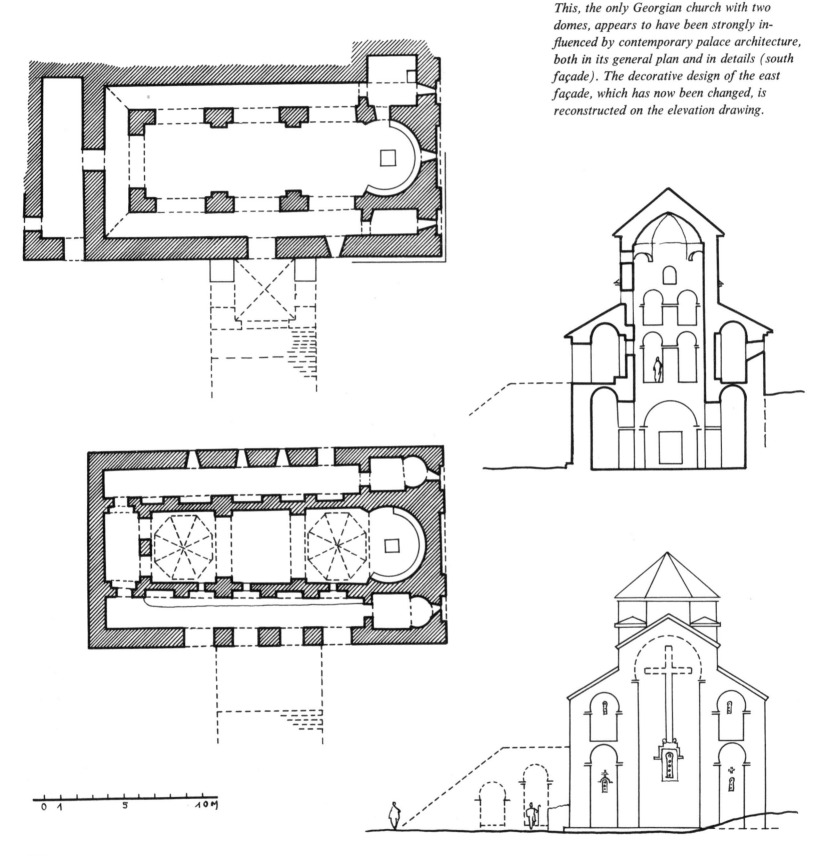

Gurjaani. Two-domed church, 8th century.
Plans of the lower and gallery levels.

Section, and elevation of the east façade (below), elevation of the south façade (right) and view from the south-west (below right). This, the only Georgian church with two domes, appears to have been strongly influenced by contemporary palace architecture, both in its general plan and in details (south façade). The decorative design of the east façade, which has now been changed, is reconstructed on the elevation drawing.

0 1   5   10 M

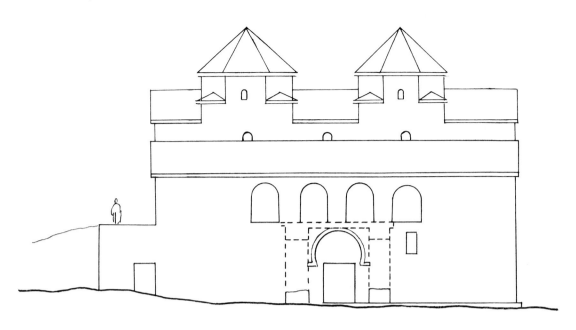

Taoskari. Centralized domed church, 8th–9th century. The centralized building had eight rectangular chambers radiating from the central bay in the form of a star; the polygonal exterior was articulated by niches, which helped to lighten the effect of the massive stonework.

Remains of the church walls, plan and elevation. (Based on the field-work of E. Takaishvili.)

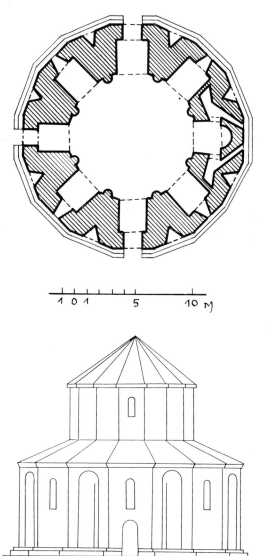

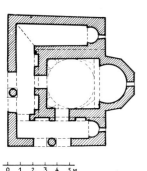

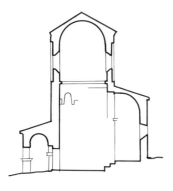

0 1 2 3 4 5м

Nekresi. Domed church, 8th-9th century. It is the emphasis placed on the individual structural elements that gives this little church its special character. The tall drum, the projecting polygonal apse and the ambulatory around three sides all contribute to its original appearance.
Plan, section, and view from the south-east.

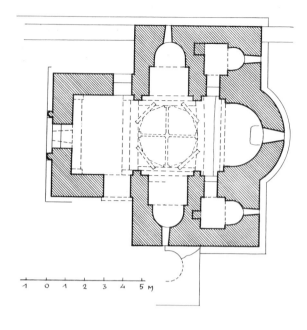

Telovani. The 'Jvarpatiosani' church (church of the True Cross), 8th century. The use of dressed stone at the corners, round the doors and windows and on the drum, while the walls are constructed of rubble masonry, is characteristic of the period. With regard to decoration, Telovani is the earliest example of the use of blind arcading on the drum. The plan (far left) shows a triconch with a projecting semicircular east apse. An unusual feature is the differing widths of the arms of the cross. Tympanum of the west door (left); view from the north-west (below left).

Sioni, near Kazbegi. Three-aisled basilica, late 9th and early 10th centuries. Plan, and view from the south-east.

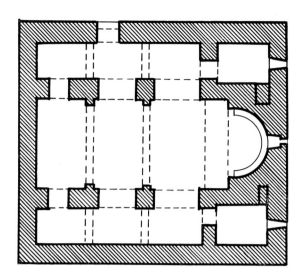

Opiza. Monastery complex. Surviving inscriptions indicate that the older buildings date from the beginning of the 9th century and were restored in the 10th century.
View from the south-east.

Doliskana. Cruciform domed church from the first half of the 10th century. Characteristically, the walls were built of rubble laid in regular courses, while dressed stones were used for the drum and the door and window surrounds. The areas thus emphasized were decorated with various reliefs, including the archangels Michael and Gabriel and the figure of the founder, King Sumbat I, with a model of the church.

Doliskana.

Left: Founder's relief on the drum, with an inscription reading 'May Christ extol our King Sumbat.'

Below left: The south window, flanked by the archangels Michael and Gabriel. Beneath the bust in the medallion to the left of Gabriel, the following words appear: 'Created by the hand of the Deacon Gabriel.' It seems likely that this is a portrait of the builder of the church.

Below: View of the church from the south-east.

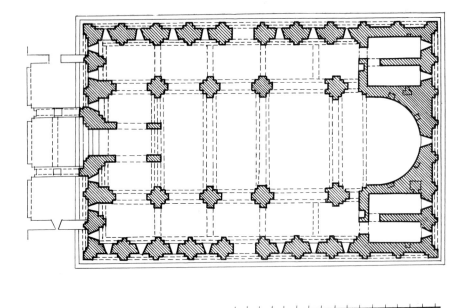

Otkhta-eklesia. Triple-church basilica from the 10th century. Plan, and view from the east, showing the two-storey aisleless church to one side.

Opposite:
Kumurdo. Domed church, AD 964. In its original form, the multi-apsed building looked from the outside like an ordinary cruciform domed church. In the second quarter of the 11th century an ambulatory was built round the west end. The ground-plan given here presents a conjectural reconstruction of the building's original appearance. A large inscription above the south door gives the date of completion and the name of the master mason, Sakotsari.
Plan; north-south section through the crossing area; remains of the dome supports; view of the ruins from the south-west.

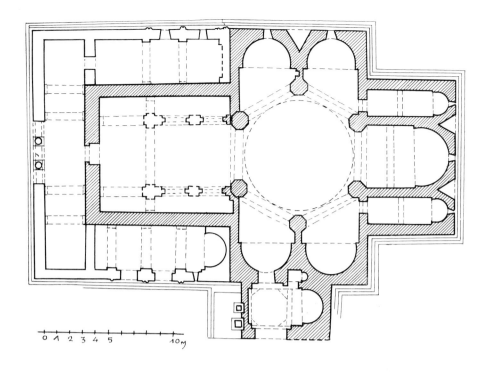

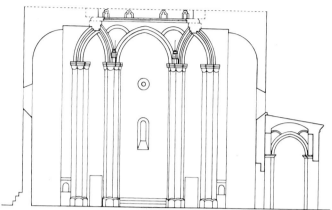

Overleaf:
*Kumurdo. Central section of the east front.
A long inscription in Asomtavruli refers to the
founder, Bishop Ioane.*

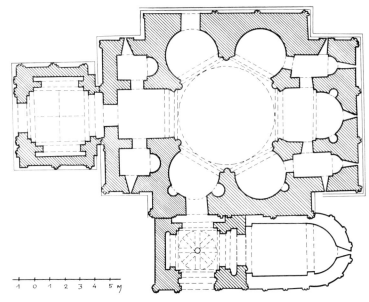

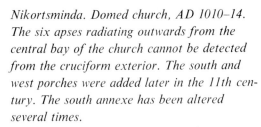

Nikortsminda. Domed church, AD 1010–14. The six apses radiating outwards from the central bay of the church cannot be detected from the cruciform exterior. The south and west porches were added later in the 11th century. The south annexe has been altered several times.

Plan, view of the tympanum over the west door and view of the church from the south. In the tympanum are portrayed Christ and the mounted figure of St George striking down the emperor Diocletian. Framing the scene is an inscription in Asomtavruli characters referring to King Bagrat III and his son Giorgi I.

Nikortsminda. Relief on the south front showing the Ascension of Christ. The composition and the explanatory inscription are
both in a highly decorated style.

Right: The ornamentation of the drum shows
the predominance of the decorative element.
Below right: Tympanum relief on the south
portal showing the Exaltation of the Cross.

Nikortsminda. View of the inside of the dome. The painting dates from the 16th and 17th centuries.

Bochorma. Domed six-apsed church, 10th century. The polygonal lower structure, with its projecting east apse and sloping zig-zag roof, was topped by a drum with blind arcading. Only a few fragments of the drum now remain.
Interior, looking east, and view from the south.

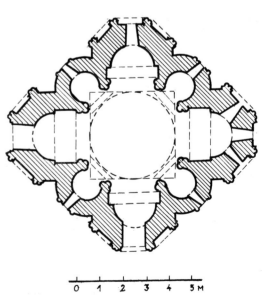

Kvetera. Centralized domed church, 10th century. This small church was built in the citadel, close to the palace. Despite its modest dimensions, the structure is monumental in appearance. Both inside and out, there is a rich diversity of formal elements.
View from the east, plan, and interior shot looking north.

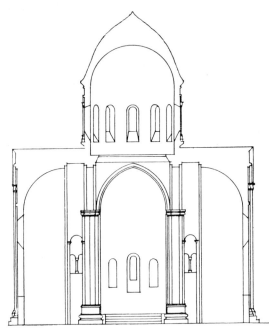

Oshki. Cathedral, built in the 970. The great triconch with its elongated western arm, by the master builder Grigol Oshkeli, was built at the behest of the Kuropalate David III, ruler of Tao, and his brother Bagrat.

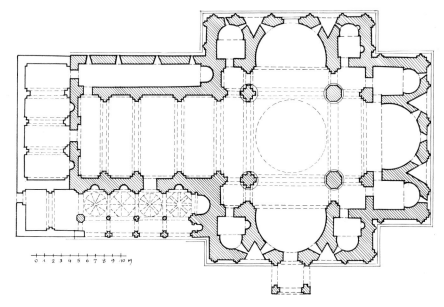

Oshki. The massive drum with its tall dome rests on four free-standing pillars. There are raised galleries at the west end and along the north side; the interior in general is remarkable for its spaciousness and simplicity. In front of the entrance to the south conch there is an open portico. The arcaded gallery along the south side of the nave exhibits interesting vaulting designs.

Interior, facing north-east (far left), east elevation and section through the crossing (centre), plan (left) and view from the south (below).

Oshki. The cathedral is richly adorned with figure sculpture and bas-reliefs.

Left: Carved ornamental decoration on the blind arcading of the drum.

Below left: Donor figures (extreme left and right) on the south wall of the eastern end.

Below: Figures of the archangels Michael and Gabriel on the blind arcading of the south wall.

Right: Capital of a pillar in the south gallery depicting the Deesis. Christ and Mary hold scrolls which originally bore inscriptions in red. Christ's halo was also painted red.

Below right: Capital of a pillar in the south gallery, with angels and cherubim.

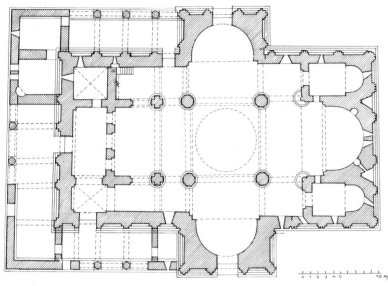

Kutaisi. The Bagrat cathedral, completed at the beginning of the 11th century.
Left and below: Reconstructed plan and view of the building without the early-11th-century porticoes.
Right: Capital and base of a pillar in the south portico.
Below right: View of the partially restored south front.

143

Kutaisi. The sculptural decoration of the cathedral is very varied in form and content. Top, left to right: Heads on the south front (above) and detail of carved decoration on the north window (below); two reliefs of mythological beasts on the west front; three capitals with animal motifs from the west portico.

Bottom, left to right: Window in the north wall, with the inscription giving the date of the building (AD 1003) just visible in the lower right-hand corner; columns of the blind arcading at the north-east corner of the north transept; the west front, after partial restoration.

Alaverdi. Cathedral from the first quarter of the 11th century.
Right: Plan. Of the ambulatory shown running round three sides, only the west part now remains.
Below: View from the south. The tall, slender drum and the dome were rebuilt in the 15th century. The defensive wall dates from the late Middle Ages.

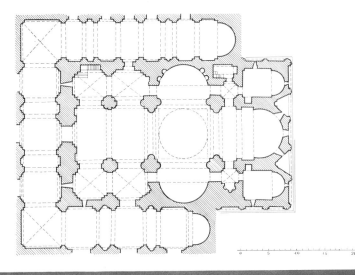

Alaverdi. Interior view, looking east. The capitals of the piers are decorated with an inverted arch motif. The surviving wall-painting includes some 11th-century fragments, but the greater part is 15th-century. The arcades of the raised gallery round the west end have been completely blocked in on the north side, and very much reduced in size on the south side.

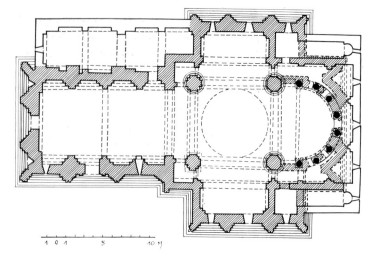

Ishkhani. Cathedral, AD 1032, with individual parts dating from the 7th and 9th centuries. The arcaded east apse is all that remains of the original tetraconch structure with ambulatory, which was similar to the church of Bana. Bishop Saban of Ishkhani, a disciple of Gregory of Khandzta, had the church restored in AD 828, and sections in the east and north date from that period. The building was completed in 1032.
Plan, north façade and arcading of the original east apse.

Ishkhani. The cornice on the drum (right), and the walled-up south door (below), showing rich ornamentation and an inscription. The inscription mentions the founder of the present church, Abbot Antoni, and two rulers, King Giorgi and the Kuropalate Bagrat.

Mtskheta, Sveti-tskhoveli. View from the church of Jvari, and (below) Sveti-tskhoveli and part of Mtskheta seen from Mount Bagineti.

Sveti-tskhoveli from the north-west. Jvari can be seen on its cliff on the further bank of the Aragvi river.

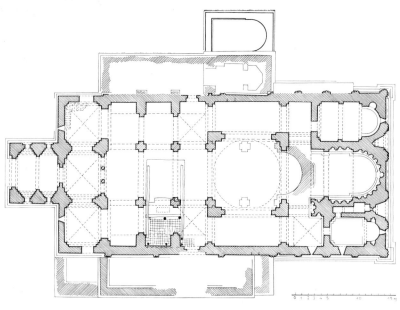

Mtskheta, Sveti-tskhoveli. Cathedral, AD 1010-29. The earlier buildings (the early-4th-century wooden church and the 5th-century basilica) are sketched in on the partially reconstructed plan.
Below: View from the north-west, showing the foundations of the north gallery. The narthex and portico were altered in the 15th century.
Right: View from the south-east, with the foundations of the south gallery.

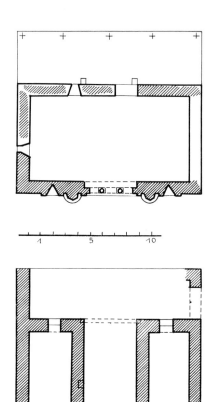

Mtskheta, Sveti-tskhoveli.
Far left: The front of the gatehouse, dating from the beginning of the 11th century.
Left: Plans of the ground and upper floors of the gatehouse.
Below left: The south-west corner of the surrounding wall, with the remains of the 11th-century bishop's palace.
Right: Gable relief on the west front showing the Majestas Domini.
Below: Interior, looking north-west. On the north wall the outlines of the original 5th-century arches have been picked out in white paint.

Mtskheta, Sveti-tskhoveli.
Interior, looking east.
The painted stone baldac-
chino on the south side of
the church, likewise called
Sveti-tskhoveli, dates from
the 15th century. The
pillars of the nave were
strengthened during the
15th-century restoration.

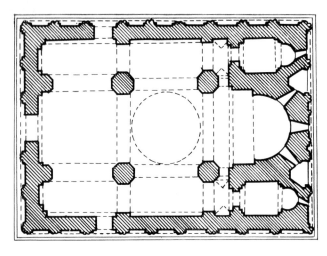

Samtavisi. Cruciform domed church, AD 1030. Ground-plan, view from the south-east, and details of the ornamental decoration on the east façade.

Samtavisi. Window with rich ornamental frame, and details of the decoration on the façades.

Mtskheta, Samtavro. Cruciform domed church from the first half of the 11th century. View from the south-east and close-up of the richly decorated drum. Dome and drum date from the 13th and 14th centuries, though the base of the drum incorporates remnants of the original. The beauty of the blind arcading on the north and south fronts deserves special note.

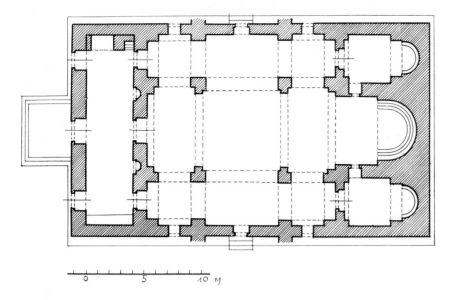

Kara Dagh ('Black Mountain'), near Antioch.
Monastery church from the first quarter of
the 11th century. Plan, and ruins of the
central-domed church, looking east.

0   5   10 M

Kara Dagh. Surviving fragments of ornamentation provide evidence of the richness of the original building.
Georgian inscription, and various pieces of carving from the dome, including the keystone (centre right) and a pendentive (below right).

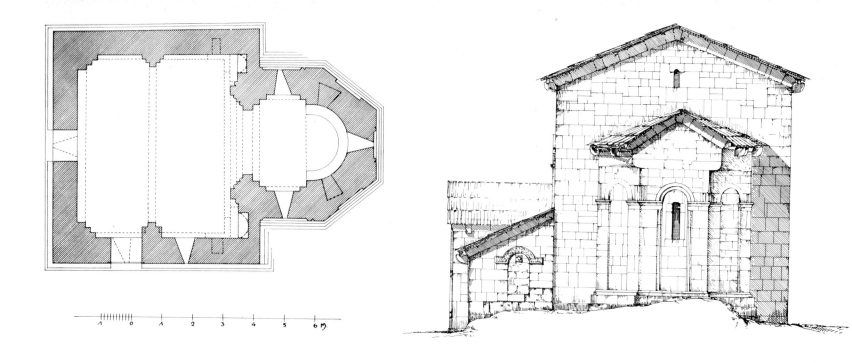

Zemo-Krikhi. Aisleless church, final quarter of the 10th century.

Above: Plan, and elevation of the east front.
Left: Bases of the pilasters to either side of the apse. The animal heads with their wide, alert eyes are highly expressive. The flat treatment is reminiscent of the animal sculptures decorating the south door at Khakhuli.
Right: Interior, looking east. The design of the east end is highly original. The low, narrow apse leaves a large expanse of wall; niches have been let into it on either side of the apse, producing a tripartite composition. The pilasters are decorated with patterns cut into the stone and painted red, white and black. In the middle of the 11th century a local feudal lord had the interior of the church painted.

Zemo-Krikhi. The wall-painting is the work of a local artist and shows close affinity with Svanetian paintings. The colouring is rich and soft, while the design shows a distinct linear emphasis. The faces are directly modelled on the people of these mountain regions. St Irene and St Marina are depicted to the right of the apse, with St Barbara and St Catherine to the left. The apse and bema show Christ throned in glory, surrounded by apostles and archangels.

Ateni. The Sion church. Wall-painting from the second half of the 11th century in the east apse and the bema. The apse vault shows the Virgin and Child with two archangels; in the arch of the bema are depicted Christ Pantocrator, John the Baptist, the prophet Zacharias, David and Aaron. The monumental figures are shown in tranquil, dignified poses, and the faces are delicately modelled.

169

Ateni. The Sion church. Wall-paintings,
second half of the 11th century.
Left: The Comforting of Joseph. The figure
of Joseph is most expressive, the hovering
angel freely drawn and spontaneous. The
inscription in Asomtavruli explains the scene.
Right: Portrait of a queen.
Below: The prophets Habakkuk and Ezekiel.
Below right: The Entry of the Just into
Paradise (fragment from the west conch).

Khtsisi. Church dating from AD 1002. View of the west window, showing the broad ornamental border decorated with a foliage motif. A beautifully carved inscription, surrounding the frame on three sides, blends harmoniously with the rest of the façade decoration to form a unified composition. The inscription names the builder, Archbishop Anania, who initiated the construction work in the year 1002, in the reign of Bagrat III.

Matskhvarishi. 12th-century wall-painting on the south wall of the church, showing St Demetrius.

In the second half of the 11th century, as mentioned earlier, the country was shaken by severe political crises. The process of unification met with resistance from inside the country as well as from foreign enemies. Byzantium in particular became a dangerous opponent at this time. The volume of building activity characteristic of the 10th and the first half of the 11th century was now radically reduced. The second half of the 11th century was taken up with the fortification of sites of strategic importance. In addition, the efforts of the people were directed towards preserving what had been built in earlier times.

The beginning of the 12th century heralded a rapid improvement in the country's situation. Under the rule of David the Builder, Georgia was transformed within a short space of time into a powerful feudal monarchy. This period saw the foundation of new cities and the restoration of old ones, and rapid construction of roads, bridges, irrigation canals and so on. Furthermore, special attention was devoted to the foundation of new monasteries and the expansion of existing ones. David the Builder founded a great monastery in Gelati, considerably enlarged the one at Shiomghvime and ordered the massive reconstruction of the cave-monastery of David-Gareja (pp. 202 –5). He was at pains to integrate the feudal monastic communities ideologically into the service of the central power.

The monastery of Gelati (pp. 181–7) was built on a generous scale commensurate with the resources of the time; it was conceived and executed on a sound economic base. At the centre of the complex was a huge domed church, and to the west of this the academy building, where instruction was given and scholars worked at the invitation of the king. Leading thinkers of the time, such as Ioane Petritsi and Arsenius, Catholicos of Georgia, worked at the academy of Gelati. Under their guidance students of the academy prepared translations of religious and secular literature, compiled commentaries and wrote works of their own. Geometry, arithmetic, astronomy, philosophy, grammar, rhetoric and music were all taught here.

A refectory was built, and cells for the monks, and evidently a palace as well. A cistern was constructed, and fed with spring water brought from a long way off through an earthenware pipeline. Near the south gate of the monastery was a hospice for visitors. The monastery precinct was surrounded by a high wall, and tradition has it that David the Builder was buried here, by his own wish, in the south gatehouse.

Just a few hundred metres away lay Sokhasteri, a domicile for monks who had taken a vow of silence. There was also, at some distance, a house for the sick and the aged.

David did not live to see the conclusion of the building of the monastery. His son Demetre had the work completed and the main church painted. Extensions were added to Gelati in the 13th and 14th centuries. The east portico of the academy, the domed church of St George to the east of the main church and the small two-storey church of St Nicholas to the west were all built at this time. The two-storey building, with a chapel on the upper level supported on huge open arches, is unique in Georgia.

At the beginning of the 16th century the Turks invaded West Georgia and set fire to Gelati. We must assume that the monastery's original wall-paintings were destroyed then. A mosaic from the apse in the main church, and fragments of the painting in the narthex, are all that survive from the 12th century. At the end of the 13th century the south chapel was painted again. Apart from this, all the wall-paintings in this church and the church of St George date from the 16th and 17th centuries. The first of the 16th-century portraits along the north wall of the main building represents David the Builder. It is probable that this portrait was painted over the original one.

Like the other churches of the monastery, the main church is built of limestone, which with time has mellowed to pale yellow, pink and, in places, grey. The buildings are decorated with blind arcades and moulded door and window frames. Ornamentation is used very sparingly here. The conical roofs and the projecting polygonal apses at the east ends of the churches indicate an intention to emphasize the artistic unity of the monastery complex.

Whereas the structure of the main church of Gelati follows the plan commonly adopted in the 11th century, with the dome at the

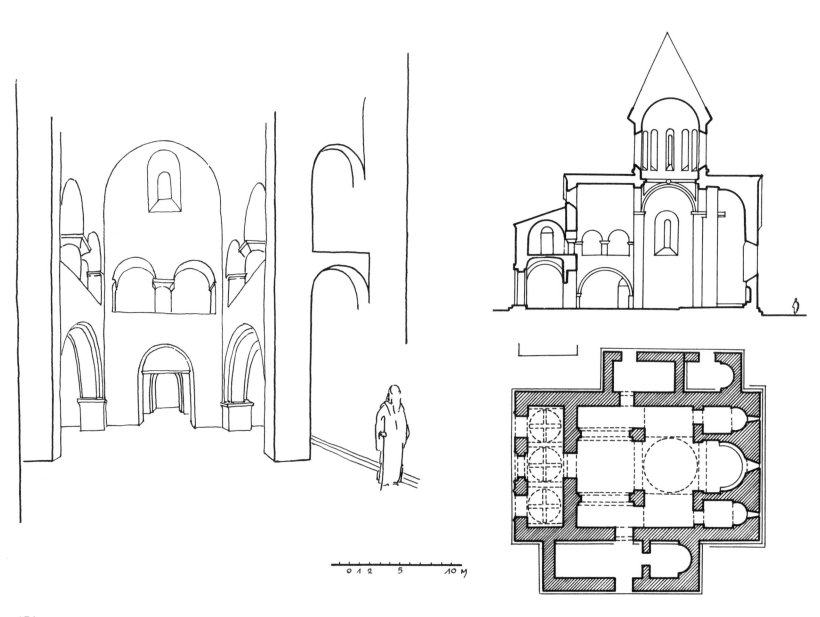

Ikorta. Plan of the church built in AD 1172.

0 1 2　5　10 M

174

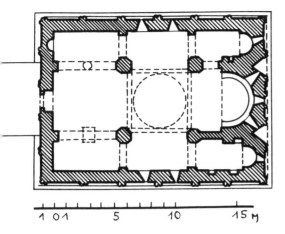

Tigva. Monastery church built in AD 1152.
View of the interior facing west, section, and
plan.
The façades of the building have little decora-
tion. The distinguishing feature of the church
is the disciplined and harmonious arrange-
ment of the architectural forms, especially in
the interior.

centre of the building resting on the corners of the apse walls in the east and on two detached piers in the west, the church of St George, while largely following the plan of the main church, nevertheless has one peculiarity which enables us to identify more clearly several characteristic features of the architecture of the early and high Middle Ages. In the church of St George, the west supports of the dome are in the form of two short, sturdy columns with capitals, the height of the latter being determined by the low arcades in the western arm of the church. Normally, such piers have abutments on two different levels, the height of those on the eastern side being determined by the arching of the dome. This produces a strong unbroken line in the bay below the dome, running from the floor right up to the dome itself, and on this flowing movement is based one of the fundamental principles of the Georgian church interior, whereby dome and drum provide the focal point round which all the other parts of the building are grouped. In the church of St George the construction of the west part, with the short west columns, produces momentarily the impression of a hall interior, but then, abruptly, the familiar image of the cruciform domed church reasserts itself. The overall concept that emerges appears to be influenced by the architectural style of several Byzantine churches from the period of the so-called second flowering, which are recorded in the literature of the time as bipartite structures combining the architectural elements of the centralized domed church and the basilica. Such a combination is rare in Georgia, though it does occur in certain 8th- and 9th-century monuments of the transitional period, when the intensive quest for new concepts meant that architectural forms were not always fully mastered. The low columns under the dome also appeared frequently at the waning of the Middle Ages, when the creative talents of the country were visibly falling off.

In 1152 a convent was founded in Tigva by the daughter of King David the Builder, who took vows and became a nun there after the death of her husband. Only the church has survived intact; all the other buildings of the convent are in ruins or have disappeared en-

tirely. The façades of the building are a warm yellowish-grey in tone, and straightforward architectural forms predominate, with virtually no decoration. The architect of Tigva created a building which is distinctive not for decorative incidentals but for the quality of its stonework, its pleasant colour and the neat finish of its smooth walls. The aesthetic effect of the cruciform domed interior is enhanced by the gallery enclosing the west end on three sides, which opens on to the interior through arches.

The tower of the monastery of Ubisi (pp. 188–9) is unusual, and indeed its excellent state of preservation makes it unique among surviving Georgian buildings. An inscription states that it was built in 1141 by King Demetre's Grand Secretary, Simeon Chkondideli. When Simeon left office he became a monk, had the tower built and began a hermit's life there.

The building has four storeys. The lower level was given over to a storeroom for provisions. On the second level is the living accommodation, a light room with a fireplace and a toilet, from which a stone staircase leads up to the third level. Here there is an altar with a painted conch. There was also a wooden balcony on this floor, and from here Simeon maintained contact with people outside. The fourth level, with its machicolations, was for defensive purposes. With blind arcades decorating its lower levels, the tall, elegant tower blends superbly both with the remainder of the monastery complex and with the surrounding countryside.

The description makes it clear that the 12th-century tower of Ubisi presents a very different picture from the 5th- and 6th-century structures designed equally as hermitages: the 40-metre-high rock pinnacle of Katskhi, for instance, had no comforts to offer to the 'stylite' saint devoting himself to a life of asceticism and self-castigation.

Another example of this type of tower can be seen at Martvili. Built at the end of the 10th or the beginning of the 11th century, it is now in a very poor state of preservation. Here there was a tall arcade on the lower level. Above this was the living accommodation, and over that a tiny aisleless church. The chronicle states that the hermit worked at his translations here. Like Ubisi, this monument, faced with dressed stone, displays all the characteristic features of the time in which it was built.

These monuments dating from the first half of the 12th century—the main church of the Gelati monastery, Tigva and the Ubisi tower—differ radically from those of the 10th and 11th centuries, whose façades had come increasingly to be adorned with a wide variety of ornament. At the beginning of the 12th century this decorative development came to a standstill, and for some time the number of buildings erected was also perceptibly reduced. The second half of the 12th century and the first half of the 13th century again witnessed a revitalization. However, we find that although the decorative forms evolved in the 10th and 11th centuries, and the numerous basic building types, continued to be used, there is little evidence of further creative development.

The domed churches in Ikorta, Betania (pp. 198–9) and Kvatakhevi (pp. 194–5), for example, are smaller than those at Gelati and Tigva or their predecessor Samtavro, and of the three only Ikorta has a gallery; in other words, the whole treatment of the church interior has been simplified. Both the internal and the external structure are dominated in each case by the tall, slender drum, the crowning element of the decorative scheme, which is covered with opulent ornamentation. The window and door frames, too, and the crosses on the façades, are richly decorated. The significance of blind arcades as a means of articulating the façades was now diminishing. They were still used here and there, but they had lost their former austerity of line and their structural quality. The motif of twin windows surmounted by a cross came increasingly into use at this time.

These 12th- and 13th-century architects relied heavily on the effects achieved by selecting stones of different colours to face the façades. Their buildings have arcaded porticoes, decorated with ornament and roofed with star vaulting, on the south side.

Apart from their structural and decorative similarities, each of these three churches has its own individual character.

The splendour of its façades makes the church in Ikorta most alluring. According to an inscription on the building, it was erected in 1172 by a high-ranking official at the court of Giorgi III. The slender and elegant contours of the church stand out clearly against the blue of the sky. The beautiful colour effects are achieved by the use of variegated stones, blue-grey with a yellow tint and violet speckled with emerald. Added to this there is the magnificent ornamentation. All this heightens the contrast between the church and the yellowish-grey of the surrounding mountains, bare of vegetation.

Blind arcades still appear on the façades of Ikorta, although their free arrangement plainly distinguishes them from those of the 11th century. Sometimes they are combined with the window surrounds, elsewhere the lines are interrupted. This variable arcading and the irregular placement of the windows produce a constantly changing effect.

Fragments of 12th-century wall-painting survive inside the building.

On a cliff to the east of the church stands the ruin of the residence once inhabited by the local feudal lord.

The striking feature of the church at Pitareti (pp. 192–3) is the range of its soft colours, which harmonize surprisingly well with the various greens of the mountain landscape. Above the violet-coloured walls rises a dome of deep ochre with insets of emerald-green stone. Here, as in other buildings of the period, the varicoloured stones are arranged in irregular, random fashion, and not in geometric patterns as on the 10th-century buildings. Blind arcading has disappeared from the façades, to be replaced by numerous individual details covered with different ornamental motifs.

A lengthy inscription on the south portico of Pitareti states that the church was built in the reign of King Giorgi IV (1213–22) by the high-ranking official Kavtar Kajipaisdze. The monument is enclosed by a double wall. The entrance tower with its belfry still survives, and there are ruins of palace buildings.

The architect of Kvatakhevi (pp. 194–5), a sensitive artist and master of his craft, found a different solution to the problem of decorating the façades. On the north façade, for example, he used the motif of an arch with stepped mouldings. The decorative elements of the east façade are virtually a repetition of

Kvatakhevi. Church dating from the end of the 12th and the beginning of the 13th century.
Details of the ornament on the drum.

those on the church of Samtavisi, with only slight alterations. The monuments of Kvatakhevi and Betania resemble each other so closely that it is quite legitimate to assume that they are both the work of the same man.

At Kvatakhevi the wall-painting has been completely lost. At Pitareti it dates from the late Middle Ages. At Betania (p. 199), however, the original wall-painting dating from the time the church was built still exists, and only a few small areas have been restored.

Beside the domed church in Betania stands a small aisleless church dating from 1196.

Other important and richly decorated churches belonging both chronologically and stylistically to this group include those in Akhtala (p. 196), Khujabi, Tsughrughasheni and the village of Metekhi.

At the beginning of the 13th century large domed churches were constructed of brick, for example at Kintsvisi (pp. 206–9) and Timotesubani (pp. 210–11). Their plan and general construction follow the architectural principles of the monuments discussed above, but their proportions are different. A distinguishing feature of these buildings is the decoration of the drum with arches of half-round bricks, accompanied at Timotesubani by blue-glazed plaques and crosses. Both buildings retain wall-paintings, dating from the time of their construction, which are among the best of their period in the whole of Georgia.

It was at this high point of its political, economic and cultural development that Georgia was invaded by the bellicose nomadic Mongol tribes from the east. They had already conquered China, India and the ancient Rus, and now they did not spare Georgia. From the 1240s onwards Georgia was under the domination of Mongol power for almost a century; only after a hundred years of unflagging resistance did it finally regain its liberty. King Giorgi V, the Splendid (1314-48), was able to secure a short-lived improvement in the country's political and economic situation, and Georgia established economic relations with the Golden Horde, Iran, several countries in Asia Minor and the north Italian city states. However, the devastation of Tamerlane's repeated incursions, and the invasions of his successors, which continued from 1384 to 1415, spelled disaster for the political, economic and cultural life of Georgia. The persistent and courageous resistance of the people provoked the conquerors into imposing gruesome penalties. Whole towns were laid waste, the most important buildings destroyed, villages burned and prisoners deported to Central Asia.

Following the invasions of the Mongol hordes, Georgia was further weakened by attacks from the Persians and the Turks. In the 15th and 16th centuries the united Georgian state disintegrated into the separate kingdoms of Kartli, Kakheti and Imereti. Further fragmentation occurred through the formation of *satavado,* provinces which were politically and economically semi-independent—Samtskhe-Saatabago, Odishi, Abkhazia and Guria.

The 16th century was characterized by ceaseless heroic resistance against the foreign conquerors. Politically isolated and economically weak, Georgia fought with its last strength to hold its own against its aggressive neighbours, the Ottomans and the Iranian Kizilbashi. Savage campaigns were conducted in the first half of the 17th century by the Persian Shahs Abbas I and Abbas II, who were aiming at the annihilation of the Georgian people. Despite bitter fighting, Kartli and Kakheti were defeated and fell under the Persian yoke. It was not until 1744, after long and terrible struggles, that the domination of the Kizilbashi was thrown off. In 1762 Kartli and Kakheti were united. The country needed a strong ally. The treaty concluded with the mighty Russian state at the end of the 18th century saved the Georgian people from physical destruction. Despite the colonial rule of Tsarist Russia, the country continued to make economic and cultural progress.

Capitalist development gradually changed the entire social structure of Georgia. Artistic concepts underwent a fundamental change. Progressive representatives of the Georgian people propagated the new ideas that were current in Russia and contemporary Europe. Georgia, which for centuries had been isolated from Europe, now began to win back its place at the side of the European countries. The creative power of the people was to be the foundation on which Soviet Georgian art was established.

The Metekhi church in Tbilisi (pp. 213–15) has a very special position among surviving medieval buildings. It stands on the rocky outcrop at the centre of the city, with the district of Isani extending eastwards and the old town of Tbilisi spread out to the north-west, on the far side of the river Kura. The church is a wonderful sight, crowning the sheer, imposing cliff above the river and merging harmoniously into the overall view.

The Metekhi church was built between 1278 and 1289 by King Demetre II, who later became known as 'the Self-Sacrificer' because of his submission to execution by the Mongols. An earlier church had stood on the site, in which, according to the chronicles, Queen Tamar had prayed for the victory of her army at the battle of Shamkhori. From the 17th century onwards, when the throne of Kartli was intermittently occupied by Mohammedanized kings and the whole of East Georgia was under extreme political pressure from Iran, Metekhi became neglected and fell into a state of severe disrepair.

The church is built of brick, the façades faced with dressed stone. Restorations undertaken in the 19th century used only brick. The plan of Metekhi differs from those of its predecessors in having four piers to support the dome and three semicircular apses projecting on the outside. This is not, however, the expression of a search for something new, but rather a sign of the times, with their tendency to return to traditional forms.

The architect arrived at interesting and unusual solutions for the façades of the monument. He rejected the use of blind arcading, with its inherent feeling of movement, instead articulating the smooth surfaces with two horizontal bands which run round all four walls and give a strong feeling of unity to the composition. Apart from the framing of the windows, the decorative scheme includes crosses and niches. The niches have no structural significance here, but are used purely for decorative effect. In direct opposition to the horizontal articulation of the façades by bands is a distinct vertical rhythm, expressed on the main apse in the thrice repeated motif of window, cross and pilaster which is further emphasized by the clustered mouldings decorating the edges. This vertical emphasis is in

keeping with the general accent on height in the proportions of the building.

The semicircular apses, in conjunction with the other shapes of the structure, produce picturesque effects and again stress the soaring proportions of the church.

The portico of the main entrance on the north side, which is contemporary with the church building, is interesting for its decoration, both outside and inside.

In the ruins of the Narikala fortress, which stood on the hill on the opposite bank of the river, the remains of a domed church have been discovered. It was smaller than Metekhi, but judging from certain details it appears to have been built at the same time and to have had some connection with the other church.

By adopting a flexible political course, Sargis Jakeli, ruler of Samtskhe, was temporarily able to establish a favourable position for his province vis-à-vis the Mongol Khan. His possessions comprised the regions of south-western Georgia beyond the gorge of Borzhomi, namely Klarjeti, Tao and Speri. The house of Jakeli chose Sapara (p. 218) as their residence. Here they built a palace, and beside a small church dating from the 10th century they erected a large domed church, a bell-tower and various other buildings. Inside the church, wall-paintings survive which include portraits of Sargis, his son Beka and other members of the Jakeli family. An inscription in the west portico names the architect, Paresaisdze.

The domed church of Zarzma was erected at the beginning of the 14th century. It, too, contains portraits of Sargis and Beka Jakeli and of the latter's sons. The monastery here dates from the early days of feudalism and was founded by Serapion Zarzmeli. A chapel was then built in the 10th century; it has an inscription naming David III Kuropalates.

The general structure of the churches in Sapara and Zarzma echoes the architectural forms of buildings from the late 12th and early 13th centuries. The essential features that distinguish these churches from the others are their proportions, their use of light and the nature of their decorative forms. The very tall, slender drums of the earlier monuments are now replaced by wider, squatter ones, giv-

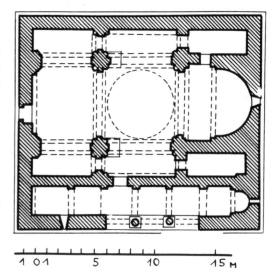

Zarzma. Domed church, early 14th century.

Tbilisi, Anchiskhati. Bell-tower in the enclosure wall, erected in 1675. Plans of the upper and lower levels, elevation of the façade fronting on to the street, and section. There is a passage running through the ground floor, and on the upper level are the living quarters of the sexton. The lower part is built of bricks, arranged in the patterns characteristic of the period.

ing the buildings a lower, more balanced appearance. Triangular niches are no longer used for the articulation of the façades. The door and window frames are decorated with a variety of ornamental motifs, but whereas the ornament of the 11th and 12th centuries was typified by lively interpretations of a wide repertoire of plant forms, the dominating elements now are geometric patterns, soberly executed with precise attention to detail.

The architectural developments of the 13th and 14th centuries can be followed in other regions of Georgia as well, though admittedly in size and quality of execution the buildings cannot compare with the churches of Sapara and Zarzma. Examples in Samtskhe are the domed structures of Chule, Bieti and Tiseli, not forgetting Sameba in the mountains at the foot of the Kazbek peak (p. 220), the aisleless churches in Skhalta, Daba and Sachino, and finally Charebi and Klivana—a late example of the three-aisled basilica. The unusual church at Khobi also deserves mention.

Georgian art of the late Middle Ages possesses a number of attributes that distinguish it from the art of the preceding era. Certainly it continued the excellent traditions that had been developed in the past, but it no longer attained the high standards of artistic achievement and the clarity and continuity in the creation of national forms which had hitherto secured for Georgian architecture its place among the outstanding achievements in the history of world art.

The long period of Iranian rule in Georgia, and the close contact that ensued between Georgian officials and the Iranian ruling class, promoted the spread of Iranian forms and Iranian taste. Stone was replaced as the predominant building material by brick, frequently arranged in patterns. The façades were now decorated with crosses, rhomboids and the like set into the walls. Everywhere the pointed arch appeared in place of the round arch commonly used before.

There is scant evidence of any original artis-

tic inspiration during this period, but Georgia did largely preserve its own architectural traditions, conferring a local flavour on the foreign artistic forms. This, in fact, appears to have been the chief concern of the time. The small selection of buildings from the 16th and 17th centuries discussed below will serve to illustrate the architecture of this period.

The second half of the 15th century was taken up with the restoration of buildings damaged by earthquakes and enemy attacks. New domes were built at this time in Samtavisi and Alaverdi. Sveti-tskhoveli, Ruisi and other churches were also restored, often with marked alterations to the structure.

Despite the depressed situation of the country, there were periods during the 16th–18th centuries when a remarkable political and economic expansion occurred in certain of the provinces. Kakheti in particular rose to prominence in the 16th century, in the reign of Leon I. Gremi became the capital, and remained so up to the time of the devastating

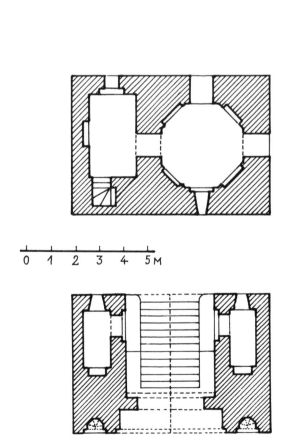

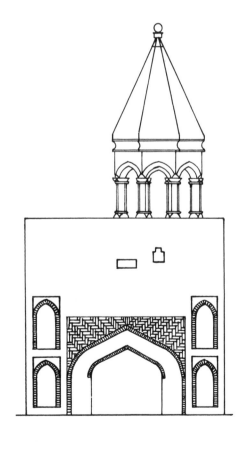

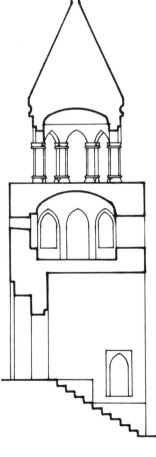

179

military incursions of Shah Abbas I, when the distinction passed to Telavi.

The best preserved part of Gremi is the citadel (p. 216), which includes the church of the Archangels and a dwelling-tower. The remains of business establishments, a public bathhouse and several parish churches survive in the town itself.

The church of the Archangels was built in 1565. It is a repetition of the traditional type of cruciform domed church with two detached piers, but with a marked emphasis on height. The wall-paintings decorating the interior date from 1577. The dwelling-tower is on three floors, with living and reception rooms, and terminates in a belfry which was added later. From the top floor of the tower there is a panoramic view of the Alazani valley and the peaks of the great Caucasus mountains.

Ananuri (p. 217), one of the most remarkable monuments of the 16th and 17th centuries, was built beside the 'Georgian military highway' in the Aragvi gorge. The gorge was controlled by the *eristavis* of Aragvi, one of the most powerful feudal families of the time. Ananuri was their residence at the end of the 17th century. The complex consists of two fortresses, the upper and the lower, the latter being badly damaged. The upper fortress contains two domed churches, a bell-tower, and another tower besides, and there is also a water cistern. The tower is an important element in the general appearance of the complex. It tapers towards the top, and has a crenellated roof. These towers were quite common in the mountain areas of Georgia such as Tusheti and Khevsureti. The smaller of the two churches is built of brick and is quite modest in appearance. The larger church, however, is faced with squared stone, has decorative ornamentation and makes a most impressive sight.

In Ninotsminda, a tall brick bell-tower (p. 219) was built in the 16th century beside the 6th-century domed church. This was a new type, which was to become more common in the following years. The tower has living rooms on three floors, with a belfry above. The living rooms are vaulted, and each is individually designed. Recessed areas in the brickwork of the façades form rectangles containing pointed arches and crosses, while the corners of the building are decorated with rows of recessed diamonds. The well-balanced structure of the bell-tower, the construction of its rooms and the decorative adornment make it in aesthetic terms one of the most remarkable buildings of its time in Georgia.

A bell-tower of a different kind was built into the wall enclosing the Anchiskhati church in Tbilisi in 1675. The low, cuboid building, with its arcaded passage and its one room on the upper level, is surmounted by a belfry with a conical roof. The unusual proportions of the structure, and the contrast produced by the juxtaposition of the brick-built lower mass with the lantern-like belfry of grey-blue stone, make the building particularly attractive.

With the decline of creative talent, the interest in older, national decorative forms increased. This is particularly evident in a number of 18th-century buildings, for example in Barakoni, Sagarejo and Largvisi (p. 197).

Gelati. View from the south of the main church of the monastery, dating from the first quarter of the 12th century, and the bell-tower from the second half of the 13th century. The blind arcading with its deeply stepped mouldings enlivens and breaks up the façades, which have virtually no other decoration.

Gelati. The monastery complex from the south-east. The main church is in the centre, with the mid-13th-century church of St George to the right. To the left of the main church are the bell-tower, the two-storey church of St Nicholas (late 13th and early 14th centuries) and the 12th-century academy building with its 13th-century portico.

The great mosaic in the apse of the main church, dating from the third decade of the 12th century.
The vault shows the Virgin and Child flanked by the archangels Michael and Gabriel. Mary's blue mantle, and the emerald-green and lilac robes of the archangels, make the figures stand out sharply against the gold background. The pictorial technique characteristic of Byzantium is here combined with the linear concept of form typical of Georgian art. This gives us reason to suppose that the mosaic was modelled on Byzantine examples by local artists who may have learned their craft in Byzantium.

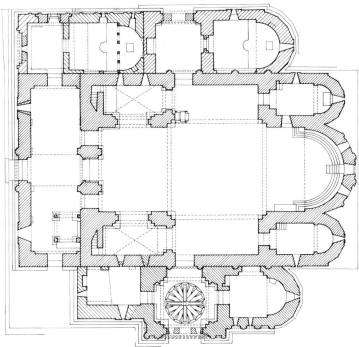

Plans of the main church (left) and the church of St George (below). The main church was originally intended to have an ambulatory round three sides, but this idea was abandoned while building was still in progress in favour of a narthex at the west end and an extension on the south side. The additional structures to the north date from the 13th and 14th centuries. There are galleries over the corner chapels at the west end of the church.

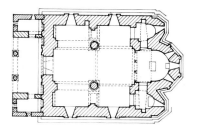

Gelati.
Left: Wall-paintings from the 17th century in the north annexe of the main church. The lower part of the south wall (below left) shows King Giorgi of Imereti with his family.
Right: Interior of the main church, looking east. The broad, spacious bay beneath the dome is the dominant feature of the church. The whole of the interior is covered with paintings. Like the apse mosaic, the paintings in the narthex date from the 12th century. Those in the main part of the church are from the late Middle Ages.

Gelati.

Right: Wall-paintings of the late 13th century in the south annexe of the main church, showing King David V (Narin) in monk's garb and in royal robes.

Below: Wall-painting dating from the first half of the 12th century in the narthex of the main church. It depicts the 3rd and 4th Ecumenical Councils, which sat in the 5th century. These scenes and their inscriptions are connected with the rivalry between the various Church factions in the Caucasus.

Far right: Interior of the church of St George, looking east. The paintings date from the 16th century and are in a comparatively good state of preservation.

Ubisi. The monastery was founded in the 9th century by the famous Georgian monk Gregory of Khandzta. Extensions were later built on to the south and west walls of the 9th-century church. Inscriptions in Asomtavruli and Nuskhuri survive on the walls, and there is a late-14th-century wall-painting in good condition.

The residential tower was erected in 1141. An inscription on the south wall names its builder and first occupant, the minister Simeon Chkondideli. The text reads: 'I, Simeon Chkondideli, miserable sinner, exalted the glory of God in building this monastery and tower, in the reign of God's anointed Demetre, King of Kings, son of the great King David. In the year 361 of the Georgian era, 535 of the Saracen era.'

The monastery precinct is divided up into a series of separate courtyards, each of which had its own particular function. The west door leads into the main courtyard of the monastery with the church, refectory and other appointments. The front of the tower opens on to this court. The second court is immediately adjacent to the tower, and includes a burial place. The third court was used for domestic purposes. The tower was restored in 1968, when certain small sections had to be rebuilt.

Founder's inscription in Asomtavruli (positioned upside-down), elevation and ground-plan of the tower, and view of the monastery from the north-west.

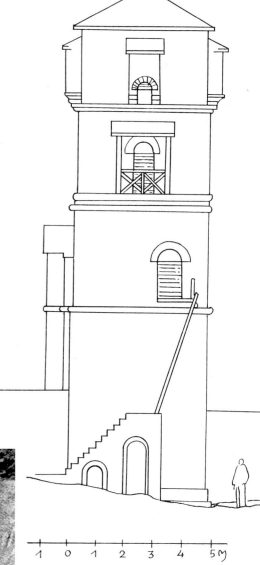

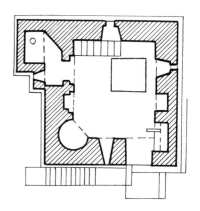

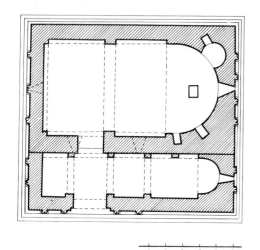

0 1 2 3 4 5 м

Tsinarekhi. Church of Magalaant-eklesia, late 12th and early 13th centuries. The name derives from the local landowners, the Magaladze family.

This aisleless church with southern annexe is built of warm yellow stone with selected blocks of pale blue and green. It is distinguished by its slender proportions and elegant decoration, with blind arcading on the east and west fronts. The surrounding wall, towers and belfry date from the 16th and 17th centuries.

Plan, close-up of the church from the southwest, and general view from the south-east.

Pitareti. Cruciform domed church, AD 1213–22. General view from the south-west. Built into the surrounding wall is a two-storey gatehouse with belfry.

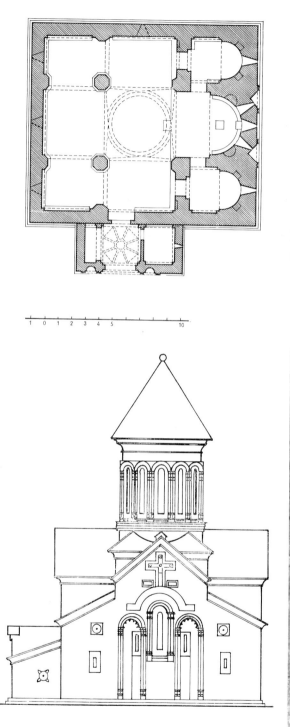

Pitareti. Plan, east elevation and view of the east front. The rich ornamental and representational decoration of the building is further enhanced by the use of variegated stones.

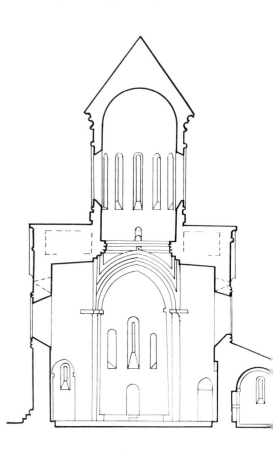

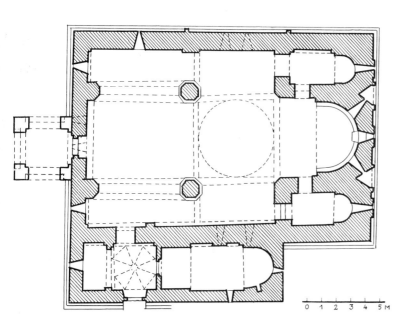

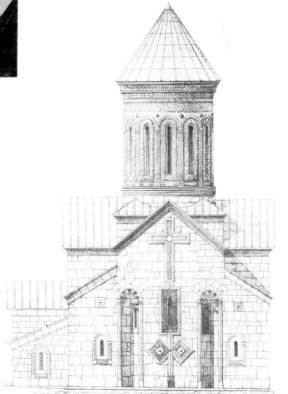

0 1 2 3 4 5м

Kvatakhevi. Cruciform domed church, late 12th and early 13th centuries. View of the drum and plan of the church (far left); section and east elevation (left); general view from the east (below).
There was originally a convent here, but at the end of the 14th century it was pillaged during the raids of Tamerlane. A number of the surviving buildings date from the

16th and 17th centuries. In 1854 the church was restored on the initiative of Prince Ioane Tarkhan-Mouravi, grandson of the last Georgian king, Giorgi XIII. The restoration, including the rebuilding of some parts which had been entirely lost, was expertly done, although the ornamentation was not replaced. At this time a hemispherical roof—an element utterly alien to Georgian architecture—was

built over the dome. As a result, when the building was restored again in 1967 the conical roof had to be pitched at a steeper angle than was originally intended (compare the photograph with the reconstructed elevation). The dominant element in the decorative scheme is the drum, which is entirely covered with ornamentation.

Akhtala. General view from the east of the monastery founded in the early 13th century by Ivane Mkhargrdzeli, a dignitary at the court of Queen Tamar. All that remains now of the monastery itself is part of the massive wall and the ruins of a tower-dwelling and other buildings. The church has lost its drum, but the richly decorated façades have survived intact. The east front repeats the composition of ornamental shaft and diamonds, window and decorated cross, with two niches flanking the apse, which first appeared at Samtavisi and subsequently became quite common.

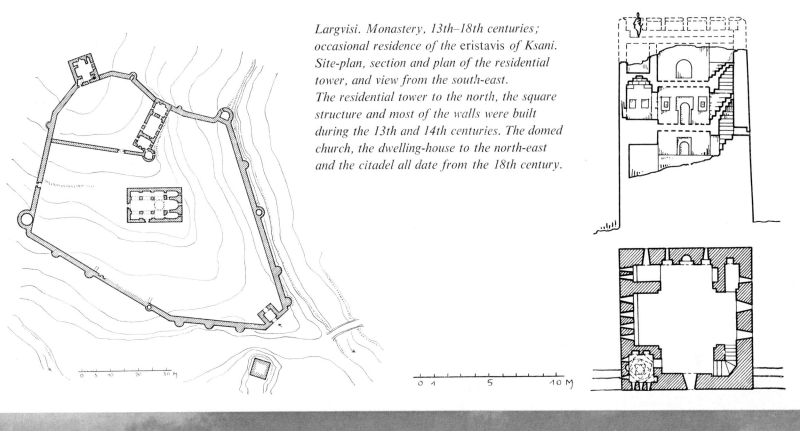

Largvisi. Monastery, 13th–18th centuries; occasional residence of the eristavis of Ksani. Site-plan, section and plan of the residential tower, and view from the south-east. The residential tower to the north, the square structure and most of the walls were built during the 13th and 14th centuries. The domed church, the dwelling-house to the north-east and the citadel all date from the 18th century.

Betania. Domed church, late 12th and early 13th centuries. View from the west (left), interior looking north-east (below left), plan (below) and elevation of the east façade (bottom).

The small church at the north-west corner dates from the year 1196. The brick extension to the main church was built over an older crypt. In the course of the restoration work carried out in 1974, gables and roofs which had been pitched at a shallower angle during extensive 19th-century repairs were restored to their original appearance.

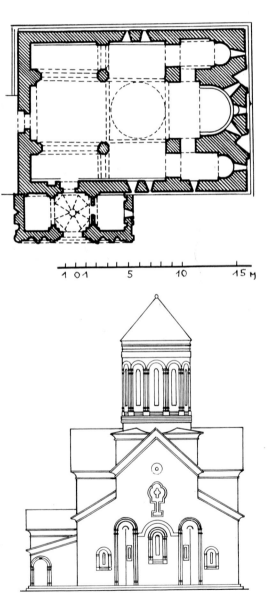

Vardzia. 12th-century cave complex.
Right: Fragments of a wall-painting from the north wall of the church, 1184–5, with representations of Tamar and Giorgi III (copy in the Georgian State Museum of Art).
Far right: Overall view of the complex from the south-west, and interior of the so-called 'Assembly Hall' ('Sakrebulo').
There were some 550 cells, cut into the rock on several levels and serving a variety of purposes, and most of them survive to this day. The front of the cliff face has collapsed, but it was chiefly passages, stairways and open porches or balconies that were lost. A portico with two arches has been erected in front of the church. The bell-tower is built of dressed stone, but the belfry has not survived.
In the 16th century the monastery was looted by the Iranian Shah Tahmasp, who, according to a contemporary chronicler, carried off untold riches.

200

David-Gareja. Metropolitan monastery of the Lavra, founded in the 6th century and extended in the 9th century and again in the 11th and 12th centuries. Ancillary monasteries—Bertubani, Natlis-mtsemeli, Dodo, Udabno and so on—sprang up along the mountain chain of the region, all using the name of the parent house. A large number of wall-paintings created by the school of artists resident here in the Middle Ages are still to be seen in the caves.

Left: The parent monastery of the Lavra, with the monks' cells. The round tower in the foreground dates from the late 17th century.

Below: Cave-monastery of Udabno. The refectory, looking north. The front part of the room has collapsed.

David-Gareja.
Left: Cave-monastery of Udabno. Interior of the refectory, looking north-east. The warm-hued figures of the wall-paintings are picked out in brilliant splashes of colour against the light background.

Below left: Cave-monastery of Bertubani. Church interior, facing east. The wall-painting dates from the years 1213–22. The south wall and part of the ceiling have collapsed, but monumental figures of the Virgin and Child and archangels survive in the apse, and there are large portraits of Queen Tamar and her son, Giorgi IV Lasha, on the north wall. On the ceiling are depicted the Exaltation of the Cross, with hovering angels, and other scenes with smaller figures.

Right: Udabno. The north side of the main church. The south wall and the ceiling have collapsed. Apart from their artistic merit, the remains of the wall-paintings (10th–11th century) are of particular interest because they include the oldest example in Georgian monumental painting of a cycle illustrating the life of a saint, in this case that of the Georgian saint David Garejeli, and are thus a record of specifically Georgian iconography.

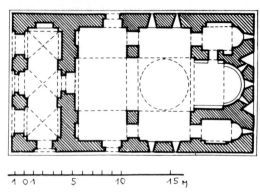

1 0.1   5   10   15 м

Kintsvisi. Cruciform domed church from the early 13th century; one of the few Georgian churches to be built of brick. The cornice and the base of the walls are of stone. The façades were left undecorated, except that the east front is relieved by two tall niches. The church has a narthex, opening out through large arches, with a gallery above it, and there are annexes to the north and south.

Inside the church is one of the finest cycles of wall-paintings to survive in Georgia from the early 13th century. Nearby, within the enclosure, are two other small churches and the remains of monastery buildings.

Plan (left), view from the north-west (below) and interior facing north-east (right). Portraits of Giorgi III, Tamar and Giorgi IV Lasha appear in the lower zone of the north wall. The altar screen dates from a later period.

Kintsvisi. Fragments of wall-painting from the north wall.

Portrait of Queen Tamar from the lower band (below left), and figure of a seated angel (below right) from between the two windows; the angel belongs to the scene of the Maries at the Tomb. Both illustrations were taken from copies in the Georgian State Museum of Art.

The Last Supper.

Timotesubani. Brick-built central-domed church, early 13th century.
Blind arcading articulates the tall drum, which is set with round turquoise-coloured tiles beneath the cornice. These contrast strongly with the bricks and with the grey of the cornice itself, producing a striking colour effect. The south annexe is a later addition. Following an ancient Georgian tradition, there is a large cross raised in relief inside the dome. An ornamental band separates this from the tall, slender figures of the Deesis and the archangels. The spaces between the windows of the drum are divided into an upper and a lower band; each section carries a representation of a saint (right). The window reveals are covered with ornamental motifs which enhance the decorative quality of the painting. The windows consist of tiny pieces of glass set in alabaster and ceramic frames.

210

Timotesubani. The wall-painting is contemporary with the building of the church.
Right: The Angel from Paradise. Detail from the Last Judgment on the west wall.
Below: An evangelist and a flying angel, from one of the pendentives.

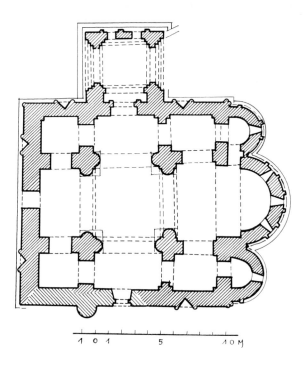

Tbilisi. The church of Metekhi, AD 1278–89.
This building differs in plan and general form
from other domed churches built at the height
of the Middle Ages. The treatment of the east
façade, for instance, with its three projecting
semicircular apses, had become rare by this
time, as had the use of four uniform clustered
piers to support the dome. Both the interior
and the exterior of Metekhi have been restored
many times over the centuries, and the present
drum and dome clearly date from a later
period.
View from the north-east. On the far side of
the river Kura lies the ancient citadel of
Narikala, with part of the old city below.

Tbilisi, Metekhi.
Left: East front. The decorative motifs on the three apses are badly worn. Evidence can be seen of the restoration work undertaken in the 17th and 18th centuries, which was carried out mainly in brick.
Below: Detail of the decoration on the east front.

Standing high up on the steep bank of the river Kura, the church of Metekhi is the focal point of the old city of Tbilisi.

Gremi. Citadel of the fortified town. The walls, a tower-house and the church survive. The church was built in 1565 by King Leon I of Kakheti. The great tower has several storeys designed for residential use; the belfry is a later addition. The town lay in the valley at the foot of the citadel, and the ruins of churches, a commercial quarter and a bath-house can still be seen.

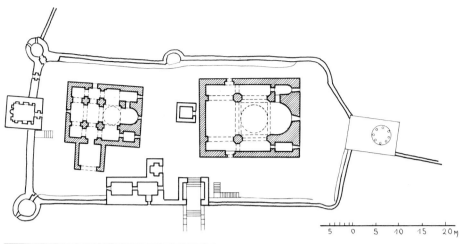

Ananuri. Complex dating from the 16th and 17th centuries. The upper fortress, enclosed by a wall with defensive towers, is the better preserved, and contains two domed churches dating from the period when the eristavis of Aragvi were at the peak of their power. The large church was built in 1689; the smaller one is older. The large rectangular tower, which stands at the highest part of the site, has several storeys; it was used for residential purposes.
Plan, and view from the south-east.

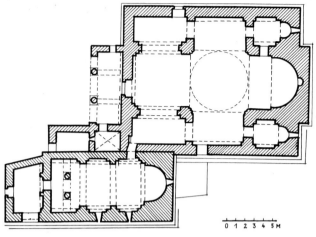

Sapara. Residence of the rulers of Samtskhe, 13th–15th centuries. The domed church, the bell-tower and the now ruined castle were all built in the late 13th and early 14th centuries; the aisleless church dates from the 10th century. The domed church was built by the architect Paresaisdze on the instructions of Beka and Sargis Jakeli; inside are wall-paintings with representations of the Jakelis from the mid-14th century. The aisleless church has interesting reliefs on the façade and raised galleries in the nave. The altar screen is now in the Georgian State Museum of Art. Plan, and view from the south-west.

0 1 2 3 4 5M

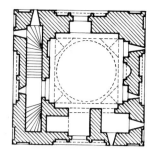

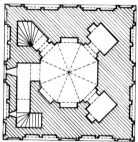

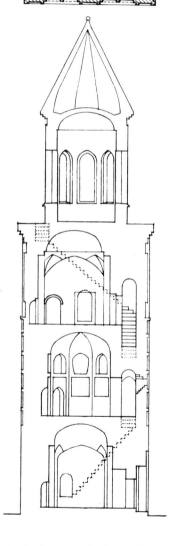

Ninotsminda. In the 16th century a bell-tower with living quarters on several floors was built inside the walls surrounding the 6th-century cathedral. The polygonal belfry, pierced by pointed arches, contrasts with the massive body of the tower. The building material, brick, also dictates the nature of the façade decoration. The living rooms have fireplaces and alcoves.
Plans of the first and second floors, section, and view from the north-west.

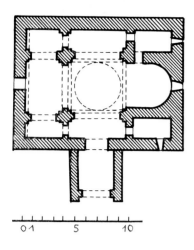

0.1 5 10

Gergeti. The church of Sameba (Holy Trinity)
and the bell-tower, 14th century. Situated at
the foot of Mount Kazbek, this building
demonstrates the close harmony which exists
between so many of the Georgian monuments
and their diverse natural settings.
Plan and view.

ART IN THE MIDDLE AGES (5th–18th centuries)
Fine arts and crafts
Stone sculpture and altar screens — repoussé work and the art of the goldsmith — enamelling — wall- and icon painting — book illumination — wood-carving, ceramics, metalwork and embroidery

In the Middle Ages, architecture was indisputably pre-eminent in Georgia, while other forms of art served as its adjuncts. This applies without reservation to sculpture and monumental painting. In the cases of high-quality metalwork, enamelling and book illumination the connection with architecture was largely a question of function, defined chiefly by activities of the Christian Church.

It should be remembered, however, that owing to the chequered course of the country's political history the preservation of works has been somewhat selective. Far fewer secular works have survived than religious ones; secular buildings and their contents were more often destroyed or carried off as booty than were churches and religious objects. Frequently the only reminder of their existence is a reference in one of the chronicles or annals. What does survive, however, is sufficient to give us a clear idea of the development and flowering of the different forms of art.

STONE SCULPTURE AND ALTAR SCREENS

The richness of Georgian sculpture is evident from the work which forms part of the façades and interiors of many of the buildings already discussed, as well as from the many impressive examples of goldsmiths' repoussé work. Since figure and pattern compositions of the highest quality were an essential feature of entire architectural periods, it is natural, after an examination of architecture, to turn first to the consideration of this particular branch of art.

Giorgi Chubinashvili has traced the stages in the development of Georgian sculpture by means of examples taken chiefly from repoussé work in precious metals. Stone sculpture was developing at the same time as sculpture in precious metals, and along similar lines. However, large figure sculptures were banned as heretical by the Orthodox Church, and this inhibited the effective development of the medium. Cramped within the confines of small-scale work, monumental sculpture could not reach the level of artistic perfection or the degree of expressiveness that prevailed in embossed work.

The starting point for sculpture is the period of late antiquity. Written sources contain some information about this period prior to the spread of Christianity. In the Georgian Chronicle we find the description of sculptures set up in Mtskheta in honour of the local heathen divinities Armazi, Gatsi and Ga. The copper figure of Armazi, according to the chronicle, was clad in a gold cuirass and had a gold helmet on its head; its eyes were of agate, and in its hands was a glittering sword. Gatsi was made of gold and Ga of silver, and they stood on either side of Armazi. The composition thus relied heavily on colour effects.

The spread of Christianity, the new ideology, entailed the destruction of heathen idols and temples. As a result, all that survives from the pre-Christian era is what was hidden underground for centuries and has now been rediscovered through archaeological research. There are a few examples of large sculptures, which are essentially imitations of Hellenistic or Sassanian models, and an enormous array of small objects worked in stone or metal which are distinctive for their rich decoration and their immensely varied ornament.

The gem from Armazis-khevi mentioned on p. 20, showing the portrait of the *pitiakhsh* Asparukh with its well-defined, individual features, stands out among these relics. Also remarkable is the sculptured ram's head adorning a necklet which likewise comes from Armazis-khevi (p. 37).

Initially, works of Christian art were a continuation of the heathen art that had preceded them, with a gradually increasing overlay of Christian ideas and attitudes. The animal motifs taken over from old heathen concepts were given a new Christian meaning, frequently by the mere addition of Christian attributes. A vivid example is the 5th-century bull's head in the baptistery of the Sion church at Bolnisi, which bears the Christian cross between its horns (p. 69).

However, the Christian Church soon learned to express its new ideas in subject compositions. Christian iconography began to spread throughout Georgia. The masters gave it their own interpretations, using the artistic resources best known to them. From the 5th to the 7th century the flat, decorative style, deeply rooted in Georgian art, predominated in sculptural works. In a few instances the influence of the art of oriental countries was evident. The rare examples of sculpture in high relief show only a summary treatment of detail, and are still inspired by the art of late antiquity. Nevertheless, there are some among them which are masterfully executed and highly expressive.

This category includes the two elongated bulls' heads, with branches of the Tree of Life in their mouths, on the east façade of Svetitskhoveli (p. 75). The heads, dating from the 5th century, stand well away from the wall and are carved three-dimensionally, with a fine, sensitive line. The ears and horns, too, were sculpted in the round, but have worn away with time. The bull's head in the Bolnisi Sion baptistery has different characteristics, and shows less attention to detail.

The relief on the capital in the apse of Bolnisi is worked differently again. The animal figures are shown in lively movement, and the portrayal is flat and markedly decorative.

Further examples of early reliefs in this flat style are those on the stele at Khandisi (p. 235) and on the cross of Kachagani (p. 237). The 7th-century Kachagani cross deserves special attention for the way in which the four angels holding the smaller cross are vividly portrayed on the arms of the cross itself, thereby uniting form and decorative composition in a convincing manner.

The 6th-century reliefs in Jvari (pp. 80–87) are of particular interest. They are an indispensable component of the façade articulation. The figures of the founders—three Kartlian rulers—are portrayed above the windows on the polygonal east apse. The central wall has the standing figure of Christ blessing the kneeling founder. Above it, the now severely damaged figure of a floating angel is let into the wall. On the side walls, angels hovering above the heads of the founders are turned towards the figure of Christ. The deliberate attempt to unify the reliefs into a homogeneous composition is further emphasized by the ornamented window hood that continues across all three surfaces.

The spaces in the three reliefs are filled with inscriptions. Here and there traces of red paint remain, which was applied directly to the stone. If the whole of the background was originally painted, then the reliefs must have had an effect quite different from the one we experience today.

The reliefs on the south façade are likewise portrayals of the founders of the church, but here they are shown together with other members of their family. They are not drawn together into a unified composition like that of the east façade, but resemble the latter in their execution. The kneeling figure on the drum, which has lost its inscription, is thought to be a portrait of the architect of Jvari.

The Jvari reliefs, particularly those on the east façade, are distinctive for their clear outlines and their emphasis on line, with the individual details being subordinate to the overall appearance. Their content has been clothed by the sculptor in essentially decorative forms.

The talent of the sculptor emerges powerfully from the Exaltation of the Cross in the arch above the south entrance. The corresponding sculpture over the small entrance is badly damaged. The focal point of the composition is the cross, the base of which opens out into leaves which spread across the lower part of the tympanum. The figures of the soaring angels, and the soft outlines of their wings extended in flight, follow the curve of the tympanum arch. The whole composition, carefully fitted into the semicircle of the tympanum, has been designed and executed with great mastery.

The Exaltation of the Cross and the portraits of the founders of the Jvari church, which still retain some of the plasticity of the forms inherited from late antiquity as well as having certain links with the art of Sassanid Iran, combine these elements with the decorative style and the linear emphasis that are characteristic of Georgia. In the hands of a talented Georgian master, the hallmarks of both cultures fused together in a distinct national form. These reliefs present an independent artistic solution.

The reliefs on the façades at Ateni (p. 89) are of various different types. Beside crudely fashioned human figures, the majority of which are found on restored parts of the walls —which has given rise recently to doubts as to whether they do in fact date from the time of the church's original construction—there are scenes of animals in a different style. On the tympanum over the north door two stags are pictured, with heads lowered to drink from a spring—a symbolic portrayal referring to apostles and saints or to the faithful. The stags are worked in low relief, but are strikingly elegant. The effect of the whole scene is both attractive and spiritual.

The hunting scene on the north façade shows a group of stags apparently frozen in fright, and a rider who has just shot the first arrow. The stags are very simply portrayed, whereas the figures of the man and the horse are carved much more carefully. The rider wears a headdress with a cloth streaming out behind, like the Sassanid horsemen.

Whereas sculpture of the 6th and 7th centuries still bore traces of features taken from antiquity and from ancient Persian art, which were reinterpreted on the basis of Georgian folk art, the sculpture of the 8th and 9th centuries deliberately shook off these influences and began to wrestle with the problems of plasticity in an entirely independent manner.

A striking illustration of the new artistic direction is provided by the relief in Opiza (p. 244), created around 826, which portrays the *eristavis* Ashot I and David. The composition extends over two stones. Christ, seated on the throne, makes a gesture of benediction over the model of a church which Ashot holds in his hands. On the other side, David is shown in prayer. All the figures are portrayed frontally, each standing isolated. Only the impressive gesture of Christ links the three figures of the composition into one scene. The relief has little plasticity; all is flat and linear. The profound expressiveness derives from the excessively large heads and hands of the figures, from Christ's gesture, and from the drapery indicated by the use of parallel lines.

At the beginning of the 10th century, the process of evolution towards an indigenous form of sculpture entered its most decisive stage of development. This was the time of transition from a flat portrayal to one where the figure is cut deeply into the stone—that is, the transition from the linear to the plastic. This process can already be seen in full spate in an example from the beginning of the 10th century, the portrayal (p. 245) of the *eristavi* Ashot II, known as Kukhi, which dates from the years between 891 and 918. The figure is 113 centimetres high and is carved in high relief, although it is kept very solid, without any detailed working of the individual parts. It originally adorned the north-west pier of the church in Tbeti. Today this relief is in the Georgian State Museum of Art. In contrast to the Opiza relief, it reproduces realistically the head-covering, the clothing and the design of the fabric. The decorative element of the relief consists in the rich pattern of the fabric.

In the second half of the 10th century, and through the 11th century, sculpture became widespread throughout Georgia. It became one of the most important components of façade decoration, and occupied conspicuous spaces above doors, around windows, on the drum and in the gables. The extensive use of reliefs on façades is illustrated by buildings in Oshki, Khakhuli, Vale and Zaki (or Zegani), by monuments in the ancient province of Kudaro—Kvaisisjvari, Kasagina and Nadarbazevi, by the Kutaisi cathedral, Nikortsminda, Sveti-tskhoveli and so on.

In the 10th century, sculpture began to appear inside the buildings. The squinches at Kumurdo and the piers at Tbeti are decorated with figures of the founders. Plastic portrayals of animals are to be found at the bases of the wall-piers near the apse at Zemo-Krikhi (p. 166), the heads of a ram and a bull decorate the apse window of the annexe of the same church, and a roundel showing the Exaltation of the Cross can be seen in the 11th-century annexe to the church in Katskhi.

As monumental wall-painting came increasingly to be used for church interiors, sculpture disappeared from these interiors. However, it became such an important feature in the decoration of altar screens that this will be dealt with separately.

Like many periods of artistic creativity, the 10th century too was characterized by the fact that, in addition to progressive trends, it also manifested unmistakable signs of orientation towards the past. This emerged in the course of the century in the not infrequently applied convention of making the head and hands disproportionately large, altering the proportions according to the relative importance of the parts, and in the use of a linear style of presentation, with its resulting strength of expression. By the turn of the century the efforts to suppress this tendency could be seen quite plainly, and in the first half of the 11th century the success of the attempts to evolve new plastic principles became evident.

The reliefs of the church in Oshki (pp. 139–41) are evidence of the diverse ways in which sculptural problems were overcome.

A dignified row of almost life-size figures appears on the south façade of the church. It consists of a Deesis, together with figures of the founders, the *eristavis* David and Bagrat, with models of churches in their hands. The figures are slender and skilfully carved. The heads are almost completely in the round, though today they are badly damaged, and the postures and gestures are lifelike. The garments of the saints fall in soft, heavy folds, and the complicated patterns on the clothing of the founders lend the whole composition a decidedly decorative tone. The monumental figures of the archangels on the upper parts of the façades are likewise in high relief, and the style is again decorative. The free delineation of the

drapery, particularly on the skirts of the garments, is quite striking.

The figures on the capitals of the piers in the south gallery are framed in friezes of foliage, and thus appear as an integral part of the decorative scheme of the capitals. A long animal frieze decorates the drum. The figures of a lion and a bull that appear by the north window of the church are completely flat and without any decorative embellishment. Thus we have here two artistic techniques side by side: the one progressive, as in the fully rounded figures of the founders and the archangels, and the other archaic, producing figures still bound to some extent by the conventions of the decorative, flat treatment.

Vale (p. 248) has a large number of reliefs dating from the final third of the 10th century. Relief compositions decorate the doorways and the windows, and occupy special places on the cornerstones of the cornices. As at Oshki, there are examples here of both bas-reliefs and three-dimensional portrayals. The reliefs at Vale have connections with sculptures in Tskarostavi and Doliskana.

The reliefs on the west cornice of the church in Korogho (pp. 246–7) have motifs of particular interest. They date from the very end of the 10th century and the first years of the 11th. Without any previous model to work from, the master produced realistic scenes of the construction of the church. The reliefs are remarkably expressive and attractive. There is no other known series of images portraying work scenes, which explains the significance of the Korogho reliefs.

The church in Nikortsminda (pp. 131–3) is richly adorned with ornamental and figurative reliefs, well preserved and still in their original positions. Here the reliefs decorate the tympana of the doors and the gables of the façades, combining with the blind arcades and the other elements of the façade ornamentation in a unified decorative scheme. Each gable relief is a complete scene, framed by an ornamental band that plainly defines its position on the façade. In these scenes which appear high up on the building, the decorative aspect is emphasized, whereas the reliefs in the tympana are more sculptural and more developed.

The distribution of the reliefs on the façades at Nikortsminda is a perfect example of the system evolved in Georgia, as distinct from the arrangement adopted in the Romanesque period in western Europe, where the reliefs were mainly concentrated around the entrance doors, creating richly decorated portals.

On the west façade of Sveti-tskhoveli (pp. 150–55) a late-11th-century relief portraying the Majestas Domini fills the triangle of the gable above the curve of the blind arch. It is a simplified representation, but worked in high relief, presumably to ensure that, despite its high position, it would catch the attention of the observer. Two angels in flight, which were later placed on the east façade of the building, and the two bulls' heads decorating the west gate of the encircling wall, date from the same period.

It is evident that the sculptural decoration of façades was subordinate in principle to the overall decorative composition. Yet it is not uncommon for individual figures to occupy random positions that do not relate to the rest of the scheme. The decoration of the façades of the Bagrat cathedral in Kutaisi, for example, which is distinguished by the rigorous disposition of its blind arcading, incorporates several isolated sculptured figures which break up the regularity of the design. The expressive figure of a griffin at the southeast corner of the church in Samtavisi (AD 1030) stands out as an effective contrast. The smooth lines of the body and the feeling of movement towards the centre of the façade make this a particularly attractive sculpture. Separate panels with representations of animals and birds adorn the façades of Khtsisi (AD 1002). Further examples could be included.

This use of sculpture shows, on the one hand, the love of the Georgian masters for free variation of the overall decorative composition and its details, and, on the other hand, their love of diverse, ever-changing artistic forms, as expressed in the abundant repertoire of ornament evolved over the centuries. In addition, these individual figures obviously had a symbolic significance which made them worthy of a special place independent of the other elements of the façades.

In the façade decoration of the Kutaisi cathedral, a striking element is provided by the capitals (p. 143) in the south and, more especially, the west portico, which date from the early decades of the 11th century. The corners of these capitals, and in some cases the centres of their faces, are decorated with human figures and animals, sometimes flat and sometimes rounded, closely interwoven with a large leaf motif. There seems to be a connection with the development of Romanesque capital sculpture, but this has yet to be submitted to scholarly research.

In accordance with church ritual, the altar area in the Georgian church was separated from the remainder of the interior, originally by a curtain, but later by an altar screen proper.

These altar screens, which were erected in Georgian churches from the early Middle Ages onwards, arrest the attention by the richness and beauty of their ornamental decoration and the high artistic standards attained in the execution of the reliefs. Imposed by the liturgy, they acquired a positive artistic function, and should be regarded as part of the overall decorative scheme of the interior.

Only a very few altar screens have been preserved in good condition. For the most part, only fragments have survived, but some of these make it possible to reconstruct the original appearance of the screen of which they were a part.

For the period up to the 10th century, there is evidence of a variety of forms of altar screen. Examples of two kinds survive: low barriers consisting of single slabs, and screens surmounted by small columns carrying arches; as a variant of the latter, there are screens where the columns rest on the ground and the spaces between are filled in with stone panels. The position of the screen seldom varies: as a rule it stands at the transition from nave to apse, possibly a fraction more towards the main part of the church.

From the 11th century onwards a further type of altar screen evolved, and it was not until the late Middle Ages that this was succeeded by a continuous wall with small openings. Georgian altar screens were not high, and because of their open arches they did not shut the altar section off from the remainder of the church or detract from the overall spatial effects of the interior. Georgian screens differ in construction from those of Byzantine, Slavic and oriental origin. They generally terminate in arches, and only in a few isolated instances are wooden beams laid across the columns. Moreover, these screens have no more than one entrance to the apse, whereas those in other Orthodox countries usually have two or three openings. The altar screens were made of stone, stucco, or very occasionally of wood. In the late Middle Ages, the use of brick was introduced. Relief carvings of patterned ornament and sometimes of figures were the usual decoration, though occasionally —as at Armazi—painting was also used. Crosses and icons were part of the decorative scheme.

At Jvari in Mtskheta there is a fragment of one of the early 6th-century screens consisting of panels with reliefs worked into them. Two fragments from the 7th and 8th centuries were found at Tsebelda (p. 242): these panels are absolutely covered with little scenes separated by ornamental bands. Examples from the 8th, 9th and 10th centuries are more numerous. Complete screens preserved intact in Armazi, Ubisi, Sioni near Kazbegi and Dzveli Shuamta, and incomplete examples in Gveldesi (p. 243) and the church of Giorgiseuli in Savane, are all already more accomplished in appearance. They are constructed on the lines of a low barrier, with small columns or a colonnade surmounted by arches, and a doorway in the centre.

Pride of place among the 10th-century screens goes to the one from Potoleti (pp. 238–39) and to the fragments from Skhieri, Salkhino and Kaberi.

Regarding individual features, the altar screens exhibit widely varying treatments. In the case of Armazi (p. 242), for instance, the dominant decorative element consists in an ensemble of paintings, with human heads looking forth from the spandrels, an entwined rope or cable motif immediately over the arches, and crosses on the panels. Gveldesi is richly adorned with reliefs and ornaments. In the altar screens at Ubisi and Sioni, the main accent is placed on the column capitals. Potoleti and Salkhino use a wide variety of patterned ornamentation.

The fragments of screens from Shiomghvime (pp. 250–1), Sapara, Khovle, Urtkhvi, Samtsevrisi, Tserovani (p. 254) and Ateni (p. 249), which date from the first half of the 11th cen-

Khtsisi. Relief from the east façade of the church, AD 1002, showing peacocks flanking a cross. The upper part of the cross is damaged.

tury, consist of large panels with broad ornamental borders worked in a delicate, complicated style. The central part of each panel is reserved for reliefs, which form the dominant element of the decoration.

Certain altar screen reliefs from the early decades of the 11th century provide the best possible examples of Georgian stone sculpture. The mastery of sculptural techniques can be seen here at its highest level of development. Figures are treated freely, with no trace of the former stiffness of posture. The bearing of bodies and heads, and the movement of the hands, ensure that the figures are fully involved in the action of the scene depicted. The contours of the figures, even in the details, are soft, flexible and expressive, and the draperies fall in light folds. The scenes are set against an architectural background.

In the Annunciation scene from Sapara (p. 252), the Virgin Mary occupies the central position. The gentle inclination of the head, the softness and warmth of her appearance suggest the anticipation of motherhood. The shapes are plastic, rounded and soft. Of the angel, only the head and one hand, delicately raised in a gesture of benediction, remain. The two figures standing on the right belong to another scene, the encounter of Mary and Elizabeth. They provide balance in the composition.

Depicted on a smaller stone at Sapara is the Presentation in the Temple (p. 253). At the centre of the scene, Mary is placing the Infant in the outstretched hands of Simeon. The dynamic moment is emphasized by the figure hurrying forward from the left. The gesture of the outstretched hand and the inclined head draw the frontal figure on the right—probably Hannah—into the action of the picture.

In this and other scenes from Sapara, and from Khovle, Urtkhvi, Shiomghvime and other churches, we see not only the masterly portrayal of figures but also the unconstrained depiction of emotional moments by purely sculptural means. The Sapara scenes are worked in light blue-green stone, and are bordered by an ornamental band of delicate and complex design.

In the 12th- and 13th-century altar screens at Meria and Gudarekhi, and at Satkhe (p. 241), where the whole screen survives intact, figure reliefs are largely replaced by ornament. At Satkhe there are only two small scenes, which are lost in the welter of ornamental decoration. Both the reliefs and the ornament are simplified and stiff compared to those of the 11th century; they do not have the lively attraction of their predecessors.

The altar screens dating from the late Middle Ages are not impressive in artistic terms. A few painted screens, however, are worthy of mention: these include the 16th-century screen in the church of St George in Gelati (p. 187), and the one in David-Gareja which dates from the 17th and 18th centuries. Its surface is divided up into rectangles framed by ornamental bands; inserted in the rectangles are icons painted on wooden panels.

REPOUSSÉ WORK AND THE ART OF THE GOLDSMITH

The work of the medieval Georgian goldsmiths is among the finest in the world. 'Apart from architecture,' writes Giorgi Chubinashvili, 'metalwork is the only branch of Georgian art which, according to all the available evidence, reached the peak of artistic perfection in the course of a thousand-year evolution. Not only did Georgian culture produce highly accomplished work in this field, but in so doing it developed its own individual style, both in overall design and in the details. In this connection, the peculiar characteristics of the smith's art enable us to form some idea of those aspects of the creative process which were forcibly repressed in other areas, for example in the development of sculpture.'

The earliest examples we have of medieval goldsmiths' work date from the 8th and 9th centuries. However, as we saw earlier, the roots of the craft in Georgia reach back into remote ages, and we may assume that such objects were being made in early Christian times, but have simply not survived.

The majority of the surviving objects are icons and crosses—processional crosses and those that stood in front of the altar—but there are also goblets, crowns, book covers, vessels, mountings and jewellery.

These items are for the most part worked in

silver gilt, and seldom all in solid gold. They are decorated with enamelling, niello and precious stones. Many have inscriptions, sometimes recalling the donor and sometimes the goldsmith. On some of the icons the faces and occasionally even the hands are painted, but very few of these paintings have come down to us. The icon of the Virgin Mary from Tsilkani (p. 280) deserves special mention; the experts believe that it dates from the 9th century and was painted in tempera and coated with a film of wax. The frame and inscription are of a later date.

The monumental icon of the Transfiguration (p. 255) from the monastery of Zarzma dates, according to its inscription, from the year 886. The icon was badly damaged, and has been restored a number of times. The ornamental frame and several details date from these restorations. Several figures appear on the icon. At the centre is Christ in the mandorla, the only complete figure to survive, and to either side of him are Moses and the prophet Elijah. The three apostles Peter, James and John are portrayed at the bottom, two of them kneeling and one standing. The linear design and the gestures, with the exaggerated size of the hands, give the work its expressive quality. Christ's garment is drawn in long, parallel, smoothly flowing folds. 'The Zarzma icon is a stylistically mature work exemplifying the artistic transition to a more refined picturesque composition where each figure has its own particular place in the design' (Giorgi Chubinashvili).

The 9th-century open-work liturgical fan from Mestia (p. 256) is also very impressive.

Another outstanding piece of work is the great processional cross of Ishkhani (p. 258), created in the year 973. The cross is 51 centimetres high and 36 centimetres wide, and the original shaft has also been preserved. The figure of Christ, with arms stretched wide, covers the small cross at the centre almost completely. The straight, fully extended limbs create a feeling of tension by their contrast with the slightly inclined head, in which suffering and sorrow are conveyed by the closed eyes and mouth. The contrasting colours of the gilded cross and the silver Christ figure further enhance the effect of the work. In its control of sculptural forms, this cross repre-

sents a notable advance on the Zarzma Transfiguration icon.

The processional cross of Breti (p. 257) was made between 994 and 1001 by Master Gabriel Sapareli. In the figure of Christ, the artist has skilfully intensified the modelling to produce truly three-dimensional effects. The bent knees stand away from the background, one foot is crossed over the other, and the curled fingers reach out into space. The complicated movement of the body and the angularity of the face are evidence of the striving for expressiveness. Whereas the lower half of the body hangs limply, the head and shoulders tower triumphantly above the nails. The reliefs at the end of each arm of the cross are the work of a different master.

The Martvili cross dates from the middle of the 11th century, and was originally gilded all over. The front face is covered with figures worked almost completely in the round. The creator of this work mastered sculptured form to perfection. The gentle, harmonious structure of these figures, the free, soft curves of their limbs and the flowing lines of the drapery replace the strongly expressive quality of the earlier crosses.

The Khobi icon of the Virgin Mary stands out among the works dating from the 10th century. It was made in 970 in memory of King Leon II. The painted face as it exists today was added later, and does not even conform to the original in outline and shape.

The icon was richly decorated with enamelled medallions and precious stones, of which the majority are now lost. There are, however, old photographs in existence which show the ensemble in its original form. One of the enamelled discs adorning the halo has survived; this dates from the early Christian period, whereas the enamelled medallions decorating the frame are of the same date as the icon itself.

The icon relies for its effect on colour—on the colour links between the gilded figure and painted face of the Virgin and the coloured medallions of cloisonné enamelling, the rows of pearls and the individual precious stones.

The early-11th-century Tsageri icon of the Virgin and Child, on the other hand, is all in repoussé work. The pale gilding gives it a dignified appearance. The austere face of the

Virgin is heavily emphasized. The frame, decorated with ornaments and precious stones, is set with embossed medallions showing half-length portraits of saints.

The richly decorated gold vessel from Bedia (p. 260) was made in the late 10th or early 11th century by order of King Bagrat III. The surface is divided up by arches into twelve compartments with a figure in each—seated figures of Christ and of the Virgin and Child, with five apostles between them on either side. Figures arranged in a row like this are characteristic of the 10th century. The drapery no longer adds to the expressiveness, nor is it yet used to indicate the bulk of the figures. Occasionally it appears to be employed simply as a device for displaying an attractive line or design.

A separate and unified body of work is formed by the plaques, almost square (30 × 35 cm) in shape, from Sagolasheni (p. 265), Shemokmedi (p. 259) and Motsameta. They are decorated with carefully embossed work depicting scenes on different iconographic themes. The ornamental frames are worked in a variety of ways.

The dedicatory inscription of the Catholicos Melkhisedek at Sveti-tskhoveli states that in this church the 'king's door' was made of gold and silver, and continues: 'I have covered the sacred throne with gold and silver, and adorned it with gems and pearls.' The annalist records that the throne of Queen Tamar in Vardzia was overlaid with gold. It is likely that the bases of the altar crosses were also adorned with embossed plaques.

The few examples that we have of these plaques date from the late 10th and early 11th centuries. They bear scenes from the New Testament. The compositions are distinguished by their monumental dignity and their decorative quality. They were produced in various workshops, and each has its own individual character.

Surviving church regalia include a number of liturgical fans. The early-11th-century fan from Shemokmedi (p. 262) is a work of great artistic accomplishment. It is made of silver and gilded. A long inscription runs the length of the outer edge, naming Ivane, son of Farsman Laklakidze. The artist who produced this work was evidently aiming at a splendid decorative effect. 'He is less concerned with the nervy, expressive look; in the harmony of the line and the movement of the forms and patterns he creates a delicate music ...' (Giorgi Chubinashvili).

The Shemokmedi icon of the Virgin and Child (p. 263) dates from the first quarter of the 11th century. The broad frame is covered with individual scenes from the lives of the Virgin and Christ. One of the inscriptions mentions the donors, members of the feudal Laklakidze family. The embossed background of the icon is completely filled with decoration. Mary and the Child, and the figures on the frame, are delicately worked in harmonious line. The original painted faces have not survived, but the raised outlines of the heads still suggest that the Mother was leaning over the Child as he nestled against her. The austere and dignified expression of the Tsageri Virgin has been replaced here by a more intimate expression of feeling.

The kind of emotional tone found in this motif was rare in Byzantium in the 11th–13th centuries. This led Giorgi Chubinashvili to the following conclusion: 'If we take into consideration the range of Georgian goldsmiths' work that we have seen, and the psychological character that permeates it, then in connection with the study of the Laklakidze Madonna the absolutely fundamental question arises as to whether this type of composition might not have originated in Georgia in the 11th century, and have found its way later to Byzantium, and from there on to Italy, where at a later stage of artistic development it acquired its familiar, rich expression.' This icon is the work of the same master who made the liturgical fan referred to above.

Portrayals of St George occurred in large numbers in Georgia. We find them in icons, wall-paintings and stone reliefs. In comparing the many examples with the depictions of St George on horseback produced in other countries, Giorgi Chubinashvili came to the conclusion 'that only in Georgia do we encounter him on such a massive scale in the 10th and 11th centuries, whereas in other countries, particularly in Byzantium, portrayals of him are virtually unknown before the 12th century. Moreover, the high degree of development and the numerous variations of

the three fundamental types in 10th- and 11th-century Georgia lead us to consider this country, rather than Byzantium or its provinces in Asia Minor, as the place of origin of both the theme and the icons themselves. It is no coincidence that, in the majority of examples, the evil fiend being cast down by St George is depicted in the form of the crowned Byzantine (or Roman) emperor. The goldsmiths were not isolated from political issues; they, like all nationally minded Georgians, were aroused by the Byzantine pressure on Georgia which began in the last decades of the 10th century. The fiend cast down by St George, the symbol of knightly, heroic courage, was given a concrete and realistic personification in the form of the political enemy, the Byzantine emperor.'

St George is portrayed either as a full-length standing figure with lance and shield, or on horseback, running his lance through the dragon, the personification of evil, identified in the minds of the people with the emperor of Byzantium. The oppressions of the period were compared with the persecution of the Christians by the eastern Roman emperor Diocletian. In some examples the latter takes the place of the reigning Byzantine emperor.

The Nakipari icon of St George (p. 271) is an impressive example of Georgian repoussé work from the early 11th century. It shows the saint on horseback running his lance through Diocletian, the persecuter of the Christians. The icon is enclosed in an ornamental frame incorporating figure medallions. The figures of St George, the horse and Diocletian, raised in relief from a smooth background broken only by an inscription, entirely dominate the scene. St George's head, with its large halo, is the focus of attention; its inclined attitude, and the saint's exalted expression, reveal him as the executer of a divine mission. The delicacy of the artist's decorative sense is evident in the way the ornamental frame has been made.

The Labechina icon of St George (p. 264) is a similar example. The silver work is partially gilded, and dates from the second decade of the 11th century. The ornamental frame has been lost. The pictorial content is similar to that of the Nakipari icon. The movement of the horse is livelier, and the artist conveys the

nervous tension of the horseman through the lance blow dealt to Diocletian. The figure of St George is modelled for maximum expressiveness. The head is worked in considerable detail, which, together with the expressive facial features, highlights the drama of the moment.

The silver disc with the representation of St Mamai (p. 261), made in the monastery of Gelati, is a magnificent work from the beginning of the 11th century. St Mamai was executed on a charge of witchcraft. The saint, named in the inscription on the disc, is shown seated on a lion, which bares its teeth menacingly. The scene does not refer to any specific episode in the life of the saint, but simply alludes to his role as protector of wild animals. In order to give extra emphasis to certain parts, the disc is partially gilded. This sculpturally outstanding piece is worked with great technical skill; the composition derives largely from the necessity of fitting the figures into the round shape of the disc. It was originally part of a larger ensemble, but the rest has not survived.

The highly expressive figure of St Mamai, and particularly the head, are worked almost in the round. The sculptural approach can also be seen in the representation of the folds of the saint's garment. The way in which his right knee stands out from the lion's body, while his foot seems to be pushed behind the animal's foreleg, is evidence of the attempt at a three-dimensional effect. The tip of the lion's tail, fashioned in the form of a leaf, and the ornamental treatment of the mane prove the strength of the decorative tendencies within the artistic traditions.

The 60-centimetre-high plaque with a representation of Simeon (p. 260) is part of a large icon from Lailashi showing the Presentation in the Temple. The figure of Simeon is gilded, while the background and the halo are not, except for a thin gold line round the edge of the halo. The head is worked in high relief. The garment envelops the figure in heavy, flowing folds. The outstretched hands, the bowed head and body and the slightly bent knee convey the awe with which Simeon accepts the child.

An icon from Eli (p. 267), made between 1030 and 1040 by the master Tevdore Gvazavaisdze, shows Christ seated on the throne. Medallions are worked into the frame. The robes of the carefully sculpted figure of Christ have somewhat angular folds, an echo of preceding periods. On the other hand, there is a perceptible attempt to portray the throne in three-dimensional terms. The composition stands out sharply from the smooth background.

The large crosses that stood in front of the altar in Georgian churches form another distinct body of works. Such a cross had been erected as early as the 4th century at Svetitskhoveli, in the church built by St Nino. These crosses stood on special pedestals, and they have been kept in their original position in a number of churches in Svaneti and other regions.

A brilliant example from Mestia (pp. 268–69) dates from the first half of the 11th century and stands 125 centimetres high. Scenes from the life of St George are portrayed on the gilded obverse; the reverse is covered with ornament. The lower part of the cross has sustained damage, and a number of the original relief plaques are missing; not long ago part of an 11th-century icon with a representation of the archangel Gabriel was rather insensitively attached in their place.

The artist of the Mestia cross has carefully selected those episodes from the saint's life which lend themselves to effective and sculpturally expressive representation. The scenes, set out in rows along the arms of the cross, are arranged not in chronological order but according to the composition of the scenes and their interrelation. Giorgi Chubinashvili has compared this artist's approach to that of the master of the upper church in Assisi, who in similar fashion selected characteristic and visually effective scenes from the life of St Francis to fit into the available spaces. 'And just as the frescoes in Assisi influenced all subsequent portrayals of the life of St Francis, so the cross of Mestia became a model for the selection and arrangement of compositions on other crosses depicting scenes from the life of St George, for example the late-12th-century Sadgeri cross or the one from Goris-jvari dating from the end of the 16th century.' The Mestia cross is distinguished by the highly skilled adaptation of the subject to the medium of sculpture, identifying its creator as 'an artist of exceptional talent at the peak of his development.'

The 11th-century Katskhi cross (p. 266) is 235 centimetres high and is in a near-perfect state of preservation. It originally stood on a base in the domed church in Katskhi, but today it can be seen in the Georgian State Museum of Art in Tbilisi. The cross is covered with gilded relief plates, and the lower part is engraved with a dedicatory inscription. Each of the scenes is surrounded by a wide decorative border. In the centre is the Crucifixion, and on the arms archangels, warriors and scenes from the New Testament.

Compared with the work of the master of Mestia, the Katskhi cross has a more pronounced decorative classical character. The garments are draped in heavy swathes, enveloping the whole figure. The figures are grouped naturalistically against the plain background, often spilling out of their allotted areas on to the ornamental surround. This means that the artist did not regard the border as the limit of the composition, but simply as a decorative element in the overall structure of the cross.

In the 12th and early 13th centuries, when Georgia was at the height of its power, a trend emerged in metalwork towards a splendid decorative treatment of pictorial images. The masters now concentrated all their energies on creating ornaments of complicated design and endless variation of form. Examples of this trend include the ornamental decoration of three mid-12th-century Deesis icons from Shiomghvime, a dish made by order of David the Builder, and a flagstaff made for Rusudan, sister of Giorgi III.

Whereas at the end of the 10th and throughout the 11th century efforts were mainly directed towards solving purely sculptural problems, with little or no attention paid to colour effects, from the 12th century onwards there was a renewed interest in colour motifs, as in the works of the 10th century, and now they were developed to their full potential.

An icon from Gelati (p. 270) with a half-length figure of Christ dates from the first half of the 12th century. The halo, background and frame are all in repoussé work; the figure of Christ was painted, but none of the original painting has survived. The frame is set with coloured enamel medallions. The rich ornamental decoration combines most effectively with the colours of the enamelling and the painted areas.

The Khakhuli icon triptych (pp. 272–3) dating from the mid-12th century, with its fusion of different artistic techniques, represents the high point of the pictorial-decorative form. In keeping with the tendencies of the period, enormous expenditure was lavished on this large icon, which is 147 centimetres high and, with wings extended, 202 centimetres wide. Of the actual icon image, nothing remains but the enamelled hands and face of the Virgin and part of the halo. The triptych into which the icon is set is completely covered with decoration executed in a wide variety of techniques. The background is totally filled with a light and freely worked ornamentation; in the central gold panel this is controlled and forms a subordinate part of the overall design, but on the silver-gilt wings, despite its flat relief-like style, it becomes the dominant element. This ornamental background is inlaid with a large number of enamel plaques, cabochon jewels, filigree rosettes and pearls, arranged in a symmetrical pattern.

Apart from a few later replacements, this monumental masterpiece of the goldsmith's work survives in its original state. The brilliant display and wealth of colour preserve their impact to this day, the effect being achieved not so much by the artistic individuality of the piece as by the fusion of so many different elements.

The Anchiskhati triptych (p. 274) was just as famous as the icon of the Virgin of Khakhuli. The bust of the Redeemer is embossed, and the face was painted. The frame is the work of the master Beka Opizari. This work was produced in the reign of Queen Tamar, at the end of the 12th century, by order of the bishop of Anchiskhati, Ioane Rkinaeli.

In the second half of the 14th century, the regents of Samtskhe had the head-piece and wings made for the icon. These are decorated with lively, carefully worked relief scenes containing many figures. The reverse of the wings dates from the 17th century.

Further items that have survived from the end of the 12th century are the repoussé covers of the Gospels from Berta (p. 275) and Tskarostavi. These were the work of the Opiza masters, the older Beshken Opizari and the younger Beka Opizari, mentioned above for his contribution to the Anchiskhati icon. Both book covers carry long inscriptions naming both the donors and the goldsmiths. Figure compositions fill the centre of the covers. The ornamental borders include inscriptions and gems, and even the subsidiary figures appear to form part of the frame.

Beshken and Beka Opizari relied on traditional stylistic principles, and their figures and ornaments were the product of the long and mighty evolution of the art of the Georgian goldsmith.

In Georgia, apart from the flag of the united state, there was also a flag for each of the individual provinces. The repoussé point (p. 275) of the flagpole that carried the Svanetian flag (the 'Lomi') has survived from the 12th century. An inflatable fabric flag in the form of a lion was attached to this pole. The figures of St Jonas and St George are portrayed on the front of the spike, and on the reverse is the figure of an archangel, with a long and beautifully written inscription.

In addition to the group of icons we have already described, where only the central figures—and occasionally even just the heads and hands—are painted, the background and frame being in repoussé, others have survived in which the entire central portion is painted and only the frame is in repoussé work. Very few icons consist entirely of painting. There are excellent examples of the art of the icon in the Georgian State Museum of Art and in the Museum of History and Ethnography in Mestia. Further examples can be found in a few churches in Svaneti.

In the late Middle Ages the standard of goldsmithing, as of architecture, dropped below its former peak of achievement. Yet there are examples from this period—the Chkhari altar cross, for instance, a copy of which was erected in Sveti-tskhoveli not long ago, or the Alaverdi triptych (p. 276)—which attain a certain sculptural expressiveness.

In the 16th and 17th centuries, artistic elements and technical methods developed much earlier continued to be widely used, but in addition new motifs and techniques now ap-

peared. The ornamental foliage, for instance, which filled the backgrounds with a dense, carpet-like cover, was now frequently engraved. Works were richly decorated with gems such as turquoise and rubies, and with pearls. These colour accents scattered over the surface greatly enhanced the effect of the work. The Alaverdi icon of the Redeemer and a vessel from Chkhorotsku (p. 277) are superb examples of this method.

In this late period, special positions were sometimes reserved on the icons for portraits of the religious or secular donors. On the Kortskheli icon of 1640 (p. 277), the kneeling figures of the *eristavi* Levan Dadiani and his wife Nestan-Darejan are introduced at the lower edge. From the 18th century onwards, motifs taken from European models began to appear in the goldsmiths' work.

ENAMELLING

The manufacture of glass and vitreous substances has been practised in Mtskheta and the surrounding areas since antiquity. This tradition has apparently been virtually unbroken since the last centuries before Christ, and some early examples of cloisonné and champlevé enamelling have survived. The bronze plaque from the belt fittings discovered in the burial place of the *pitiakhsh* Asparukh (2nd century AD) at Armazis-khevi, for instance, was enamelled. A ring with cloisonné decoration was found in a 4th-century grave. Enamelled objects were also being made in the 6th century: a small decorative plaque embellishing the Khobi icon of the Virgin dates from this period. The encolpion from Martvili (p. 278) dating from the 8th or 9th century, with its portrayal of the Deesis, is in cloisonné work, in rich colours against a translucent emerald-green background. A few small examples have survived from the 10th century: the cross of King Kvirike attached to one wing of the Khakhuli icon, and a pectoral cross from the monastery of Martvili. In the 12th century, enamelled items seldom appeared as independent works in their own right; the technique was used chiefly to provide colour in a larger context, for example in the medallions of icon frames or the halos in the icons themselves.

Three enamelled panels from Gelati (p. 279, above) which depict scenes containing many figures provide examples of the art of enamelling in the 12th and 13th centuries. Cloisonné work continued to be produced in the late Middle Ages, and the larger enamelled panels with the portrayals of St George on horseback (p. 279, below) must have been made in the 15th or 16th century. Enamelled works often bear inscriptions in Greek as well as in Georgian, even if they were made by Georgian artists.

WALL- AND ICON PAINTING

Georgian architecture dealt at an early stage with the most important questions of the distribution of interior space by creating a variety of buildings of the domed and basilica types. The clarity and precision in the construction of the architectural forms was underlined particularly by the beautiful workmanship of the masonry, which consisted of perfectly squared stones. The surface of such a wall is an artistic element in its own right. Moreover, as mentioned earlier, colour was used in a variety of ways in the interior of the buildings.

Mosaics were already used in the semi-domes over the altars at Jvari and Tsromi. Then there was the use of colour to accentuate the stonework in certain places, such as the windows and the apse, by tracing the joints in red, black or white paint, sometimes in one continuous line and sometimes as a dotted line. In Tsromi the red and black sketch lines of the mosaic in the apse are still visible. In Ateni there are remnants of a chequered pattern traced in red (p. 89). The relief crosses in the domes may also have been coloured for emphasis.

The artistic construction of the interior gave prominence to those very features which were later to be fully developed in Georgian mural painting: the important elements were design and the emphasis on line.

In the course of many centuries a large quantity of monumental painting was produced in Georgia, including a number of striking, artistically outstanding works. A large number of paintings have been entirely lost, and there are only small fragments of many more. Nothing survives from the pre-feudal period, when as far as we can tell wall-paintings were used to decorate buildings of all kinds. Faint traces of colour have been discovered on the plaster of the domed hall in Armazis-khevi. Apart from a few meagre remnants, there are no examples of façade painting either, which clearly was not much used in Georgia. The explanation lies no doubt in the Georgians' love of stone with its highly expressive surface, which they exploited with delicacy and skill, and perhaps also in the climate of the land, which made the permanence of such paintings a doubtful proposition.

Façade paintings, whether covering large areas of the wall or accentuating parts of the structure, do still exist on a few monuments dating from the 8th and 9th centuries—Akura, Tsirkoli, Armazi, and so on. Later examples survive at Oshki, Khakhuli and Ishkhani, and figure compositions still adorn parts of church façades in Svaneti, as at Iprari (11th century), Lagami and Chashashi (14th century), Lasht-khveri (17th century) and elsewhere.

The mosaic from the altar niche at Tsromi (p. 93) is remarkable both for its age (it dates from the 7th century) and for its artistic quality, which is evident from the fragments that remain. These fragments, which have been removed and housed in the museum in Tbilisi, make it possible, in conjunction with the preliminary sketch and thorough comparative studies, to produce a more or less reliable reconstruction of the mosaic.

Holding an unfurled scroll in his left hand, his right hand raised in blessing, the figure of Christ was depicted on a gold background in the centre of the conch, flanked by the apostles Peter and Paul, who were turned to face him. The apostles were notable for their life-like postures and the natural drapery of their garments. This scene—the Delivering of the Law—has iconographic and stylistic connections with early eastern Christian tradition. A broad ornamental band along the bottom completes the composition.

In the 8th and 9th centuries, architecture was in the so-called transitional phase of its development, when new objectives were formulated and cheaper building materials came into general use. These materials—boulders, rubble and porous tufa—encouraged the tendency to cover the walls with plaster, which then came gradually to be decorated. In Armazi, Sioni in Ertso and Telovani, parallel or intersecting lines were etched into the plaster and then filled with colour.

Altar screens have already been discussed in connection with sculpture. In the church at Armazi there is a screen (p. 242) dating from 864, made of plastered tufa and painted with designs in brick-red. The heads placed between the arches, executed in a flat, linear style, produce a most expressive effect by the simplest of means. The painting on the Armazi altar screen is one of the earliest surviving Georgian wall-paintings containing human figures, and one of only a few that survive from this period in the whole of the Middle East.

An interesting example of early mural painting is provided by the small peacocks depicted on the wafer-thin stucco of the side walls of the apse at Zemo-Krikhi.

The 8th and 9th centuries—the period of Arab rule in Kartli, characterized by periodic activity on the part of liberation movements and the exaction of gruesome penalties by the conquerors—saw an upsurge of national consciousness. A number of works were produced at this time in the literary form known as the 'Life and Acts', dedicated to the founders of the Georgian monasteries. Single episodes from these 'Lives' were also depicted in wall-paintings. This was how the main church of Udabno (p. 205) and other churches in the monastery complex of David-Gareja, for example, came to have single scenes or an entire cycle illustrating the deeds of David Garejeli.

At the beginning of the 10th century these wall-paintings acquired great significance in the decorative schemes of church interiors. Nevertheless, it was still only the altar section that was highlighted by means of painting. The Dodo monastery in David-Gareja and the first layer of the wall-painting in Nesgun provide examples. The figures are drawn in a flat, linear style, which in terms of the portrayal of the human figure represents the same level of independent development as can be seen in sculpture in the 8th and 9th centuries.

In the late 10th and early 11th centuries, pictorial compositions began to be used throughout the church interior. Wall-painting acquired great importance. Furthermore, from the 11th century onwards it played a dominant role in the architectural design of the interior by emphasizing the structure of the building as a whole.

This desire to cover the walls with painting did not merely express an aesthetic need, but illustrated both the progressive development of national traditions and the influence of the Byzantine theory of painting in the 10th century.

The surviving examples have enabled Tina Virsaladze to assess the development of the style and iconography from the 11th to the 13th century, and to detect several schools of painting.

During this period, Georgian painting differed from that of Byzantium. It developed along the same lines as the other branches of Georgian art, and underwent—somewhat belatedly—the same creative upsurge as occurred in architecture and sculpture from the end of the 10th to the second quarter of the 11th century. The choice of subject-matter for the main apse was entirely independent in iconographical terms. The Deesis motif occurred frequently, both in the simple version with Christ, Mary and John—as in the main church of the Udabno monastery in David-Gareja (10th or 11th century) and at Iprari (11th century)—and also in the version extended to include the archangels and seraphim, which can be seen at Zemo-Krikhi (11th century) and Pavnisi (12th century). At this time the favourite Byzantine motif for the apse was the Virgin and Child. In Georgia the tradition of using crosses in the dome persisted, as at Kintsvisi and Timotesubani; at Ishkhani and Manglisi they are supported by angels. This treatment of the dome is common only in Georgia.

By contrast with the characteristic conception and execution of Byzantine painting, Georgian wall-painting is predominantly linear, deriving its effect from the emphatic expressiveness of the line; these paintings are distinguished by their strong emotional aura, their restraint and their homogeneous colouring.

During the period from the 11th to the first half of the 13th century, the development of style passed from the severely monumental to the dynamic and the decorative. In the buildings of the 10th and 11th centuries and the first half of the 12th century, wall-painting is characterized by a clear compositional arrangement of the scenes and a harmonious balance which sometimes approaches perfect symmetry. The horizontal rows of pictures are mostly emphasized by ornamental bands or simply by coloured lines, which are firmly subordinated to the architectonic structure of the interior.

At the end of the 12th and the beginning of the 13th century, a new principle emerged in the arrangement of the pictorial zones. Single figures interrupt the horizontal rows by projecting upwards or downwards, and the bordering lines are then drawn around them, as at Kintsvisi and Timotesubani. The registers are no longer so strictly governed by the arrangement of the interior. Within this relaxed framework, the wall-painting of the period generally tends to be dynamic and decorative, rejecting strict, 'classical' clarity.

The mosaic in the conch of the main church of Gelati (p. 183), depicting the Virgin and Child with the archangels Michael and Gabriel, dates from the first decades of the 12th century. Certain features of the mosaic suggest that the artist was a Georgian who had passed through the school of Constantinople.

It is interesting to trace the stylistic changes in the wall-paintings decorating the altar sections of churches during the 11th and 13th centuries. In the 11th century, for example, at Ateni, the dominant position in the painting was occupied by the huge, static figures of the Church Fathers. At Betania, where the wall-painting in the altar area dates from the beginning of the 13th century, the figures are not to scale. The general construction of the painting produces an illusion of movement, increasing as it travels upwards from the calm, frontal figures of the Church Fathers through the slight activity of the apostles to the violent movement in the row of prophets. A narrow band separating the registers is interrupted by the figures of the deacons at the apse windows. The half-length figures below the windows also break up the regular horizontal line of the composition.

The portrayal of the figures changes, too. The stiff, squat figures of the late 10th and early 11th centuries, as at Oshki and Khakhuli, are gradually modified during the second half of the 11th century and the early 12th century and become elegant, with majestic movements. The faces are delicately modelled and the drapery reveals and accentuates the shapes of the bodies. The paintings of this period are distinctive for their expressiveness of movement and delineation and their emotional quality—see, for example, Ateni (pp. 169–71), Zemo-Krikhi (p. 168), the narthex of the main church at Gelati (p. 186), the works of the Svanetian artist Tevdore at Iprari, Lagurka and Nakipari and the paintings at Matskhvarishi (p. 172).

Some decades ago it was recognized that monumental painting in fact reflected the achievements of the Georgian sculptors in the early 11th century.

There is a group of wall-paintings from the late 12th and early 13th centuries at Betania (p. 199), Vardzia (p. 200), Timotesubani (pp. 210–11) and, more particularly, Kintsvisi (pp. 207–9) which are highly artistic. The delineation and the forms become gentler and more elegant, the combination of colours is sophisticated, the lines are softly rounded and flowing. Yet for all that the paintings have lost something of the strength that permeated the earlier frescoes.

Several schools of painting can be identified in Georgia from the 11th to the 13th century. The paintings in Ateni, Kintsvisi, Timotesubani and elsewhere belong to the metropolitan school. Those from Racha and Svaneti—the frescoes in Zemo-Krikhi and the works of the artist Tevdore, mentioned above, in Matskhvarishi—belong to a separate school. Finally, the wall-paintings in the David-Gareja monastery complex fall into another, quite distinct, category. All of these schools imbued their paintings with the flavour of their highly individual styles.

The fresco painting of the fully developed medieval period has left us with a series of portraits of individuals from both the secular and the religious spheres, especially of people on whose initiative buildings were erected, extended or painted. In accordance with the attitudes and customs of the feudal society of that time, the subjects bear all the characteristic marks of the upper stratum of the population.

As a rule, the north wall of a building was the place favoured for such portraits, not least perhaps because of its advantageous position directly opposite the main south portal, and on account of the good lighting from the windows of the south wall. However, portraits of founders do occasionally appear on the south and west walls.

These portraits may be found both in churches and in individual chapels. The figures are mostly portrayed full-length, in an attitude of prayer, and the most important figures are usually singled out from the rest by differences in size and posture. Most individuals are shown with their bodies slightly turned, expressing some emotion.

Of the founder-portraits that survive from this period, those of Queen Tamar, King Giorgi III and King Giorgi IV Lasha at Vardzia (p. 200), Betania (p. 199), Kintsvisi (p. 208) and Timotesubani are outstanding.

Queen Tamar was celebrated as fair and womanly by her contemporaries Chakhrukhadze and Shota Rustaveli, and was described by the annalist as follows: 'Many women display power, but not as she does. Not by cabals does she regulate the life of her people, but with wisdom and the force of truth and purity, of calmness, generosity and grace, and by the exercise of justice.'

All four existing portraits of Tamar reflect this assessment of her, despite the fact that the conventions of medieval painting imposed limits on the manner of portraiture. In Vardzia she is depicted in her youth, and in the other wall-paintings she is shown as a woman and ruler in her prime.

The wall-paintings of the 13th and 14th centuries display new features assimilated from the so-called 'Palaeologian' Byzantine style. There are noteworthy examples at Ubisi (painted by the artist Damian), Sapara, Zarzma, Martvili and Tsalenjikha (executed by the artist Kir Manuel Eugenikos of Constantinople), and in the chapels at Gelati and Khobi.

The remains of the late-13-century wall-painting in the south chapel of Gelati (p. 186) contain details that plainly indicate when it was painted. The movements of the figures are free and natural. The figures are richly modelled with strong, bright highlights.

The wall-paintings in Ubisi, dating from the end of the 14th century, contain figures captured in vigorous motion and in complicated attitudes. They are angular and expressive. The lines of the drapery are sharp, and the copious use of white paint heightens the expressiveness. The compositions are filled with figures, and typical backgrounds consist of mountain landscapes or complex architectural scenes.

These characteristics endure, and are plainly evident in the 15th-century paintings at Nabakhtevi and Alaverdi. The Nabakhtevi frescoes, with their light backgrounds, are softer and more decorative in colouring.

Apart from the paintings which follow the new trends detailed above, there is a further group which perpetuates the traditions of an earlier time in a somewhat debased form, as for example the wall-painting from the end of the 13th century in the church of the Annunciation at David-Gareja.

A large number of 16th- and 17th-century frescoes have survived in Georgia. During this period Georgia was cut off from the other European countries with whom she had previously shared a common development. The evolution of Georgian art did not continue along the normal, predictable lines, and naturally this is reflected in mural painting.

The 16th-century paintings in the main perpetuate the traditions of the preceding age. The style is now distinctly linear. Examples can be seen in the church of St George at Gelati (p. 187) and in Dzveli Shuamta, Gremi and Nekresi.

17th-century wall-paintings—as in the west arm and the north chapel (p. 184) of the main church at Gelati, the south-west annexe of Khobi, and at Bobnevi—depict scenes and figures on a noticeably smaller scale. The monumental character is reduced accordingly. The drawing is conventional, and the colour is pale and weak, though occasionally characterized by the combination of several stronger tones. The works of individual masters reveal a certain variety.

The monumental paintings on secular themes that have survived from the 17th cen-tury in Lashtkhveri deserve special mention. Amirani, whose name figures prominently in Georgian legends from early antiquity onwards, is shown on the façade of the church battling with the dragon and with the 'Devi' or giant. The scene is an illustration of the *Amiran-Darejaniani* of Mose Khoneli, a contemporary of Rustaveli.

In the late Middle Ages there was a marked increase in the number of portraits of donors. As in earlier times, a place was reserved for them on the north wall of the building, and not infrequently on the south and west walls as well. The distinguishing features of these portraits are their flatness and the deliberate, expressive outlines. The figures are portrayed frontally; the three-quarter profile current from the 11th to the 13th century, which created an illusion of movement towards the altar, is with a very few exceptions now replaced by stiff and frozen postures.

BOOK ILLUMINATION

The oldest examples of Georgian writing that have come down to us date from the 5th century. These are the inscriptions, mentioned earlier, in the mosaic floor of the Georgian church near Bethlehem (p. 42) and on the architrave of the door in Bolnisi (p. 69). Apart from this, fragments of 5th- and 6th-century manuscripts (palimpsests) have survived which are not merely important works for the study of early Christian literature, but are also impressive examples of a highly developed bookmaking craft.

In succeeding centuries, hundreds of beautiful manuscripts were copied and illuminated, mostly in the scriptoria of the monasteries, both inside Georgia itself and in Syria and Palestine, on Mount Sinai and Mount Athos and elsewhere.

The material used was well-prepared parchment; there is no evidence of the use of paper before the 11th century. From the earliest times, Georgian manuscripts were made in the form of the codex, that is as books with separate quires bound into a single binding. Several of the manuscripts have embossed covers. For the writing itself, inks of the most diverse colours were used, ranging from rich black to golden ochre. The Georgian calligraphers were restrained in their use of decoration, and included very little vermilion.

The visual appeal of these handwritten books begins with the liveliness of the script itself; the varying pressure of the calligrapher's pen made the ink flow more or less strongly to produce a richly differentiated range of colour tones.

The early manuscripts are without adornment, but the arrangement of the text on the page, the choice of ink colours and the introduction of occasional large capitals already reveal that striving for artistic form that was to reach such a high level of development in later times.

The oldest surviving illuminated manuscripts date from the 9th and 10th centuries. Earlier manuscripts are mentioned in literary sources; the Georgian Annals, for instance, refer to a richly adorned Gospel book produced in the 5th century for Vakhtang Gorgaslani. In the second half of the 10th century —that is in the period when indigenous artistic traditions were reaching their definitive form— new elements were introduced such as headpieces, illuminated capitals and the figures decorating the signs of abbreviation.

In the manuscript illuminations produced in Georgia, as in other countries of the Christian world, two basic artistic styles can be discerned: the 'graphic' style, using outline drawings in a combination of light colours (e. g. the Song Book of Mikael Modrekili, the Synaxarion of Jibisdze, the astronomical treatise of 1188 and the Yenashi and Urbnisi Gospels), and the 'picturesque' style, with strong colours applied in several layers, frequently using gold on vermilion (e.g. the Gospel books of Gelati and Vani, the Second Jruchi Gospels and the Synaxarion of Ekvtime Mtatsmindeli). The two styles were current simultaneously for several centuries, and were used in manuscripts of a modest, popular type as well as in rich volumes of a very high standard of artistic accomplishment.

Traces of Hellenistic influence can be detected in the illustrations in the graphic style that appear in such early manuscripts as the Adishi Gospels (p. 284) of AD 895 and the First Gospels of Jruchi (p. 285) of AD 940.

The mature example presented by the Byzantine manuscript format had a decisive influence on Georgian manuscripts. Renée Schmerling, who studied Georgian manuscripts for many years and investigated basic issues of technology and aesthetic form, wrote that, in the late 10th and early 11th centuries, Georgian manuscripts preserved their national character less in the aesthetic conception of the individual decorative elements than in the relationship between these decorations and the various sections of the text. Here we see the innate character of the Georgian people at work, upholding their national creative traditions against a wide variety of strong external influences.

During the 11th century, the composition of Gospel books matured into an established artistic format. Heading the manuscript were canon-tables, at the beginning of each Gospel was a full-page illustration of the evangelist, and ornamental motifs and illuminated capitals decorated the chapter headings and the beginning of the text. Great importance was attached to these in the production of a manuscript page. The calligraphers created a great variety of initial letters; in the early stages, the capitals were strong and monumental in outline, but later they were given rich, decorative shapes.

The 11th and 12th centuries were as fertile with regard to the perfection of artistic book design as for the continuing development of wall-painting. At this time magnificent codices such as the Gelati Gospels (p. 287) were produced in the tradition of the Constantinople school. Other illuminated manuscripts are suffused with a more independent, national interpretation of aesthetic form and colour; noteworthy examples include the Mestia Gospels, the 'Flower Triodion' or decorated Lenten service book, and the Second Jruchi Gospels. The astronomical treatise illustrated with signs of the zodiac is unique: copied in 1188, it is the earliest surviving manuscript of secular content.

The Gelati and Second Jruchi Gospel manuscripts are richly adorned with miniatures: the Jruchi codex contains 359, the one from Gelati 244. Occasionally several illustrations appear on one page. A lot of gold was used in these miniatures and illuminated capitals.

Each of the seven miniatures from the Illuminated Triodion (p. 292) to have survived undamaged occupies a whole page. A simple compositional structure is here combined with a refined, elegant style and a soft colour range; the general approach is reminiscent of monumental painting. The manuscript is thought to have been produced in a scriptorium in central Georgia, perhaps at Gelati.

The miniatures in the Second Jruchi Gospels, and especially one group that are all the work of the same master, are distinguished by their linear emphasis, their restrained colouring and the expressive impact which derives not merely from the movements and gestures, but also from the basic structure of the compositions—some of the figures break through the borders of the pictures, and all move freely within a framework of complex architectural forms.

The miniatures in the manuscript of the works of Gregory of Nazianzus (p. 288), dating from the late 12th or the early 13th century, are likewise full-page. The text is written in a beautiful Nuskhuri script which strongly affects the aesthetic character of the entire codex, while the miniatures are set apart from other contemporary work by their monumental decorative quality.

The illuminator of the astronomical treatise of 1188 (p. 286) demonstrates the characteristic Georgian feeling for the plastic expressiveness of line in a flowing and harmonious manner.

In terms of decoration, the distinctive quality of the manuscripts dating from the 13th century and after is their search for new artistic methods. The classical structure of the composition is now progressively replaced by a freer arrangement of the figures. Increasingly, details project beyond the frame, while the decorations find their way into the text itself. The design of the initial letters becomes more complex and varied, and they increase in number. The Largvisi and Yenashi Gospels illustrate these tendencies, as does the Gospel book now in Moscow.

The design of the majority of books from the 16th and 17th centuries reveals the influence of Iranian miniature painting, which now asserts itself in defiance of ancient Georgian tradition, as for example in the illustra-

tions to Shota Rustaveli's epic poem *The Man in the Panther's Skin* or to *Zilikhaniani*. Among this group of manuscripts are some in which there is a strikingly free and self-sufficient approach to calligraphic problems and to the compositional structure of the entire codex, including the colour effects. A good example of this too is the 17th-century manuscript of *The Man in the Panther's Skin* copied and illustrated by Tavakarashvili. A growing interest in European models is evident at this time.

Georgian manuscripts have survived in their thousands, but no doubt this is only a part of the total output produced by the scribes, calligraphers and artists, nameless masters of a fertile branch of Georgian art.

In 1629 the first Georgian printed books were published in Rome. In 1709, a Georgian printing-house was set up by King Vakhtang VI in Tbilisi, with the aid of a Georgian Church leader, writer and translator, Metropolitan Antimos Iverieli, who was at that time living in Wallachia (Romania). From then on the development of book production was analogous with that in the rest of Europe.

WOOD-CARVING, CERAMICS, METALWORK AND EMBROIDERY

Wood-carving has long played an important role in the general decorative scheme of buildings in Georgia—in the columns and beams of domestic dwellings of the *darbazi* type, in doors, furniture and so on. As one of the oldest cultural activities, wood-carving is rooted in folk inspiration, and yet it developed as a professional craft. The quality of the carved wooden objects that survive from the 10th and 11th centuries is outstanding, and they can easily bear comparison with other forms of art.

In this respect it is no doubt significant that wood-carving borrowed ideas and motifs, both ornamental and figurative, from stone and metalwork. Occasionally there is evidence of the process being reversed, with wood-carving influencing stone sculpture. This influence can be detected mainly in the 8th, 9th and 10th centuries, that is to say during the period of fervent quest for new decorative forms. The

10th-century altar screen of Potoleti (pp. 238–39), for example, bears close similarities to decorations carved in wood.

Beautiful 10th- and 11th-century doors in carved wood have been preserved in various historical regions of Georgia. The doors from Otsindale (p. 293) and Jakhunderi (p. 291) have surfaces divided up into panels, rectangular, square or round in shape, which are filled with ornament and figures. The ornament is extremely varied and produces a most decorative effect. The surface of the door from Chukuli (p. 292), dating from the first quarter of the 11th century, is divided into separate panels by means of frames decorated with open-work bosses. The panels themselves are filled with portraits of saints in low but carefully worked relief. The door is covered with a wealth of ornament, including some which is highly original, and its overall composition is based on the contrast between the flat figures and the ornamental elements in *à-jour* work.

An early-11th-century beam which formed the top of the altar screen at Melesi has ornament covering its front face. In the centre, above an enclosed square panel, there is a small inscription in Asomtavruli. Trailing stems with large, soft, freely drawn leaves run outwards from the centre to both sides. This beam is all that remains of the Melesi altar screen; the columns on which it rested, and the other parts of the screen, are lost.

These examples from Chukuli, Otsindale, Jakhunderi and Melesi give some idea of wood-carving in the 11th century. There are many more examples that could be included, from this and more recent periods and from various areas, for the art of wood-carving continued to flourish until very recently.

Building on the achievements of antiquity, many Georgian crafts—pottery, glass-making, production of metal articles, weaving and so on—developed much further during the Middle Ages. The items made were destined mainly for daily use, although some of them were utilized in building or filled certain functions of divine service.

Glazed ceramics (pp. 294–5) were widely used. Vessels of differing shapes, small oil-lamps and even roof tiles, floor tiles and elements of façade decoration were coated with slip and glazes. A variety of techniques were employed for their decoration, including sgraffito and resist work using both slip and coloured glazes.

In the late Middle Ages the manufacture of majolica became very widespread. A few examples have survived of open-work ceramic discs which were set into windows. Some of them can still be seen today in their original places, for example in the church of St George at Gelati and in Timotesubani, Khobi and Kortskheli.

Glass-making, too, was known in Georgia from antiquity. Glass products figure prominently among archaeological finds, and include vessels, seals, window panes and jewellery—rings, bangles, and beads. The manufacture of glass and ceramic wares has continued without interruption up to the present day.

The rich traditions of metalworking were also pursued successfully throughout the feudal age. Weapons made of high-grade steel, with decorated blades and handles, have survived, together with pieces of armour such as chain-mail and helmets, embellished with ornament, and a wealth of articles for everyday and liturgical use. Two of these articles which are worthy of special mention are the bronze foot of a candlestick decorated with lion figures (p. 296) and a 12th-century silver jug with a niello inscription naming King Giorgi III (p. 296).

Georgian textile products were known from the earliest times. They not only served to meet the general demand from within the country, but were also much sought after for trade purposes. Only isolated examples of this once rich fund of material have come down to us. Small fragments of old fabric have been preserved on the back of a few icons and processional crosses.

Reliefs and paintings from the 10th century onwards provide a fairly clear picture of the clothing worn by the feudal aristocracy, which was made of rich and sumptuously decorated materials. Some of the fabrics were evidently home-produced, while some were imported wares.

We have examples of embroidered textiles for the whole of the period between the 13th or 14th and the 19th centuries, and indeed the tradition of artistic embroidery is still alive today in the mountain regions. The embroidered articles were used for clothing, purses and head-coverings, and also for religious purposes, for example in liturgical vestments (pp. 297–98) and tapestries depicting the mourning of Christ.

The embroidery threads were produced and dyed locally. Coloured silk threads, silver threads with and without gilt and coloured braid were all used. From the 18th century onwards, tinsel, ultra-fine gold and silver wire, glass beads and chenille were imported from western Europe. The work was done in satin stitch with gold, silver and silk threads. The embroideries, produced by skilled seamstresses, are colourful, with well-chosen combinations of shades. They are as individual and as national in feeling as the products of other branches of the arts, and reflect the tastes of the periods in which they were made.

This survey of the immense legacy of Georgian art has sought, despite the inevitable limitations of the space available, to demonstrate the essential features of the different art forms.

Through the centuries, art in this region on the borders of Europe and Asia has followed a distinctive national evolution and travelled a complex and independent road. At certain points in this long history, peaks of artistic achievement have been attained in various spheres, and in this way the Georgian people have made a valuable and unique contribution to the art of the world.

Khandisi. Fragment of a stele from the second half of the 6th century. Such stelae were quite common throughout Georgia as votive monuments; this one originally terminated in a cross and stood on a square base. Christ is portrayed on the front, and below him the Virgin and Child; on the sides, angels and saints. The general approach is decorative, with a flat and linear style of execution. Below: Detail of the figure of Christ.

*Lamazi-gora, near Bolnisi.
6th-century stone cross with
relief ornament. The stone
has been worked into the
shape of a foliated cross
decorated with lilies.
S. Janashia Museum (State
Museum of Georgia).*

Kachagani. Stone cross with a representation of the Exaltation of the Cross, first half of the 7th century. The original base of the cross is missing.
The movement of the angels is light and delicate; harmony and tranquillity are achieved in the artistic interpretation of the composition. The relief is decorative and linear in character.

Potoleti. 10th-century altar screen.
It has been possible to rebuild the screen
almost in its entirety from the fragments that
survived, but it has not yet been established
whether the columns carried arches or whether
an architrave, possibly of timber, was laid
across them.
Georgian State Museum of Art.

239

Ozaani. Fragment of a stucco altar screen, now coloured pinkish-yellow, which can be dated from its style of execution to the 10th or the early 11th century. All that survives is a part of the right-hand panel. The ornamental infill of the arch takes the form of a foliated stem growing out of a full-bellied jug or vase; after attractive circumvolutions, the stem ends in a cross. This motif stands out from others because of the originality and spontaneity of its design.

Patara Oni. Altar screen from the first half of the 11th century.
The stucco screen, which stood in a small aisleless church, was destroyed recently, and only a few fragments of the carved decoration have survived. The richly ornamented work was painted in black and brick-red. In material and construction, the screen corresponded with other examples from the same period (Sveti, Savane, Jrbuchi, Likhne, Dzveli Shuamta and others).

Armazi. 9th-century altar screen.
Detail of the painting (after a copy in the
G. Chubinashvili Institute for the History of
Georgian Art, Academy of Sciences of the
Georgian SSR).

Tsebelda. Fragment of a 7th-century altar
screen. Several of the motifs are characteristic
of early Christian iconography. Despite the
high relief of the scenes, the overall effect is
flat and graphic.
Georgian State Museum of Art.

Gveldesi. Panel from an 8th-century altar
screen. The design fills the entire surface, and
is executed in the flat, decorative manner that
characterized the stylistic development of the
sculpture of that period.
Georgian State Museum of Art.

Gveldesi. Small column, 8th century. Height
36 centimetres. On three of the surfaces,
human figures in arched frames are carved in
low relief. The figures, which have dis-
proportionately large heads, seem frozen in
their stiff postures; their clothing is indicated
by rather arbitrary patterns of close parallel
lines.
Georgian State Museum of Art.

243

Opiza. Relief panel of c. 826 AD showing Ashot I and David, rulers of Tao-Klarjeti, in the presence of Christ. All the figures, as well as the model of the church that Ashot holds, have inscriptions in Asomtavruli to identify them. Christ has laid his right hand on the church in blessing.

Tbeti. Figure from a pier in the church of AD 891–918. The man is Ashot II of Tao-Klarjeti, portrayed in traditional manner as the founder of the church, but the model which he held has been lost. Part of the head, the face, the hands and the feet are all missing. The ruler wears magnificent garments, with lions and stags decorating the cloak. The figure was originally accompanied by an inscription.
Georgian State Museum of Art.

Bedia, near Sukhumi. Fragment of a relief from the second half of the 10th century. The tall, slender figures were originally framed by arches. The surviving small columns with their foliated bases are reminiscent of the arch motifs appearing in the canon-tables of manuscripts, which may have inspired the sculptor of this panel. The awareness of spatial depth which can be detected in the perspective foreshortening of the hands and feet represents an important step forward in the development of Georgian sculpture in the 10th century.
Georgian State Museum of Art.

Korogho.

Below: View of the church (late 10th and early 11th centuries) from the west, showing the carved cornice. The tower was used for defence, and the ruined building beside it was the place of assembly for the elders.

Right: The cornice, with its scenes from the building of the church. On either side, the workmen are shown moving up towards the figure of the Virgin in the point of the gable. From left to right, the following scenes appear: a workman hewing stone; a large block being pulled by animals; the preparation of mortar (?); the mortar being carried to the building site (?); small stones being transported on a hand sledge; the founder with a model of the church; the consecration of the church, with a priest on the right and (possibly) the architect on the left; an overseer (?); men carrying stones on their backs; the splitting of a large block; a woman bringing food.

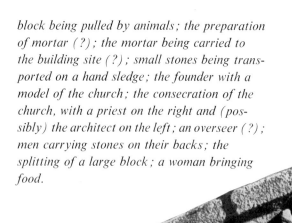

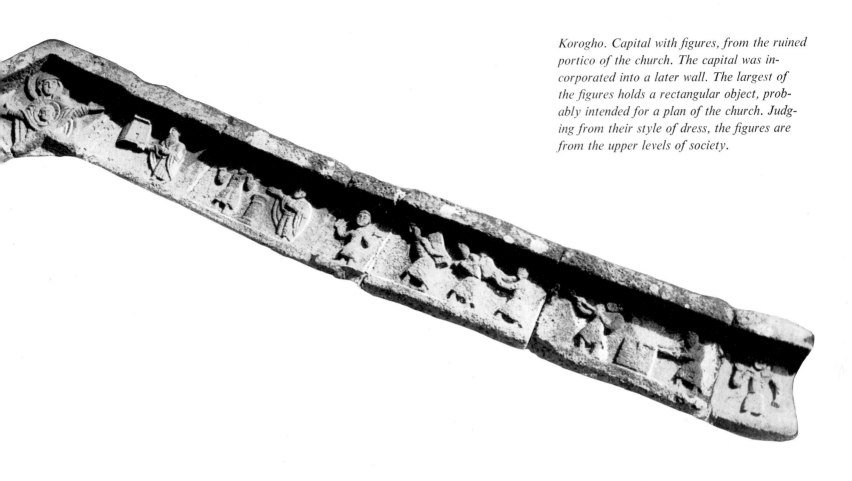

Korogho. Capital with figures, from the ruined portico of the church. The capital was incorporated into a later wall. The largest of the figures holds a rectangular object, probably intended for a plan of the church. Judging from their style of dress, the figures are from the upper levels of society.

Vale. Tympanum over the west door of the church. Last quarter of the 10th century.

*Ateni. Fragment of an altar screen from the
first half of the 11th century.
The panel is entirely covered with a pattern of
leaves, carved in sharp and clean relief, which
serve as a background to the inset icons of
the evangelists Luke and Mark. Originally
pale green, the stone has darkened with age.
Georgian State Museum of Art.*

Shiomghvime.
Left: Panel from an altar screen dating from the first quarter of the 11th century. The scene, the Hospitality of Abraham, is symbolic of the Trinity.
Georgian State Museum of Art.

Centre: Detail of the left-hand angel.
Right: Detail from a small column, early 11th century. The head is carved in the round and attached to the pillar at only one point at the back of the head. The attraction of the face with its big eyes lies in the purity and gentleness of the delicately worked features.
Georgian State Museum of Art.

Sapara.

Left: Part of a panel from the altar screen, first quarter of the 11th century. The blue-green stone slab originally had a broad ornamental border all the way round. The central part contains two scenes, the Annunciation and the meeting of Mary and Elizabeth. The Annunciation shows Mary seated in front of a building; the angel approaches her with head inclined.

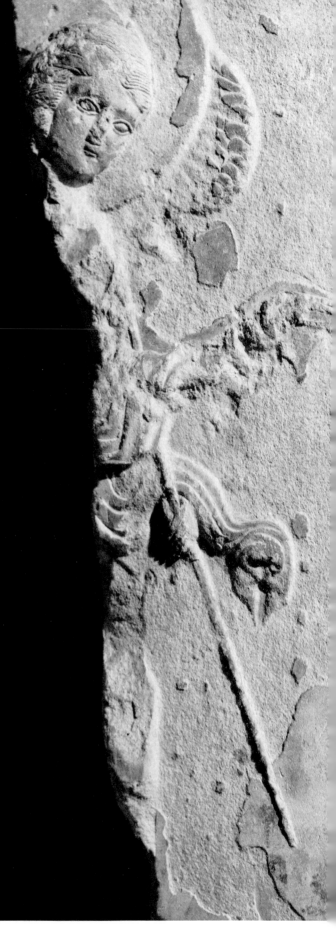

The figures of Mary and Elizabeth in the second scene are isolated somewhat by the line of the building, but the Virgin's outstretched hand serves to unify the composition. By means of thematic links, the group of the two women serves to emphasize the soft femininity of the figure of the Virgin.
Georgian State Museum of Art.

Centre: The surviving fragment of the angel from the Annunciation. The sensitive lines of the head, carved in high relief, the delicate delineation of the face and hand and the soft flowing folds of the garment all testify to the great skill of the artist.

Right: Part of a second panel from the altar screen, showing the Presentation of Christ in the Temple. Despite its poor state of preservation, the vivid expressiveness of the figures and the sculptural skill of their creator are still evident.
Georgian State Museum of Art.

Tserovani. Fragment of an altar screen from the first half of the 11th century. The ornamental border is remarkable for its elegant design and intricate workmanship. The stone is pale yellow in colour, though traces of reddish-brown paint can still be seen on the smooth chamfer.
Georgian State Museum of Art.

254

Mestia. Open-work liturgical fan in silver-gilt. 9th century.
Svaneti Museum of History and Ethnography.

Breti. Processional cross, AD 994–1001. Silver-gilt. Height 52 centimetres, length of haft 32 centimetres. The lower arm of the cross broke off at some time and was shortened during a subsequent restoration. The smooth surface between the figures is filled with inscriptions; those on the lower part of the cross include references to King Bagrat, the son of Gurgen, and to the goldsmith, Gabriel Sapareli.
Georgian State Museum of Art.

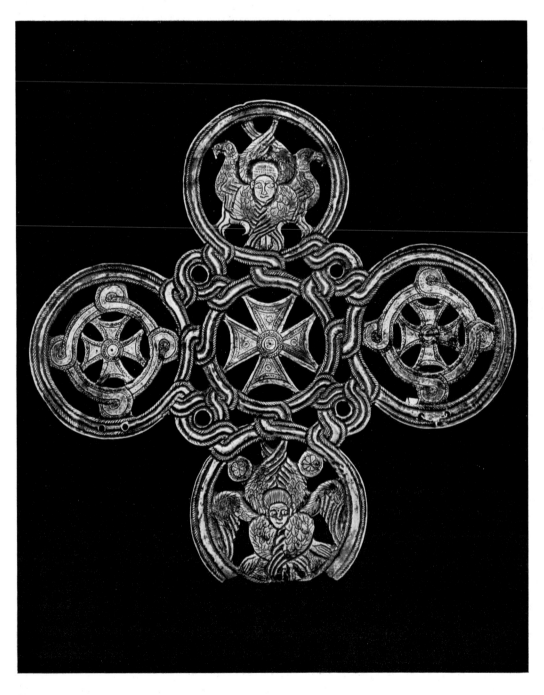

Ishkhani. Processional cross, AD 973. The figure of Christ with outstretched arms dominates this masterpiece of medieval metalwork. The date of the commission and the name of the donor, Bishop Ilarion of Ishkhani, appear in an inscription in Asomtavruli script across the arms of the cross. Georgian State Museum of Art.

Shemokmedi. Early-11th-century embossed panel showing three scenes merging into one another: the Deposition, the Entombment and the Arrival of the Women at the Sepulchre. The composition includes inscriptions in Asomtavruli.

The figures, which stand out sharply from the smooth background, are alive with sculptural expressiveness. The upper part of the panel has been restored; the inscription attached here in the place of the original border refers to Prince Mamia Gurieli and his consort Tinatin (1598–1625). Georgian State Museum of Art.

Bedia. Gold vessel from the end of the 10th century or the first years of the 11th. The body of the vessel is adorned with twelve raised figures set in arched frames. Georgian State Museum of Art.

Lailashi. Embossed silver plaque, c. 1020 AD. Height 65 centimetres. The figure of Simeon in this panel, which originally formed part of a larger icon of the Presentation in the Temple, is one of the largest surviving examples of an embossed human figure. The priest, whose robes hang in heavy folds, is shown bending forwards slightly in anticipation of the part he is to play. For its time, it is a work of great expressiveness, though technically crude. Georgian State Museum of Art.

Gelati. Silver roundel, partially gilded, show-
ing St Mamai. Early 11th century. Originally
part of a larger ensemble, this piece is clearly
the work of a highly skilled goldsmith who
devoted particular care to three-dimensional
effects and the indication of spatial depth.
Georgian State Museum of Art.

Shemokmedi. Silver liturgical fan, partially
gilded, from the beginning of the 11th century. Height 56.5 centimetres. Both sides of
the quatrefoil fan are covered with repoussé
work. The individual scenes, carefully balanced

and skilfully adapted to the circular format,
are framed in broad ornamental borders.
Their arrangement tends to emphasize the
central section. The relief figures are subordinate to the overall rhythm of movement

discernible in the composition. The fan was made for Ivane Laklakidze, possibly by the same artist who produced the icon of the Virgin for the Laklakidze family. Georgian State Museum of Art.

Shemokmedi. Silver-gilt icon of the Virgin from the first quarter of the 11th century. 80 × 64 centimetres. The original painted faces of the Virgin and Child have been lost. The broad repoussé frame is made up of fifteen panels, each depicting a number of figures in a scene from the Gospels. The arrangement of the piece reveals the endeavour to create a balanced composition from asymmetrical and freely varied elements. The skill of the master is likewise evident in the gentle, harmonious lines of the figures and their garments. Georgian State Museum of Art.

Labechina. Icon of St George running his lance through the Emperor Diocletian. Repoussé work, early 11th century. Georgian State Museum of Art.

Sagolasheni. Five embossed silver-gilt panels from the late 10th or early 11th century. Average dimensions 30 × 35 centimetres. The composition of the scenes is primarily decorative in character. The outlines of the

individual figures are kept very simple, the artist's interest clearly centring on the plastic forms themselves. Georgian State Museum of Art.

*Katskhi. The 11th-century silver-gilt cross which stood before the altar of the domed church. Illustrated are the central section (left), showing the Crucifixion, and the right arm (below), with Christ's Descent into Hell and the Dormition of the Virgin.
Georgian State Museum of Art.*

*Eli. Embossed icon from the fourth or fifth decade of the 11th century depicting Christ Pantocrator.
Svaneti Museum of History and Ethnography.*

Mestia. Silver-gilt cross from the first half of the 11th century with scenes from the life of St George. The cross is 125 centimetres high and was made to stand in front of the altar. Several of the panels are not in their original positions, and the figure of the arch-angel Gabriel, which comes from an 11th-century icon, was attached quite recently to the lower part.

Overall view, and close-ups of the upper part and the two original plaques from the lower section.

Svaneti Museum of History and Ethnography.

Gelati. Icon of the Redeemer, first half of the 12th century. The painted face has not survived. The enamelled medallions on the frame bear inscriptions in Asomtavruli. Georgian State Museum of Art.

*Khobi. Gold pectoral cross of Queen Tamar,
late 12th or early 13th century.
Obverse (below) and reverse.
Georgian State Museum of Art.*

*Nakipari. Early-11th-century embossed icon.
St George slaying the Emperor Diocletian.
A long inscription in Asomtavruli names the
goldsmith as Asat Gvazavaisdze.
Svaneti Museum of History and Ethnography.*

Khakhuli. Triptych from the first third of the 12th century, incorporating older elements. The central part of the triptych consists of gold, the wings of silver-gilt, with precious stones, pearls and enamelling. Width including opened wings 202 centimetres; height 147 centimetres.

All that remains of the 10th-century icon of the Virgin Mary is the enamelling of the face and hands, now preserved in Tbilisi. The triptych had been transferred to the monastery of Gelati, but in 1859 it was fraudulently removed and triptych and icon were split up and dispersed.

The central icon, which measured 54 × 41 centimetres, was the largest example of medieval cloisonné enamelling surviving at that time.

An inscription on the right wing refers to King Demetre I, on whose instructions the magnificent triptych was created.

Detail of the right wing. Crosses and medallions, most of them the work of Georgian enamellers but a few produced by Byzantine masters, are set into a background of intricate foliage decoration and precious stones.

10th-century cross with cloisonné enamelling, originally made as a reliquary. The two halves were later separated and applied to either wing of the triptych. On the left wing is the half shown here, with a full-length figure of Christ and heads of the evangelists Matthew and Luke and of Saints Peter and Paul. The inscriptions in Greek and Georgian on either side of the figure of Christ mention King Kvirike. On the right wing is a portrayal of the Crucifixion.
Georgian State Museum of Art.

*Anchiskhati. Silver-gilt triptych made at the
end of the 12th century on the instructions of
Bishop Ioane Rkinaeli. The frame is the work
of the master goldsmith Beka Opizari.
Georgian State Museum of Art.*

Svaneti. Tip of a Svanetian flagpole or ceremonial banner staff from the late 12th or early 13th century. Portrayed here are St Jonas and St George; on the reverse is an archangel.
Svaneti Museum of History and Ethnography.

Berta. Repoussé Gospel cover, late 12th century.
Beshken Opizari, the goldsmith, is named in one of the inscriptions.
K. Kekelidze Institute of Manuscripts, Academy of Sciences of the Georgian SSR.

Chkhorotsku. Gold vessel dating from the second half of the 16th century. Georgian State Museum of Art.

Kortskheli. Icon of the Prophets, 1640. An inscription in the secular Mkhedruli script identifies the figures in the lower panel as the patron, Levan Dadiani II, and his wife, Nestan-Darejan. Georgian State Museum of Art.

Martvili. 8th- or 9th-century encolpion with a representation of the Deesis in cloisonné enamel. The repoussé wings date from a later period.
Georgian State Museum of Art.

Gelati. Three gold plaques with cloisonné enamel insets, 12th or 13th century. Height 17 centimetres, width 10 centimetres. These three plaques originally formed part of a much larger ensemble; the remaining eight, formerly in the Petersburg collection of M. P. Botkin, are no longer traceable. The scenes depicted are (left to right) the Raising of Lazarus, the Presentation in the Temple and the Descent of the Holy Spirit.
Georgian State Museum of Art.

Gelati. Two gold plaques with cloisonné enamel insets, 15th or 16th century. 17 × 13 centimetres and 14.5 × 11.6 centimetres. Both panels show St George fighting the dragon and bear inscriptions in Greek and Georgian scripts.
Georgian State Museum of Art.

Tsilkani. Icon of the Virgin and Child, 9th century. Encaustic with some tempera. The frame, the inscription and some other parts date from considerably later.
Georgian State Museum of Art.

Mestia. Icon of the Virgin and Child with St Barbara, 9th or 10th century.
Svaneti Museum of History and Ethnography.

Khe. Icon with a half-length figure of an angel, 11th century, from the church of Kvirike and Ivlita. The frame is embossed silver.

Tskhumari. 12th- or 13th-century icon of the Crucifixion.
Svaneti Museum of History and Ethnography.

Ubisi. 14th-century triptych.
Georgian State Museum of Art.

284

Adishi. The evangelists Luke and John, from the Gospel Book of AD 897. The Gospels were written in the monastery of Shatberdi by the scribe Mikael.
Svaneti Museum of History and Ethnography.

Jruchi. First Gospel Book, AD 940. A note in the manuscript reveals that it was copied by the scribe Grigol at the monastery of Shatberdi, but that the canon-tables were the work of the artist Tevdore. The manuscript, which is written in bold, handsome Asomtavruli characters, is executed in sepia ink, as are the eight surviving canon-tables.

The figures are characterized by the delicacy and expressiveness of their line. The overall composition of the miniatures shows eastern Hellenistic influences.
K. Kekelidze Institute of Manuscripts, Academy of Sciences of the Georgian SSR, N 1660.

Astronomical treatise, AD 1188. Zodiac sign of Leo. This page contains examples of all three Georgian scripts: the text is written in Nuskhuri, the line above the lion in Asomtavruli and the note in the margin in Mkhedruli. K.Kekelidze Institute of Manuscripts, Academy of Sciences of the Georgian SSR, A 65.

The Synaxarion of Zakarias Valashkerteli, dating from the first half of the 11th century. The manuscript was written in Constantinople, probably in a Georgian monastery; part of it is missing, but seventy-four miniatures survive which reveal certain links with early Christian models. The miniatures are clearly the work of a highly skilled artist. The one shown here depicts the Miracle of the Loaves and Fishes. K.Kekelidze Institute of Manuscripts, Academy of Sciences of the Georgian SSR, A 648.

Gelati. 12th-century Gospel Book. This magnificent manuscript is decorated with canon-tables, vignettes and a large number of miniatures. The miniatures are decorative in character and dynamic in design. The text is written in Nuskhuri. K.Kekelidze Institute of Manuscripts, Academy of Sciences of the Georgian SSR, A 908.

Illustration from a copy of the collected works of St Gregory of Nazianzus dating from the end of the 12th and the beginning of the 13th century. St Mamai, seated on a huge lion, is represented as the protector of wild animals. Around him are genre scenes symbolizing spring: digging, planting trees, tending sheep, and so on.
K. Kekelidze Institute of Manuscripts, Academy of Sciences of the Georgian SSR, A 109.

Alaverdi. Gospel Book, AD 1054. The manuscript was copied by the scribes Simeon, Giorgi and Dvali at the Georgian monastery on the Black Mountain near Antioch. It is written in beautiful Nuskhuri characters and decorated with illuminated capitals, vignettes and miniatures. Shown here is the final illustration of the canon-tables, a floriated cross with inscriptions in Greek and Georgian (Asomtavruli).
K. Kekelidze Institute of Manuscripts, Academy of Sciences of the Georgian SSR, A 484.

Bichvinta. Gospel Book from the first half of the 13th century. All that remains of the manuscript is two miniatures of evangelists, in which the attempt to preserve independent Georgian traditions can be discerned. Illustrated here is the miniature of St Luke.
K. Kekelidze Institute of Manuscripts, Academy of Sciences of the Georgian SSR, N 2120.

Martvili. St Luke, from the Gospel Book of AD 1050. The manuscript is decorated with miniatures and illuminated capitals. The miniatures are in rich colours throughout.
K. Kekelidze Institute of Manuscripts, Academy of Sciences of the Georgian SSR, S 391.

Largvisi. Gospel Book, 13th century. St Luke.
K. Kekelidze Institute of Manuscripts, Academy of Sciences of the Georgian SSR, A 26.

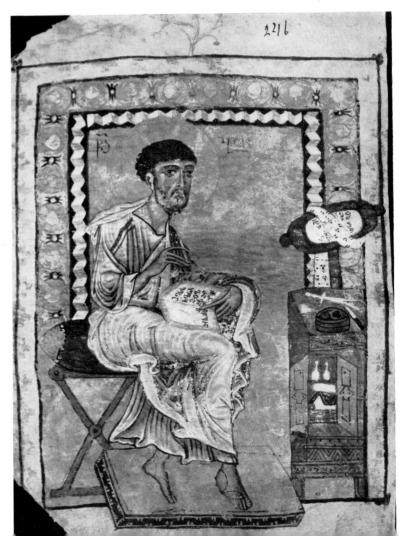

The 'Flower Triodion' from the first half of the 12th century. The manuscript may have been produced in the monastery of Gelati. Seven miniatures, without any text, are all that remain today. Their composition is distinguished by the severely simple arrangement of figures and architectural backgrounds, the gestures of the figures and the distribution of details. This manuscript is one of the finest works of medieval book illumination. Doubting Thomas (left) and Christ and the Woman of Samaria.
K. Kekelidze Institute of Manuscripts, Academy of Sciences of the Georgian SSR, A 734.

Jakhunderi. Detail of a wooden door from the first quarter of the 11th century. The borders originally held panels carved with relief figures, only one of which now remains. The central part and the corners were decorated with open-work bosses, but none of these have survived.

Chukuli. Wooden door from the first quarter of the 11th century, richly decorated with relief carvings of human figures and ornamental pierced bosses.
S. Janashia Museum (State Museum of Georgia).

Savane. Two fragments of doors from the
11th century.
Georgian State Museum of Art.

Otsindale. Detail of a wooden door from the
first quarter of the 11th century.
Georgian State Museum of Art.

Mtskheta. Roof tiles from Classical antiquity. S. Janashia Museum (State Museum of Georgia).

Mtskheta, Sveti-tskhoveli. Ceramic floor tiles. Four fragments with coloured decoration on a base of white slip, finished with transparent glaze (9th-11th century), and one undecorated tile from the floor of the church of St Nino (early 4th century).

Fragment of a bronze matrix from Selobani with the figure of an archangel, for use in repoussé work; three roof tiles from Eredvi, Achanua and the Bagrat cathedral in Kutaisi (10th and 11th centuries); ceramic tile from the bishop's palace in Samtavisi (10th–11th century).

Kaspi. Ceramic dish, 12th–13th century. The figure of a lion, framed in foliage, is etched into the white slip. The surface is covered with a transparent glaze.
S. Janashia Museum (State Museum of Georgia).

Tbilisi. Pottery plates and vase, 12th–13th century. The ornament is incised into the white slip and covered with a transparent glaze.
S. Janashia Museum (State Museum of Georgia).

Martvili. Foot of a bronze candlestick, 7th century (?).
Georgian State Museum of Art.

Mestia. 12th-century silver jug with niello decoration. The inscription in Asomtavruli names King Giorgi III.
Svaneti Museum of History and Ethnography.

Tsaishi. Embroidered omophorion, made in 1312 by Tamar Kherkheulidze as an orarion and dedicated to the icon of Anchiskhati in the church of Ancha. In 1358 it was transformed into an omophorion by Natela Jakeli, who added two inscriptions and an ornamental border. In 1652 Tamar Jolia of Tsaishi reworked the figures and added pearls, precious stones and another inscription. The embroidery is worked in satin stitch with gold and silver thread, coloured braid and silk thread.
Georgian State Museum of Art.

Ruisi. Embroidered epitrachelion, 17th century. Made as a votive offering by Mariam, the wife of King Rostom of Kartli, it is worked in satin stitch using gold and silver threads, bright braid and coloured silks. Georgian State Museum of Art.

Bibliography

Abramishvili, Guram: *Davit Garejelis tsikli kartul kedlis mkhatvrobashi.* (The cycle of David Garejeli in Georgian mural paintings. Georgian text, Russian and English summaries.) Tbilisi, 1972.

Academy of Sciences of the Georgian SSR, Giorgi Chubinashvili Institute for the History of Georgian Art: *Ars Georgica. Kartuli khelovneba.* (The art of Georgia. Collected papers published by the Institute. Georgian and Russian texts, German and French summaries.) Vol. 1, etc., Tbilisi, 1942–

Academy of Sciences of the Georgian SSR, I. A. Javakhishvili Institute of History, Archaeology and Ethnography: *Didi Pitiunti.* (Reports on the archaeological excavations at Pitiunt or Bichvinta, on the Black Sea coast of Abkhazia. Georgian text, Russian and English summaries.) Vol. 1, etc., Tbilisi, 1975–

– *Vani.* (Reports on the archaeological excavations of 1947–69 at Vani, in Western Georgia. Ed. Otar Lortkipanidze. Georgian text, Russian and English summaries.) Vol. 1, etc., Tbilisi, 1972–

Aladashvili, Natela: *Monumental'naya skul'ptura Gruzii. Figurnye rel'efy V–XI vekov.* (Georgian monumental sculpture. Figure reliefs of the 5th–11th centuries. Russian text, English summary.) Tbilisi, 1977.

– *Nikordsmindis reliepebi.* (The bas-reliefs on Nikortsminda church. Georgian text, Russian and German summaries.) Tbilisi, 1957.

– 'Rel'ef iz Opizy s izobrazheniem Ashota Kuropalata' (A bas-relief from Opiza portraying Ashot Kuropalates.) in *Soob-shcheniya Akademii Nauk Gruzinskoi SSR* (Bulletin of the Academy of Sciences of the Georgian SSR), vol. 15, no. 7, Tbilisi, 1954. (Georgian and Russian versions.)

– (with Gayane Alibegashvili and Aneli Vol'skaya): *Rospisi khudozhnika Tevdore v Verkhnei Svanetii.* (The wall-paintings of the artist Theodore in Upper Svaneti. Russian text, English summary). Tbilisi, 1966.

Alibegashvili, Gayane: *Chetyre portreta tsaritsy Tamary.* (Four portraits of Queen Tamar. Russian text, German summary.) Tbilisi, 1957.

– *Khudozhestvenny printsip illyustrirovaniya gruzinskoi rukopisnoi knigi 11 – nachala 13 vekov.* (The artistic principle of the illustration of Georgian manuscript volumes, from the 11th to the beginning of the 13th century. Russian text, French summary.) Tbilisi, 1973.

– 'Pamyatniki srednevekovoi stankovoi zhivopisi' (Monuments of medieval panel painting) in *Srednevekovoe iskusstvo. Rus'. Gruziya* (Medieval art, Russia and Georgia. Russian text.) Moscow, 1978.

Allen, W. E. D.: *A History of the Georgian People.* London, 1932.

Amiranashvili, Shalva: *Beka Opizari.* (Biography of the medieval Georgian master of metalworking. Russian text.) Tbilisi, 1956.

– *Les Émaux de Géorgie.* Paris, 1962.

– *Georgian metalwork, from Antiquity to the 18th century.* London, 1971.

– *Gruzinskaya miniatyura.* (Georgian miniature painting. Russian text, English summary.) Moscow, 1966.

– *Istoriya gruzinskogo iskusstva.* (History of Georgian art. Russian text.) Vol. 1 only published, Moscow, 1950; also revised and extended edition, complete in one volume, Moscow, 1963.

– *Istoriya gruzinskoi monumental'noi zhivopisi.* (History of Georgian mural painting. Russian text.) Vol. 1 only published, Tbilisi, 1957.

– *Kartveli mkhatvari Damiane ... Georgian painter Damiane.* (Georgian, Russian and English texts.) Tbilisi, 1974.

– *Khakhulis karedi.* (The Khakhuli triptych. Georgian, Russian and English texts.) Tbilisi, 1972.

– *Medieval Georgian Enamels of Russia.* New York, 1965.

– *Ubisi. Masalebi kartuli kedlis-mkhatvrobis istoriisatvis.* (The church of Ubisi. Materials on the history of Georgian fresco painting. Georgian and Russian texts.) 2 vols., Tbilisi, 1929.

– *Vepkhis-tqaosnis dasurateba ... Miniatures of the XVI–XVIII centuries to the poem, 'The Knight in Tiger's Skin'.* (Georgian text, with Russian, English and French summaries.) Tbilisi, 1966.

Andghuladze, Nugzar: *Tiris monastris khurotmodzghvruli ansambli ... L'Ensemble architectural du monastère de Thiri.* (Georgian text, with Russian and French summaries.) Tbilisi, 1976.

Apakidze, Andria: *Goroda drevnei Gruzii.* (Cities of ancient Georgia. Russian text.) Tbilisi, 1968.

– (with G. Gobejishvili, A. Kalandadze and G. Lomtatidze): *Mtskheta. Itogi arkheologicheskikh issledovanii.* (Mtskheta. Results of the archaeological excavations. Vol. 1: Monuments of Armazis-khevi, discovered in the seasons 1937–46. Russian text, English summary.) Tbilisi, 1958.

Ars Georgica *see* Academy of Sciences of the Georgian SSR.

Avalishvili, Z. D.: 'A fifteenth-century Georgian needle painting in the Metropolitan Museum, New York' in *Georgica*, vol. 1, no. 1, London, 1935, pp. 67–74, 2 plates.

Azarpay, Guitty: *Urartian Art and Artifacts. A chronological study.* California University Press, 1968.

Bagrationi, Prince Vakhushti: *Description géographique de la Géorgie, publiée d'après l'original autographe par M. Brosset.* (Georgian and French texts.) St. Petersburg, 1842.

Baltrušaitis, Jurgis: *L'Église cloisonnée en Orient et en Occident.* Paris, 1941.

– *Études sur l'art médiéval en Géorgie et en Arménie.* Paris, 1929.

Barnaveli, Sara: *Kartuli droshebi.* (Georgian royal standards and military banners. Georgian text.) Tbilisi, 1953.

– *Sakartvelos sabetchdavi da skhva gliptikuri masalebi.* (Georgian seals and other engraved stones and gems. Georgian text, Russian and French summaries.) Tbilisi, 1965.

Berdzenishvili, N. A., and others: *Istoriya Gruzii.* (History of Georgia. Russian text.) Vol. 1, Tbilisi, 1962.

Beridze, Vakhtang: 'L'Architecture géorgienne' in *Bedi Kartlisa, Revue de Kartvélologie*, vol. XXV, Paris, 1968, pp. 129–43.

– *Dzveli kartuli khurotmodzghvreba.* (Ancient Georgian architecture. Georgian text, Russian summary.) Tbilisi, 1974.

– *Dzveli kartveli ostatebi.* (Masters of Old Georgian art. Biographical studies. Georgian text.) Tbilisi, 1967.

– *Gruzinskaya arkhitektura, s drevneishikh vremen do nachala XX veka.* (Georgian architecture, from ancient times to the beginning of the 20th century. Russian text, French summary.) Tbilisi, 1967.

– *Nekotorye aspekty gruzinskoi kupol'noi arkhitektury so vtoroi poloviny X v. do kontsa XIII v.* (Some aspects of Georgian domed architecture from the second half of the 10th century to the end of the 13th century. Russian text, French summary.) Tbilisi, 1976.

– *Samtskhis khurotmodzghvreba, XIII–XVI saukuneebi.* (Architecture of Samtskhe province, from the 13th to the 16th century. Georgian text, Russian and German summaries.) Tbilisi, 1955.

– *Tbilisis khurotmodzghvreba, dslebi 1801–1917.* (Architecture of Tbilisi, from 1801 to 1917. Georgian text, Russian and French summaries.) 2 vols., Tbilisi, 1960–63.

– (with Levan Rcheulishvili and Renée Shmerling): *Tbilisis Metekhis tadzari.* (The Metekhi church in Tbilisi. Georgian text, Russian and French summaries.) Tbilisi, 1969.

– (and others): 'Iskusstvo Gruzii' (The art of Georgia) in *Istoriya iskusstva narodov SSSR* (History of the art of the peoples of the USSR. Russian text.) Vol. 2, Moscow, 1973, pp. 173–254.

Blake, R. P., and Sirarpie Der Nersessian: 'The Gospels of Bert'ay: an Old-Georgian MS. of the tenth century' in *Byzantion*, vol. 16, Boston, 1944, pp. 226–85, 8 plates. Reprinted in shortened form in Sirarpie Der Nersessian, *Études Byzantines et Arméniennes: Byzantine and Armenian Studies*, vol. 1, Louvain, 1973, pp. 199–226, and vol. 2, plates 35–8.

Brière, Chanoine Maurice: 'Une broderie géorgienne à Detroit', extrait des *Cahiers Archéologiques*, vol. VIII, Paris, 1956, pp. 245–8.

Burney, Charles, and David M. Lang: *The Peoples of the Hills: Ancient Ararat and Caucasus.* London and New York, 1971.

Chopikashvili, N. V.: *Kartuli kostiumi, VI–XIV ss.* (Georgian costume of the 6th–14th centuries. Georgian text.) Tbilisi, 1964.

Chubinashvili, Giorgi N.: *Arkhitektura Gruzii* (The architecture of Georgia), vol. 3 in *Vseobshchaya Istoriya Arkhitektury* (General history of architecture), Leningrad and Moscow, 1966. (Russian text.)

– *Arkhitektura Kakhetii.* (The architecture of Kakheti province. Russian text.) 2 vols., Tbilisi, 1956–9.

– 'Arkhitekturnye pamyatniki VIII i IX vekov v Ksanskom ushchel'i' (Architectural monuments of the 8th and 9th centuries in the Ksani valley) in *Ars Georgica*, vol. 1, Tbilisi, 1942. (Russian text, French summary.)

– 'Bolnissky Sion' (The Sion cathedral in Bolnisi) in *Izvestiya Instituta yazyka, istorii i material'noi kul'tury im. N. Ya. Marra* (Bulletin of the N. Ya. Marr Institute of Language, History and Archaeology), vol. 9, Tbilisi, 1940. (Russian text, German summary.)

– 'Georgia, Art of' in McGraw-Hill *Encyclopedia of World Art*, vol. 6, 1962, cols. 137–52, plates 111–15. With a bibliography.

– *Gruzinskoe chekannoe iskusstvo. Issledovanie po istorii gruzinskogo srednevekovogo iskusstva.* (Georgian repoussé work. A study on the history of Georgian medieval art. Russian text.) 2 vols., Tbilisi, 1959.

– 'Iranskie vliyaniya v pamyatnikakh arkhitektury Gruzii' (Iranian influences on the architectural monuments of Georgia) in *Proceedings (Doklady) of the 3rd International Congress on Iranian Art and Archaeology*, Moscow and Leningrad, 1939. (Russian text, French summary.)

– *Pamyatniki tipa Dzhvari.* (Monuments of the type of the Jvari or Holy Cross church at Mtskheta. Russian text, French summary.) 2 vols., Tbilisi, 1948.

– *Peshchernye monastyri David-Garedzhi.* (The cave monasteries of David-Gareja. Russian text, French summary.) Tbilisi, 1948.

– *Tsromi.* (A study of the early medieval church at Tsromi. Russian text.) Moscow, 1969.

– *Voprosy istorii iskusstva. Issledovaniya i zametki.* (Problems of art history. Researches and notes. Russian text.) Vol. 1, Tbilisi, 1970.

Chubinashvili, Niko: *Gruzinskaya srednevekovaya khudozhestvennaya rez'ba po derevu.* (Medieval Georgian decorative wood-carving of the 10th and 11th centuries. Russian text.) Tbilisi, 1958.

– *Khandisi ... Chandisi. Das Reliefproblem am Beispiel einer Gruppe georgischer Stelereliefs des letzten Viertels des V., VI. und der ersten Hälfte des VII.Jhs.* (Russian text, German summary.) Tbilisi, 1972.

– *Samshvildsky Sion.* (The Sion cathedral in Samshvilde. Russian text, German summary.) Tbilisi, 1969.

– 'Zedazeni, Klikis dzhvari, Gviara' (a study of these three early medieval monuments) in *Ars Georgica*, vol 7A, Tbilisi, 1971, pp. 27–66, 13 plates. (Russian text, French summary.)

Chubinishvili, Tariel: *Amiranis Gora ... Materials on the ancient history of Meskhet-Javakheti.* (Georgian text, Russian summary.) Tbilisi, 1963.

– *Mtkvrisa da Araksis ormdinaretis udzvelesi kultura.* (The most ancient culture of the region of the two rivers Mtkvari and Araxes. Georgian text.) Tbilisi, 1965.

Davatishvili, Ketevan: *Drevnegruzinskaya vyshivka.* (Old Georgian embroidery. Georgian text.) Tbilisi, 1973.

Dolidze, Vakhtang: *Garbani. Kartuli khurotmodzghvrebis IX–X ss. dzegli Khevshi.* (Garbani church. A monument of Georgian architecture of the 9th–10th centuries in Khevi district. Georgian text, Russian summary.) Tbilisi, 1958.

– 'Satkhis khurotmodzghvruli dzegli' (The Georgian medieval church at Satkhe) in *Ars Georgica*, vol 7A, Tbilisi, 1971, pp. 131–62, plates 43–54. (Georgian text, Russian and French summaries.)

Dubois de Montpéreux, Frédéric: *Voyage autour du Caucase, chez les Tcherkesses et les Abkhases, en Colchide, en Géorgie, en Arménie et en Crimée. Avec un atlas.* 6 vols. and atlas, Paris, 1839–43.

Dzeglis Megobari. (The friend of the ancient monument. Organ of the Georgian Society for Protection of Cultural Monuments. Georgian text, Russian summaries.) No. 1, etc., Tbilisi, 1964–

Erlashova, Sophia M.: *Keramika i chekanka Gruzii/Georgian pottery and chasing on metal.* (Russian and English texts.) Leningrad, 1975.

Gabashvili, Tsiala: *Portalebi kartul arkiteturashi.* (Portals and doorways in Georgian medieval architecture. Georgian and Russian texts.) Tbilisi, 1955.

Gagoshidze, Yulon: 'Yazychesky khram' (The pagan temple) in *Dzeglis Megobari*, no. 35, Tbilisi, 1974. (Georgian text, Russian summary.)

Gamrekeli, Vakhtang: 'Dvaletis karni tsentralur Kavkasionze' (The Dvaleti Gates on the Central Caucasus) in *Dzeglis Megobari*, no. 5, Tbilisi 1965, pp. 23–33. (Georgian text, Russian summary.)

Gaprindashvili, Givi: *Ancient Monuments of Georgia: Vardzia. History, Architecture, Wall-painting, Applied arts.* (English, Russian and Georgian texts.) Leningrad, 1975.

Garaqanidze, M.K.: *Gruzinskoe derevyannoe zodchestvo.* (Georgian architecture in wood. Russian text.) Tbilisi, 1959.

Gink, Károly, and Erzsébet Tompos: *Grúzia. Kincsek, várak, kolostorok.* Budapest, 1973.

Gomelauri, Ina: *Ertadsmindis tadzris arkitektura.* (The architecture of Ertatsminda church. Georgian text, Russian and French summaries.) Tbilisi, 1976.

Inadze, Meri: *Prichernomorskie goroda drevnei Kolkhidy.* (The coastal towns of ancient Colchis. Russian text.) Tbilisi, 1968.

Janberidze, Nodar: *Pamyatniki arkhitektury Gruzii/Architectural monuments of Georgia.* (Russian and English texts.) Leningrad, 1973.

Japaridze, V.V.: *Keramikuli dsarmoeba XI–XIII ss. Sakartveloshi.* (Ceramic production of the 11th–13th centuries in Georgia. Georgian text, Russian summary.) Tbilisi, 1956.

Javakhishvili, A.I. and Zakaraia, P.P.: Iskusstvo drevnei Gruzii (The art of ancient Georgia) in *Istoriya iskusstva narodov SSSR* (History of the art of the peoples of the USSR. Russian text.) Vol. 1, Moscow, 1971, pp. 196–205.

Jobadze (Djobadze), Vakhtang Z.: 'Notes on Georgian Minor Art of the Post-Byzantine period' in *Journal of the Walters Art Gallery, Baltimore, Maryland*, vol. 23, 1960, pp. 97–117.

– 'The donor reliefs and the date of the church at Oshki' in *Byzantinische Zeitschrift 69, 1976*.

– 'The Sculptures on the Eastern Façade of the Holy Cross of Mtzkhet'a' in *Oriens Christianus*, Wiesbaden, vol. 44, 1960, pp. 112–135; vol. 45, 1961, pp. 70–77; with 15 plates.

– 'Vorläufiger Bericht über Grabungen und Untersuchungen in der Gegend von Antiochia am Orontes' in *Istanbuler Mitteilungen*, vol. 15, Tübingen, 1965, pp. 218–42, plates 51–6.

Khidasheli, Manana: *Brinjaos mkhatvruli damushavebis istoriisatvis antikur Sakartveloshi.* (On the history of artistic bronze-working in Geogia in antiquity. Description of open-work bronze belt buckles, with animal figures. Georgian text, Russian summary.) Tbilisi, 1972.

Khuskivadze, Leila: *Levan Dadianis saokromtchedlo sakhelosno.* (The icon workshop of Prince Levan Dadiani, 17th-century ruler of Mingrelia. Georgian text, Russian and English summaries.) Tbilisi, 1974.

Khuskivadze, Yuza: *Kartuli saero miniatura, XVI–XVIII saukuneebi.* (Georgian secular miniature painting of the 16th–18th centuries. Georgian text, Russian and English summaries.) Tbilisi, 1976.

Kondakov, Nikodim, and D. Z. Bakradze: *Opis' pamyatnikov drevnosti v nekotorykh khramakh i monastyryakh Gruzii.* (Description of monuments of antiquity in certain Georgian churches and monasteries. Russian text.) St Petersburg, 1890.

Kuftin, Boris: *Arkheologicheskie raskopki v Trialeti.* (Archaeological ecxavations in Trialeti. Russian text, Georgian and English summaries.) Vol. 1 only published, Tbilisi, 1941.

– *Materialy k arkheologii Kolkhidy.* (Materials on the archaeology of Colchis. Russian text.) 2 vols., Tbilisi, 1949–50.

Kushnareva, Karina, and Tariel Chubinishvili: *Drevnie kul'tury yuzhnogo Kavkaza.* (Ancient cultures of the southern Caucasus. Russian text.) Leningrad, 1970.

Lang, David Marshall: 'A Georgian embroidery panel in Hull' in *Bulletin of the School of Oriental and African Studies,* University of London, vol. XXVII, part 3, 1964, pp. 612–15, 2 plates.

– *The Georgians.* London and New York, 1966.

– *Lives and Legends of the Georgian Saints.* 2nd ed. London, 1976.

Lezhava, Giorgi, and Maria Jandieri: *Arkhitektura Svanetii.* (The architecture of Svaneti. Russian text.) Moscow, 1938.

Lortkipanidze, Inga: *Nabakhtevis mkhatvroba.* (The mural paintings of Nabakhtevi church. Georgian text, Russian and French summaries.) Tbilisi, 1973.

Lortkipanidze, Margarita: *Sakartvelos sakhelmdsipo muzeumis gemebi.* (Catalogue of the engraved gems in the Georgian State Museum. Georgian text, Russian summary.) Vol. 1, etc., Tbilisi, 1954–

Lortkipanidze, Otar: *Dzveli Kolkhetis kultura.* (The culture of ancient Colchis. Georgian text, Russian and English summaries.) Tbilisi, 1972.

– 'Monuments of Graeco-Roman culture on the territory of Ancient Georgia' in *Archeologia,* vol. XVII, 1966, pp. 49–79.

Machavariani, Elene: *Kartuli khelnadserebi ... Georgian Manuscripts.* (An illustrated album, with colour plates. Designed by Zurab Kapanadze. Georgian, Russian and English texts.) Tbilisi, 1970.

MacLean, Fitzroy: *To Caucasus, the end of all the Earth.* London, 1976.

Maisuradze, Zakaria: *Gruzinskaya khudozhestvennaya keramika XI–XIII vv.* (Georgian artistic ceramic ware of the 11th–13th centuries. Russian text, Georgian captions.) Tbilisi, 1954.

– *Ozaanis keramika.* (The ornamental tiles of Ozaani church. Georgian and Russian texts, German summary.) Tbilisi, 1959.

Marr, N. Ya.: *Zhitie sv. Grigoriya Khandzt'iiskogo ... s Dnevnikom poezdki v Shavshiyu i Klardzhiyu.* (Life of St Gregory of Khandzta ... together with a diary of a journey to Shavsheti and Klarjeti. Georgian and Russian texts.) St Petersburg, 1911.

– (with Ya. I. Smirnov): *Les Vichaps.* Leningrad, 1931.

Melikishvili, Giorgi: *Nairi-Urartu.* (A study of the civilization of Urartu. Russian text.) Vol. 1 only published, Tbilisi, 1954.

Melikset-Bek, Leon: *Megalituri kultura Sakartveloshi.* (Megalithic culture in Georgia. Georgian text, Russian summary.) Tbilisi, 1938.

Melitauri, Konstantine: *Vardzia.* (An account of the medieval cave town and monastery. Russian and English texts.) Tbilisi, 1963.

Menabde, Levan: *Centres of Ancient Georgian Culture.* (English version.) Tbilisi, 1968.

Mepisashvili, Rusudan: *Arkhitekturny ansambl' Gelati.* (The architectural ensemble of Gelati. Russian text, French summary, Tbilisi, 1966.

– 'Beris saqdari: X saukunis sameklesiani bazilika' ('Beris saqdari': a triple basilica of the 10th century) in *Ars Georgica,* vol. 7A, Tbilisi, 1971, pp. 91–110, 11 plates. (Georgian text, Russian and French summaries.)

– 'Polupeshcherny pamyatnik IX v. v sel. Bieti' (The semisubterranean monument of the 9th century in the village of Bieti) in *Ars Georgica,* vol. 6A, Tbilisi, 1963. pp. 29–55, plates 9–26. (Russian text, French summary.)

– 'Rel'efy rubezha 10–11 vekov so stsenami stroitel'stva v khrame u seleniya Korogo' (Reliefs of the 10th–11th centuries, showing scenes of building works, carved on Korogho village church) in *Sovetskaya Arkheologiya* (Soviet archaeology), no. 4, Moscow, 1969. (Russian text, French summary.)

– (with Vakhtang Tsintsadze): *Arkhitektura nagornoi chasti istoricheskoi provintsii Gruzii – Shida Kartli.* (The architecture of the mountainous portion of the historic province of Georgia – Shida or Inner Kartli. Russian text, German summary.) Tbilisi, 1975.

– (with Vakhtang Tsintsadze): *Kutaisi, Geguti, Gelati.* (A study of three leading architectural monuments of West Georgia. Russian and English texts.) Tbilisi, 1966.

Mshvenieradze, D. M.: *Stroitel'noe delo v drevnei Gruzii.* (Construction techniques in ancient Georgia. Russian text.) Tbilisi, 1952.

Neubauer, Edith: *Altgeorgische Baukunst. Felsenstädte, Kirchen, Höhlenklöster.* Vienna and Munich, 1976.

Piotrovsky, Boris: *Urartu. The Kingdom of Van and its Art.* (Translated from the Russian and edited by Peter S. Gelling.) London and New York, 1967.

Privalova, E. L.: *Pavnisi.* (A study of the medieval church at Pavnisi and its frescoes. Russian text, French summary.) Tbilisi, 1977.

Qenia, Rusudan: *Khakhulis ghvtismshoblis khatis karedis motchediloba*. (The ornamental chasing of the Khakhuli icon triptych of the Holy Virgin. Georgian text, Russian and French summaries.) Tbilisi, 1972.

Rcheulishvili, Levan: 'Rati Eristavt-eristavis nageboba Trialetis Akhalkalakshi' (The church of Grand Duke Rati at Akhalkalaki in the Trialeti district) in *Ars Georgica*, vol. 7A, Tbilisi, 1971, pp. 111–130, plates 35–42. (Georgian text, Russian and French summaries.)
– 'Nekotorye aspekty arkhitektury chernomorskogo poberezhiya' (Some aspects of the architecture of the Black Sea coast) in *Srednevekovoe iskusstvo. Rus'. Gruziya* (Medieval art, Russia and Georgia. Russian text.) Moscow, 1978.
– *Tigva. Sharvanis dedoplis Tamaris aghmshenebloba*. (Tigva, a monastic foundation erected by the royal princess Tamar in the 12th century. Georgian text, Russian and German summaries.) Tbilisi, 1960.

Rustaveli, Shota: *The Knight in Panther Skin*. (A free translation in prose by Katharine Vivian, with eight colour plates reproduced from a 17th-century manuscript.) London, 1977.

Sanikidze, Tamaz: *Gergetis khurotmodzghvruli ansambli/L'ensemble architectural de Guergueti*. (Georgian text, Russian and French summaries.) Tbilisi, 1975.

Severov, N.P., and G.N. Chubinashvili: *Kumurdo i Nikortsminda*. (Description of two Georgian medieval churches. Russian text.) Moscow, 1947.

Shervashidze, L.A.: *K voprosu o srednevekovoi gruzinskoi svetskoi miniatyure*. (On the question of Georgian medieval secular miniature painting. Russian text, French summary.) Tbilisi, 1964.

Shmerling, Renée: *Kartul khelnadserta mortulobis nimushebi*. (Examples of Georgian manuscript illumination. Georgian and Russian texts.) Tbilisi, 1940.
– *Khudozhestvennoe oformlenie gruzinskoi rukopisnoi knigi IX–XI vv.* (The artistic design of the Georgian manuscript codex of the 9th–11th centuries. Russian text.) Vol. 1, Tbilisi, 1967.
– *Malye formy v arkhitekture srednevekovoi Gruzii*. (Secondary features in Georgian medieval architecture. Russian text.) Tbilisi, 1962.
– *see also* bibliography of the writings of the late Renée Shmerling, compiled by T.V. Barnaveli, in *Ars Georgica*, vol. 7A, Tbilisi 1971, pp. 234–7.

Smirnov, Ya.I.: *Der Schatz von Achalgori*. Tbilisi, 1934.

Sokhashvili, Givi. *Samtavisi. Masalebi tadzris istoriisatvis/Samtavisi. Materials on the history of the monument*. (Georgian text, Russian and English summaries.) Tbilisi, 1973.

Strzygowski, Josef: *Die Baukunst der Armenier und Europa*. 2 vols., Vienna, 1918.

Sumbadze, L.: *Gruzinskie darbazi*. (The Georgian *darbazi* house. Russian text.) Tbilisi, 1960.

Taqaishvili, E.S.: 'Antiquities of Georgia' in *Georgica*, I, nos. 4–5, London, 1937, pp. 96–116, 26 plates.
– *Arkheologicheskaya ekspeditsiya 1917-go goda v yuzhnye provintsii Gruzii*. (The archaeological expedition of 1917 to the southern provinces of Georgia. Russian text.) Tbilisi, 1952.
– 'Four Basilican Churches of the Qvirila valley' in *Georgica*, I, nos. 2–3, London, 1936, pp. 154–173, 28 plates.
– *Khristianskie pamyatniki* (Christian monuments in Georgia. Report on his 1902 expedition), fasc. 12 in *Materialy po Arkheologii Kavkaza* (Materials on the archaeology of the Caucasus), Moscow, 1909. (Russian text.)

Thierry, J.-M.: 'Çengelli Kilise' in *Bedi Kartlisa, Revue de Kartvélologie*, vol. XXIII–XXIV, Paris, 1967, pp. 177–83, 2 plates.

Thierry, N. and M.: 'L'Église géorgienne de Pekresin (Turquie)' in Bedi Kartlisa, *Revue de Kartvélologie*, vol. XXVI, Paris, 1969, pp. 93–101, 4 plates.
– 'Notes d'un voyage en Géorgie turque' in *Bedi Kartlisa, Revue de Kartvélologie*, vol. VIII–IX, Paris, 1960, pp. 10–29. Continued as 'Notes d'un deuxième voyage en Géorgie turque' in Bedi Kartlisa, vol. XXV, Paris, 1968, pp. 51–65, 4 plates.

Tsereteli, Giorgi: *Udzvelesi kartuli dsardserebi Palestinidan ... The Most Ancient Georgian Inscriptions from Palestine*. (Georgian, Russian and English texts.) Tbilisi, 1960.

Tsintsadze, Vakhtang: *Bagratis tadzari/ Khram Bagrata/The Cathedral of King Bagrat*. (Georgian and Russian texts, English summary.) Tbilisi, 1964.
– 'Katskhis sveti. V–VI sauk. khurotmodzghvrebis dzegli' (The Pillar of Katskhi. A 5th–6th-century monument of Georgian architecture) in *Dzeglis Megobari*, no. 3, Tbilisi, 1964, pp. 52–5, 1 plate. (Georgian text, Russian summary.)
– *Tbilisi. Arkhitektura starogo goroda i zhilye doma pervoi poloviny XIX stoletiya*. (Tbilisi. Architecture of the old city, and dwelling houses of the first half of the 19th century. Russian text.) Tbilisi, 1958.
– 'Ubisis sveti' (The tower of Ubisi) in *Dzeglis Megobari*, no. 18, Tbilisi, 1969, pp. 34–7, 2 plates. (Georgian text, Russian summary.)

Tsitsishvili, Irakli: *Kartuli arkitekturis istoria*. (History of Georgian architecture. Georgian text.) Tbilisi, 1955.

Uvarova, Countess Praskov'ya: *Khristianskie pamyatniki* (Christian monuments), fascs. 4, 10 in *Materialy po Arkheologii Kavkaza* (Materials on the Archaeology of the Caucasus), Moscow, 1894, 1904. (Russian text.)

Virsaladze, Tina: *Rospisi ierusalimskogo krestnogo monastyrya i portret Shota Rustaveli*. (The frescoes of the Holy Cross Monastery in Jerusalem and the portrait of Shota Rustaveli. Russian text, French summary.) Tbilisi, 1973.

Vol'skaya, Aneli: *Rel'efy Shiomgvime i ikh mesto v razvitii gruzinskoi srednevekovoi skul'ptury*. (The bas-reliefs of Shiomghvime and their place in the development of Georgian medieval sculpture. Russian text, German summary.) Tbilisi, 1957.
– *Rospisi srednevekovykh trapeznykh Gruzii*. (The frescoes of medieval Georgian monastery refectories. Russian text, French summary.) Tbilisi, 1974.

Wessel, Klaus: *Byzantine enamels from the 5th to the 13th century*. Irish University Press, 1969.

Winfield, David: 'Some early medieval figure sculpture from north-east Turkey' in *Journal of the Warburg and Courtauld Institutes*, vol. XXXI, London, 1968, pp. 33–72, plates 4–32.

Zakaraia, Parmen: *Ananuri*. (Illustrated guide, with text in Georgian and Russian.) Tbilisi, 1967.

– *Aragvisa da Tergis kheoba*. (Historical and architectural guide to the Aragvi and Terek valleys. Georgian text.) Tbilisi, 1972.

– *Drevnie kreposti Gruzii*. (Ancient Georgian fortresses. Russian text.) Tbilisi, 1969.

– *Dsughrughasheni*. (A monograph on this early medieval church. Georgian text, Russian summary.) Tbilisi, 1952.

– *Kakhetis saportipikatsio nagebobani*. (Fortified buildings of Kakheti province. Georgian text, Russian summery.) Tbilisi, 1962.

– *Nakalakari Gremis arkitektura*. (Architecture of the ruined city of Gremi. Georgian text, Russian and French summaries.) Tbilisi, 1975.

– *Nakalakari Urbnisis khurotmodzghvreba*. (Architecture of the ruined town of Urbnisi. Georgian text, Russian summary.) Tbilisi, 1965.

Zdanevich, Ilia: *L'Itinéraire géorgien de Ruy Gonzales de Clavijo et les églises aux confins de l'Atabégat*. Paris, 1966.

Index

308

Acknowledgments are due to the following
for providing the photographs on the pages
shown:

G. Chubinashvili Institute for the History of
Georgian Art, Academy of Sciences of the
Georgian SSR: 32, 39t, 79b, 84t, 88b, 93b,
131l, 159–61, 196, 201b, 215, 218, 237,
240b, 248, 250, 261l, 293l
Georgian State Museum of Art, Tbilisi: 21,
29, 95–8, 126, 127bl, 127r, 129r, 138, 139,
140b, 149b, 258
S. Janashia Museum (State Museum of
Georgia), Tbilisi: 69t
Vakhtang Djobadze, Los Angeles: 164, 165
Rusudan Mepisashvili, Tbilisi: 121, 129l,
186t
Vakhtang Tsintsadze, Tbilisi: 26, 27, 51,
54–5, 58, 67, 72, 74, 75l, 75tr, 90, 128, 135,
144bl, 144tr, 144br, 145tr, 145b, 154t, 155t,
172, 188, 197, 198t, 210, 240t, 242t, 256
David Winfield, Oxford: 122, 127t, 140t,
140m, 141, 148, 149t

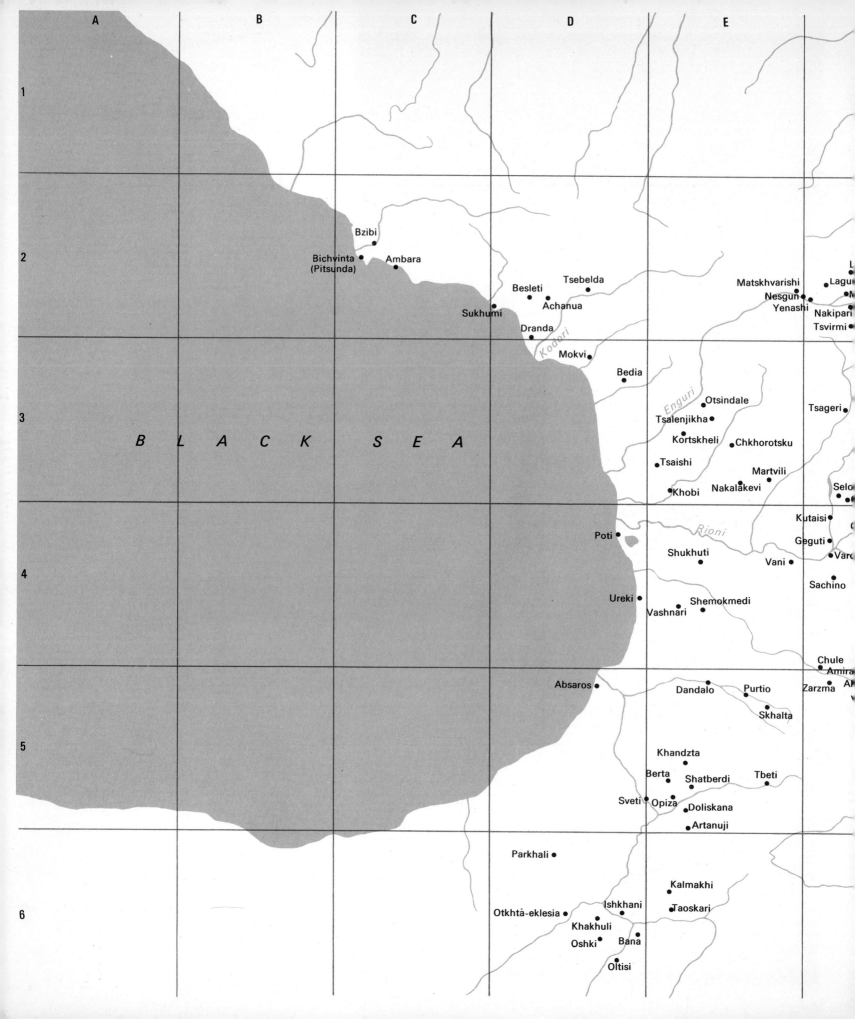

A | B | C | D | E

1

Bzibi

2

Bichvinta
(Pitsunda) Ambara

Besleti Tsebelda Matskhvarishi Lagu
Achanua Nesgun M
Sukhumi Yenashi Nakipari
Dranda *Kodori* Tsvirmi

Mokvi

Bedia

Enguri Otsindale Tsageri

3 Tsalenjikha

Kortskheli Chkhorotsku

Tsaishi Martvili Selo

Khobi Nakalakevi

B L A C K S E A

Kutaisi

Rioni Geguti Varo

Poti

Shukhuti Vani Sachino

4

Ureki Shemokmedi

Vashnari

Chule
Amira
Absaros Dandalo Purtio Zarzma AN

Skhalta

5 Khandzta

Berta Shatberdi Tbeti

Sveti Opiza Doliskana

Artanuji

Parkhali

Kalmakhi

Ishkhani Taoskari
6 Otkhta-eklesia

Khakhuli

Oshki Bana

Oltisi